Fone 654-1363

As Soon ... Your finish ... Please Return to Wm S Young



# GREAT RAIL TRIPS OF THE WORLD

CHARLES & BABETTE JACOBS

DOUGLAS BUNN—Cover Design

PAUL, RICHMOND & COMPANY—PUBLISHERS
73-465 Ironwood, Palm Desert, Ca. 92260
Phone: 619-346-4792

ISBN 0-912640-35-9



$9.95

India's *Desert Queen* powers one of the world's most stately trains — *Palace On Wheels.*

# AUTHOR'S INTRODUCTION

This book has been many years in the making — the result of scores of train trips in the United States and Canada, in Europe and Egypt, Australia and New Zealand, Mexico and South America, the Far East.

For us, it began as a child, long before the Air Age, in the dusk of winter evenings when the *Hiawatha,* a blur of lights, hurtled by with a deep-throated blast from its steam-belching locomotive on its adventurous way from Chicago to Milwaukee and points west — as thrilling to us as a shuttle blast-off to today's generation.

It continued on rail trips over the Chesapeake & Ohio to Virginia where, we recall, kerchiefed black ladies greeted hungry passengers with trays of inviting, golden brown Southern Fried Chicken . . . on the Florida East Coast to Jacksonville, Daytona to Miami . . . on the Illinois Central to New Orleans . . . the *Overland Limited* to Oakland . . . all to the wails of lonely steam whistles in the dark of night — whoo-whoo-whoo-o-o — a plaintive sound that haunts us still, one that can't be duplicated by diesel and electric locomotives.

Those were the days when Pullman cars had open sections of facing seats that, at night, porters made up into lower and upper berths with dark green curtains on each side of the center aisle for privacy. Wealthier passengers took a spacious drawing room (with private toilet) that, together with one or two smaller bedrooms occupied one end of the Pullman; men's and ladies' washrooms were at the other.

Crack *Limiteds* had an observation-lounge car (with open air platform) at the tail end, a dining car (source of perpetual wonderment and delight) somewhere in the middle.

During our college years came rides between Chicago and New York on two historic trains: *Broadway Limited* and *Twentieth Century Limited.* And then, later on, vacation trips to California on the most glamorous trains of their day: Santa Fe's star-studded *Chief* and *Super-Chief.*

We traveled thru Europe during the *Belle Epoque* of the 1920s and '30s, when train travel was at its zenith, when the *Orient Express, Train Bleu, Fleche d'Or* and other legendary trains were the epitome of luxury travel. In those days, hotel buses and attendants awaited your train's arrival in Florence and Rome, for example, to transfer you and your luggage (which might well include a wardrobe trunk) to the hotel. These, by the way, were the days when the Grand Tour was still in vogue, when one often spent up to a month or more (as our family did) *in a single city.*

Those were the days when you crossed to Egypt by steamer, rode from Alexandria to Cairo, then overnight to Luxor and on to Aswan, by train — literally the only way to go.

*One of the frustrations which must be endured stoically by modern tourists trying to see the world before it's too late is the numbing speed with which important arrivals are thrust on them. There is no longer time to travel hopefully. Transit by air has become about as stimulating and educational as a shot of sodium pentothal.*

*This is not to denigrate aviation's contribution to human welfare. There are conceivable — if not readily discernible — advantages in being able to eat breakfast in Paris and keep a dinner date in New York. But I am firm in my belief that the majority of globetrotters today learn less about Spaceship Earth from their encapsulated journeys across oceans and continents than they would glean from making bicycle tours in their home countries.*

*However, since very few people with a persistent itch to seek faraway places are likely to settle for a bicycle tour, what alternatives are there to hurtling through the stratosphere at 600 miles an hour?**

Which is exactly what this book is all about.

* This observation, which reflects much of our feeling, was written by Osmar White, well-known Australian author/journalist.

## JOYS OF RAIL TRAVEL

"To travel is to live," wrote famed Danish story teller, Hans Christian Andersen. And since it's been more than 100 years since he made that statement, he was referring to steam train and steamship — possibly horse and buggy as well.

It matters little that the steam has gone out of trains and ships — travel is still alive and well. But is it, as Osmar White asks, as intriguing as in Hans Christian Andersen's day?

It certainly can be . . . with careful planning . . . by using best available means of transport.

Remember, until each of us sees the world for ourselves in our own ways, it remains undiscovered no matter how many others have been there before us . . . and the thrill of that discovery remains as satisfying to us as it did to our ancestors.

Remember, too, that though we travel thousands of miles during a lifetime, *they must last forever.* Make the most of them.

We've found that's exactly what train travel tends to do — it adds an extra dimension. The 'remoteness' of stratospheric jets from earth contrasts sharply with the 'nearness' of trains — they provide more depth, more intensity, more closeups of mountains, plains, deserts, seashores, towns and, most satisfyingly, *people.*

Were it not for trains . . .

We'd never have seen babushka-clad peasant women looking like protypes of Mother Russia, straw-hatted Indian women of the Peruvian altiplano, Chinese farmers tilling rice paddies with water buffalo.

Nor farmers of other lands going about their daily tasks, bringing produce and supplies to market by backpack, horse and wagon, mule, camel, truck, bicycle or motor scooter.

Nor would we have been so overwhelmed by the scenic beauty of our trips had we been looking *down* instead of *across* and *up.*

And, for certain, we could not have savored the leisurely pace, the convenience of arriving in city centers with their nearby hotels.

We've just read a review of an unusual book of 100 photographs, with accompanying text and captions, titled *The Red Couch.* Its two progenitors, Kevin Clark and Horst Wackerbarth, spent five years hauling an eight-foot long, red velvet couch across the U.S. — up mountains and skyscrapers, thru mud, rain and snow, in order to photograph various types of people — each, of course, seated on the couch.

Well, you can have similar experiences — not with a red couch but on a red *Glacier Express,* an orange TGV, a silver *Indian-Pacific* or *California Zephyr,* a blue *Orient Express* or any of many other Great Rail Trips described in the following pages . . . a multitude of vignettes, portraits, landscapes and seascapes that will last a lifetime — and beyond.

# Table of Contents

# TRAINS OF THE PAST . . .

In the days of The Iron Horse, following completion in 1869 of the Union Pacific railroad, express trains attained hitherto unheard of speeds of 20 mph resulting in the demise of the pony express, stagecoach and covered wagon. During snowstorms, passengers assisted crew in clearing the tracks.

Railroads — actually wagons drawn by horses on wooden rails — date back to the mid-17th century. By mid-18th century, iron rails had been laid. In July of 1814, George Stephenson[1] of England successfully tested a steam locomotive; in 1829, his *Rocket* attained the incredible speed of 29 mph; four years before, he was responsible for developing the first public railroad the world had ever known: the 20-mile Stockton & Darlington. In 1830, a 130-mile railroad operated between Liverpool and Manchester. In 1835, Germany's Nurnberg to Furth line was opened. By 1870, most of Europe's major domestic routes had been constructed, although some additional ones were built later, notably the international Simplon tunnel route that was completed in 1906, a major engineering feat.

As a result of this activity, and the development of Pullman and Wagons-Lits cars (see Orient Express section), it was possible for travelers to tour Europe in a style befitting royalty. Luxury trains, which saw their heydays in the 1920s and '30s, vied with trans-Atlantic ocean liners in opulence and speed. Anyone who was anything — and thousands more who weren't — rode thc rails across Europe, west to east and north to south.

On the other side of the Atlantic, Silas Whitney's gravity- and horse-powered tramway on Boston's Beacon Hill was the first form of railroading in the United States. Christmas Day of 1830 saw the first train of cars pulled by a locomotive, an achievement of the South Carolina Canal and Railroad line. In 1833, the world's longest line (136 miles) under one management was in operation. Sleeping cars came into being, crude as they were, in 1837; stateroom cars (called Gothic) were operating by 1856. And then George Pullman stole the show.

By 1853, passengers were able to travel entirely by rail from New York City to Chicago, and in 1854 they could do so from Chicago to Rock Island, Illinois and the Mississippi River; in 1856, Illinois Central had laid 700 miles of track to Cairo, Illinois.

Just as railroads made possible the rapid developments of the Industrial Revolution in England, so did they contribute to the Winning of the American West. On May 10, 1869 at Promontory, Utah the Union Pacific and Central Pacific RRs met to complete the first transcontinental railway. That was followed, in 1881, by the Atchinson Topeka and Santa Fe route from Kansas City to Deming, New Mexico which connected in 1883 with the Southern Pacific from San Francisco to El Paso and New Orleans. In 1893, the Northern Pacific completed its Ashland, Wisconsin-Portland, Oregon route and Great Northern likewise from St. Paul to Seattle. By 1909, Chicago Milwaukee & St. Paul extended track to the Pacific Coast. In fact, by 1916, there were 254,000 miles of track in service thruout the U.S. — a total far exceeding that of today.

Domeliner cars were first built in 1945, proved extremely popular over western U.S. routes such as Union Pacific's *City of Los Angeles* and *City of San Francisco*. Hi-level cars were put into service by Santa Fe in 1957; the present bi-level Amtrak cars in 1979.

Canada was also a transcontinental pioneer with the opening in 1885 of Canadian Pacific Railway's Montreal to Vancouver route.

[1] Stephenson was responsible for developing the 4′ 8½″ track (size of wagon axles) which became standard gauge, currently used by major national railroads except the following: Argentina, Chile, India, Spain and Portugal (5′ 8″); Japan, New Zealand and South Africa (3′ 6″); Finland, Soviet Union (5′); Ireland (5′ 3″).

British Rail's APT — Advanced Passenger Train

# TRAINS OF TODAY . . .

Generally, equipment of major rail systems are the fastest, most comfortable in the history of railroading. Starting in 1964 with Japan's bullet trains and culminating in France's 160 mph TGVs in the 1980s, domestic railroads were able to compete favorably with airlines, particularly in convenience and price. Today, not only Fearful Flyers but vacation and business travelers generally are riding the rails in increasing numbers.

There are valid reasons for that. Despite the past tendency to think of trains as land-based jumbo jets — a means of getting from one destination to another — more and more travelers realize that riding the rails is a pleasant, comfortable way to do their sightseeing.

That being the case, which trains should one ride? Which are the tops in luxury? What are the most scenic rides? The most unusual? The best routes?

Above all, how does one plan Great Rail Trips?

Answers to those and many other questions are spelled out in the pages that follow. But here's a sneak preview:

**Top Luxury Trains**

South Africa's *Blue Train* is usually the choice of connoisseurs as the top of the tops, closely followed by *Istanbul Orient Express, Venice Simplon Orient-Express* and India's *Palace On Wheels.* On a less lavish, more functional modern scale are Australia's *The Alice* and *Indian-Pacific.*

Orient Express programs are enjoying huge success, particularly with American travelers, intrigued by Agatha Christie, who "simply must do it once." The cars are far more lavish than anything else on wheels, excepting *Palace On Wheels,* and the service far exceeds anything available on other European trains. So, of course, do the fares. But what intrigue. What delicious food. What nostalgia.

*Authors' Note:* It has always been our policy, in all our books, to 'tell it as it is.' So, here is a contrarian opinion about luxury train trips from a Vice President-Operations of a prestigious, deluxe tour operator:

* * * * * * * * * *

"The problem I have with these train trips is that invariably people are disappointed. They are, I believe, overpriced and, worse than that, oversold. *Blue Train* fares are a little better than those of the *Orient Express* because there has not been as much brouhaha made over that particular train.

"A similar thing would have happened with *Palace On Wheels* which we offered last year on one of our India tours but the railway people changed the train's itinerary considerably after our brochure was printed so we were unable to operate it. I was just as glad because in talking to some tour groups that had returned from trips which included *Palace On Wheels,* it was, apparently, far, far from being anywhere near a Palace On Wheels. In fact, Indian Railways people have indicated to me that they may not promote the train that much in the U.S. as they do not think the train will ever be up to American standards, are concentrating on promoting it in Europe.

"I think both the rail companies and passengers are at fault with the disappointment many have experienced — the rail people for overselling their trains and passengers for not understanding the limitations of sleeping car accommodations: they tend to judge them by hotel standards and, of course, there's no way a train can ever come close to what a hotel might offer regardless of how hard the operator tries to do so.

"I trust that you will mention this as only then will passengers have a more realistic expectation and, therefore, more enjoyable experiences."

* * * * * * * * * *

*Final Authors' Note:* It is true that fares on luxury train trips are high and that accommodations cannot be compared to those of a hotel or cruise ship. No question, persons considering taking an *Orient Express, Palace On Wheels* and similar trains should weigh the disadvantages against the unique experiences they offer — and the memories.

On the other hand, do not confuse the foregoing with the many other train trips described herein. Primarily, it's sleeping car accommodations that create disappointments.

# . . . ALL AROUND THE WORLD

Key To Cities
1-Vancouver; 2-Seattle
3-San Francisco
4-Los Angeles; 5-Chicago
6-Montreal; 7-New York
8-New Orleans
9-Mexico City; 10-Lima
11-Cuzco; 12-La Paz
13-Santiago
14-Buenos Aires; 15-Madrid
16-Paris; 17-London
18-Bergen; 19-Oslo
20-Copenhagen
21-Stockholm; 22-Helsinki
23-Leningrad; 24-Moscow
25-Rome; 26-Istanbul
27-Cairo; 28-Aswan
29-Johannesburg
30-Cape Town; 31-Irkutsk
32-Khabarovsk; 33-Nakhodka
34-Ulan Bator; 35-Beijing
36-Hong Kong; 37-Niigata
38-Tokyo; 39-Fukuoka
40-Pakistan; 41-New Delhi
42-Bombay; 43-Colombo
44-Calcutta; 45-Bangkok
46-Penang; 47-Kuala Lumpur
48-Singapore; 49-Perth
50-Tarcoola; 51-Alice Springs
52-Cairns; 53-Darwin
54-Sydney

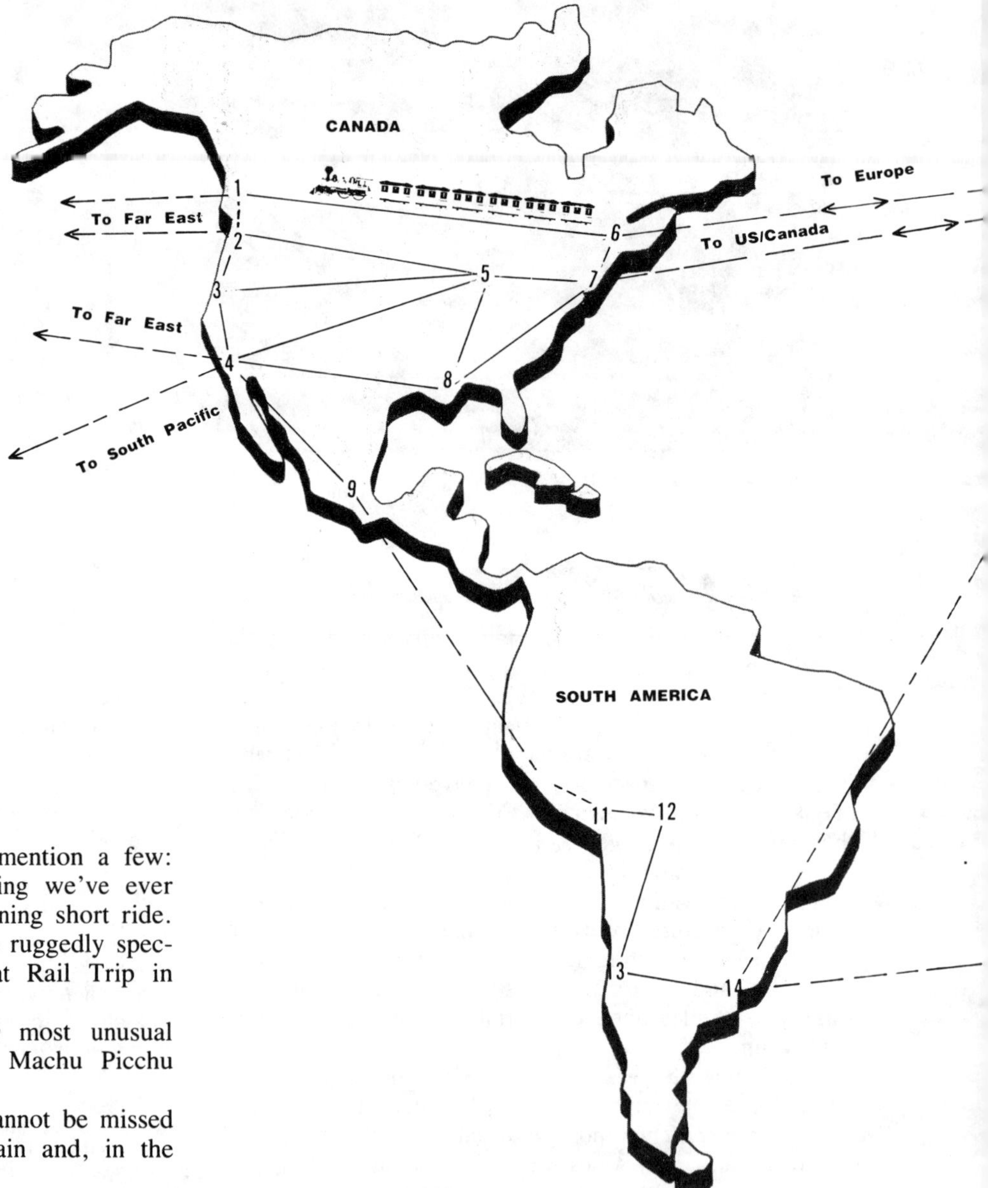


**Most Scenic & Unusual Rides**

They fill a book — this book. To mention a few: Norway has two of the most thrilling we've ever taken. Garmisch to Innsbruck is a stunning short ride. The highland seascapes of Scotland are ruggedly spectacular. All of Switzerland is a Great Rail Trip in itself.

South America offers three of *the* most unusual trips: Quito to Guayaquil, Cuzco to Machu Picchu and Cuzco to Puno.

Western United States and Canada cannot be missed by anyone seeking magnificent mountain and, in the U.S., desert beauty.

In Australia, the ride from Sidney to Alice Springs on *The Alice* is one of our most favorite.

India is a kaleidoscope of sights and sounds, but to see and hear them in comparative comfort, take *Palace On Wheels.*

**WHERE ENGLISH-FOREIGN CITY NAMES DIFFER***

Athens—Athina
Belgrade—Beograd
Bucharest—Bucaresti
Cologne—Koln
Copenhagen—Kobenhavn
Florence—Firenze
Geneva—Geneve
Genoa—Genova
Hook of Holland—Hoek van Holland
Lisbon—Lisboa
Lucerne—Luzern
Milan—Milano
Moscow—Moskva
Munich—Munchen
Ostend—Oostende
Prague—Praha
Rome—Roma
Salonica—Thessaloniki
The Hague—Den Haag
Vienna—Wein
Warsaw—Warszawa

*These native names are also different in French, Italian, German, Spanish and other languages.

**Planning Your Great Rail Trips**

For American and Canadian rail travelers, Europe has always been, and should be, their prime destination. Conversely, Europeans should make theirs the United States and Canada.

There are innumerable European routing possibilities; some of the bettter ones are listed in our Europe section. But the main problem is how to travel wisely and well within the time limits of your vacation. In particular . . .

*Don't try to see all of Europe in two or three weeks.*

*Concentrate on seeing one or two countries in depth. Last year, we spent a month riding the rails in Switzerland.*

*And for enjoyable travel, don't burden yourself with excess or heavy luggage.*

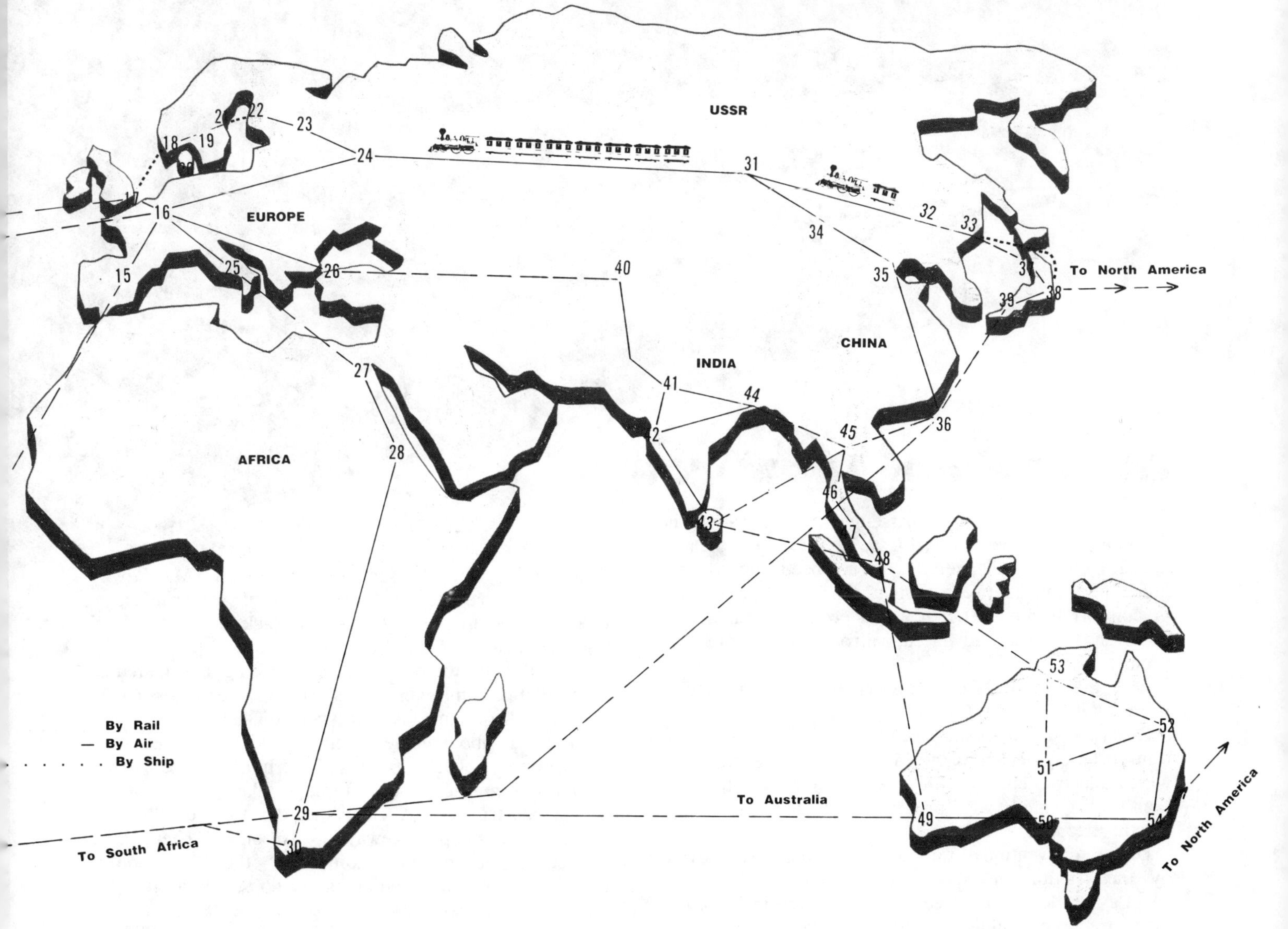


As to the rest of the world, you'll find plenty of suggestions in each of the area sections.

**Around The World By Rail**

With trans-ocean air assists, this is a perfectly viable option.

Accustomed as you are to traveling long distances by air, it may come as a surprise to see how much of the world can be seen from a train.

As our schematic map clearly indicates, there are a number of route options, from literally traveling Around The World to the equivalent of doing so. Starting from either coast of the United States or Canada, and crossing the continent by rail, here are a few of the most attractive routings:

1) By air to London, ship to Bergen, rail to Oslo and Stockholm, ferry to Helsinki, train to Leningrad and Moscow. Board *Trans-Siberian Express* for the long ride to Nakhodka, followed by ship to Yokohama or air to Niigata and train to Tokyo. Then (a) return to North America west coast by air; (b) fly to Australia and return home from there; (c) fly to Hong Kong, train to Beijing for return home by air. Or (d) fly to South Africa, go overland to Egypt then fly to Rome to cover Italy and Switzerland by train, winding up in Paris. Else (e) fly from Cape Town (after riding the *Blue Train*) to Buenos Aires and back home along the west coast of South America.

2) By air to Paris to catch the *Istanbul Orient Express,* then by air from Istanbul to Pakistan, train into India, air to Bangkok for the train to Singapore. Fly to Hong Kong and then ride the rails thru China and Mongolia to Siberia and Russia, then on to Helsinki, Stockholm, Oslo and Bergen. Return home from England after crossing the North Sea by ship.

3) Fly across the Pacific to New Zealand and Australia. Take *The Alice* from Sydney to Alice Springs, then return by air from Darwin to India, China or Japan to use any of the previously listed options.

Those, plus their many possible variations, are what dreams are made of (despite never ending a sentence with a preposition).

# *The Train of Tomorrow**

A new era in ground passenger transportation is dawning, one where wheel-less, rail-less and nearly noiseless trains will literally fly at speeds up to 250 miles per hour between distant cities with a degree of comfort, safety, efficiency and economy unmatched by even the most advanced railroad systems in existence today.

It is the era of Magnetic Levitation —MagLev for short.

Regarded as a quantum leap into the future of transportation technology, MagLev is a system in which electric energy is converted directly into motion to lift, guide and propel ultra-modern trains by electro-magnetic attraction.

Unlike conventional railroad trains that are moved by the friction of steel wheels against steel rails, MagLevs ride contact-free about half an inch *above* their track or guideway on a powerful magnetic wave. There are no wheels, axles, drive shafts, gears or other moving parts in the suspension and propulsion system. Instead, the cars are lifted and guided by a series of magnets in their undercarriage, and propelled by a long stator synchronous induction motor mounted on the guideway.

The inherent advantage of the MagLev system is that it eliminates all frictional contact between the vehicle and guideway, and therefore the wheel-to-rail interface which is the principal limiting factor in further development of high speed rail systems. The result is that this radically new type of train is able to provide downtown to downtown inter-city service along corridors up to 500 miles long in about the same time it takes to make the same trip by air, and will do so regardless of weather conditions.

While a super speed MagLev system might seem extremely expensive, it can be implemented for about the same cost as a new, advanced high speed rail system such as the Japanese Shinkansen or French TGV. Operating and maintenance costs, however, are much lower.

Transrapid 06, a second generation MagLev development, has begun three years of performance and endurance tests on a 20-mile track in Emsland, West Germany. Consisting of two 98-passenger vehicles, this prototype is currently being considered for installation on several U.S. intercity corridors — Las Vegas-Los Angeles, Milwaukee-Chicago.[1]

Each car is about 90 feet long, 12 wide and weighs approximately 105,000 lbs. Carbodies are an aluminum semi-monocoque type similar to aircraft fuselage construction. A control cab is located at one end, an inter-car passageway at the other. There is an electric equipment cabinet in the cab end bulkhead, while other equipment is housed underfloor in typical rail car fashion.

Low speed testing of the TR-06 began in 1983, following use of the TR-05 at the 1979 International Transport Exhibition in Hamburg. It is expected that test runs of 250 mph will be achieved in 1985.

While a speed of 256 mph has been demonstrated for a rail vehicle in a carefully controlled environment, most experts agree that wheel-on-rail has about reached its practical operating speed potential.[2] MagLev, on the other hand, has no wheel-to-rail contact, no metal-to-metal friction or wear. As development continues, MagLev speeds could well be increased to double or even triple those that the most advanced high speed rail system will ever be able to achieve and may well provide *average* speeds in excess of *maximum* speeds of today's fastest rail systems.

*** Photo and information furnished by The Budd Company, Troy, Michigan, manufacturers of rail cars, which holds exclusive rights to market the German MagLev in the U.S.**

[1] There are 18 other regional corridors in which high speed train or super-speed MagLev systems "could be cost effective, energy efficient and potentially profitable."

[2] According to The Budd Company.

# TRAINS OF THE FUTURE . . .

As noted, we've already seen a renaissance on rails that's resulted in today's high-speed transport. So what can be expected from the future?

For one thing, a variety of answers since developments are nationalistic. Each country has a different idea of what high-speed should be — even what constitutes a train.

In order to attain higher speeds, cars must also be redesigned, as France did with its TGVs. And that's exactly what at least two rail systems, Amtrak and German Rail, are doing — prototypes for the 1990s. Both projects emphasize roominess and wide-angled views of the countryside based on a standard body shell which can be fitted for almost any purpose, class or style.

Amtrak's, for example, will feature a variety of modules for conversion to sleeping car, diner, coach or lounge. In sleepers destined to replace current Heritage cars, a double row of windows will permit upper berth passengers to enjoy the view as they sip their morning coffee. About the same height as Heritage, the new ones will be wider and shaped differently — sides will slope out from the bottom and then back in at the top. Sleepers will have 14 two-person compartments, each with toilet and basin, plus three bedrooms with washroom, toilet and shower — and a lower berth wide enough for adult and child.

In Europe, most major rail systems are planning innovations, such as tilting cars around bends. Britain's Advanced Passenger Train (APT), which runs at 125 mph, is being redesigned as the InterCity 225: an electric, tilting train at speeds of 140 mph by 1990. Yet Norway has already put tilting trains in service (but not at such high speeds) and Sweden is developing a 125 mph tilting train for use on existing track by 1990.

German Federal Railways is developing a new generation electric model (InterCity Experimental, or ICE) for a maximum speed of 220 mph; it consists of four interior cars plus driving units at each end. Passenger cars will have:

An information and entertainment system allowing each passenger access to train information, onboard services and choice of musical programs.

New airconditioning/heating system.

Airline-style (closable) overhead luggage bins.

Adaptability to first or second class seating.

In Scandinavia, Swedish State Railways (SJ) plans a range of new, high-comfort coaches and sleepers, latter with private toilets and showers; restaurant cars will have self-serve and waiter-served areas.

Danish State Railways (DSB) plans lightweight, fast, three-car trains that operate from either end, can be moved quickly onto (and off) its inter-island ferries.

Artist's concept of Amtrak's prototype passenger cars with distinctive double rows of picture windows. A $2.7 million contract was awarded Budd Co. to construct the outer shells. Amtrak hopes to be running some of these new cars in 1985-86.

Because of current emphasis on speed, comfort and economy, 41 railroads on five continents have committed $13.3 *billion* to modernize their equipment and infrastructure. Included are some 5,000 passenger cars, 534 electric and 800 diesel locomotives, 328 self-propelled, electric trainsets and better than 41,000 freight cars.

However those, as well as the TGVs, are improvements or extensions of today's technology. What is far more exciting is the development of an experimental 250 mph magnetic levitation (Maglev) car by a German consortium. In the Far East, Japan Railways and Japan Air Lines are each developing Maglev prototypes (we've seen the elevated track on which they are tested); at the World Science Fair in Tsukba, near Tokyo, JAL is demonstrating its HSST (High Speed Surface Transport) this year. It has already been tested at 321 mph.

In the United States, feasibility studies have been started on Maglev and conventional high speed systems for Los Angeles-San Diego, Tampa-Orlando-Miami and Las Vegas-Los Angeles — latter in the super-speed category of around 250 mph. Studies are contemplated for Chicago-Milwaukee, New York-Montreal, Philadelphia-Pittsburg, Chicago-Detroit. Congressmen of Midwest states, West Virginia and Kentucky hope to pass a bill allowing them to cooperate in a joint feasibility study linking cities in those states by high speed trains.

The bottom line? Look for the train of the future to fly silently a few millimeters above the ground like a plane without wings.

# EUROPE RAIL TRAVEL

## CONTINENTAL RAIL SYSTEM

Comprised of 23 national rail lines of both Western and Eastern European countries, it's an intricate network that not only works but does so extremely well; its performance is both convenient and reliable. If politicians of those nations cooperated the way their rail officials do, there'd be instant detente.

For the tourist, this network is a bonanza for it's both inexpensive (with or without a EURAILPASS) and wide-ranging. When combined with British Rail, it enables vacationers and business travelers alike to ride the rails from the north of Scotland to the north of Scandinavia, from France to Turkey, from the Atlantic to the Pacific and the China Sea. In all, a Pandora's box of adventures limited only by the time at one's disposal.

For the most part, this train network is a commuter affair — a means of getting from one city center to another easily and quickly without the expense and time of getting to and from airports. But for those who come from afar, it's the Glamor Girls that have the track appeal: the *Train Grande Vitesse* (TGV) of France, the *Glacier Express* of Switzerland, the TEE Rapidos of Italy, the *Rheingold Express* of Germany and, especially the *Nostalgic Orient Express* to Vienna and Istanbul, the *Simplon-Orient-Express* to Venice and the *Trans-Siberian Special.*

In the following pages, we'll pinpoint not only these Great Rail Trips but also everything you need to know about train travel in Europe, Siberia, Mongolia and on into China. Read on.

## EUROPEAN TRAINS

Basically, there are intra- and inter-country rail routes. Depending on the country, domestic trains are classed as Fast (slowest), Express (fast), Rapido (fastest) or merely by number. France has the TGV, world's fastest train. Far as we know, there's no such thing as a Local regardless of how many stops a train may make.

Inter-country rail routes, a combined operation of two or more national railroads and their equipment, offer these express services:

### Trans-Europ Express (TEE)[1]

Fast, electrified, airconditioned day trains requiring first class tickets, plus special supplements that include a reserved seat for which prior reservation is normally required.

French/Belgian trains of 6 to 12 cars carry 230 to 460 passengers in compartments (usually of 6) or open car seating (usually one seat facing another on one side of the aisle, rows of two facing seats on opposite side). Meals served at seats in open saloons (cars) at extra cost; specify if desired when reserving seats.

French (SNCF) Railways also has 7- to 9-car trains for 230 to 320 passengers in compartments; meals served in 48-seat dining cars.

German Federal Railways (DB) of West Germany carry 300 to 461 passengers in 6 to 9 cars with compartments or open seating. A 42-seat dining car is attached.

Swiss Federal Railways (SBB) trains of 5 cars carry 168 in open seating — and very comfortably, too. 48-seat dining car attached.

Italian State Railways (FS) has some very luxuriously upholstered compartments as well as open seating in trains of 4 to 10 cars, 144 to 452 seats. Meals served in dining car.

On all trains with restaurant cars, reservations are solicited personally by an immaculately uniformed Head Steward.

### International Inter-City (IC)[2]

These day trains, usually airconditioned, are next to the best bets after TEE, particularly since these first *and* second class coach trains are more widely used.

Supplements are payable in both classes except in Switzerland where there are no reserved seats.

Second class compartments may have four seats abreast, open cars two seats on both sides of the center aisle.

### TGV—*Train Grande Vitesse* (High Speed Train)

With the exception of multi-daily runs between Paris-Lausanne and Paris-Geneva, *le train le plus rapide du monde* runs between Paris and the south of France.

### Trans Europ Night (TEN)[3]

Whether it be nuit, nacht or notte, at night you can "dream your way to your destination" in a sleeper. Not a bad idea considering the high cost of good hotel accommodations.

Members of the TEN pool (those initials appear on the newer cars) are Austria, Belgium, Denmark, France, West Germany, Italy, Luxembourg, Holland and Switzerland. Some cars are owned by the International Sleeping Car Company (Wagons-Lits) and leased to the pool or to the railways; prior to 1972, Wagons-Lits operated all sleeper services. Cars built since then are owned by the railroads.

[1] Some of the most celebrated: *Rheingold* from Amsterdam to Basel (also Munich during summer); *Colosseum, Vesuvio* and *Ambrosiano* from Milan to Rome and Naples; *Ile de France* and *Rubens* between Paris and Brussels; *Gottardo* from Zurich to Milan. All vice-versa, too.

[2] There are about 25 such expresses running between Holland-Germany-Austria; Germany-Switzerland; London to the French Riviera; Amsterdam-Brussels and Brussels-Paris; Paris to Cologne, Frankfurt, or Zurich; Geneva to Milan. Included are such famous name trains as *Johann Strauss* and *Prinz Eugen* between Hamburg-Vienna; *Mediolanum* from Dortmund to Munich and Milan; *Rembrandt* between Amsterdam-Frankfurt; *Mont Blanc* between Hamburg / Frankfurt and Geneva; *Merkur* from Copenhagen to Hamburg-Cologne-Karlsruhe.

[3] TENs *do not* carry restaurant cars. We found that out the hard way — from Zurich to Zagreb with Zilch (except for one chocolate bar between the two of us).

## STANDARD CONTINENTAL SLEEPING CARS

**Above:** Double Compartment. Requires first class rail ticket, double sleeper supplement.
**Below:** Single Compartment. First class rail ticket, single sleeper supplement.

**Below:** Tourist 3-berth Compartment. Second class tickets, Tourist sleeper supplement.

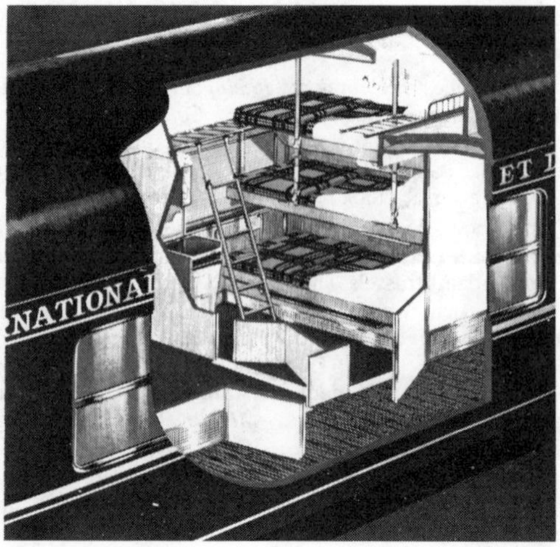


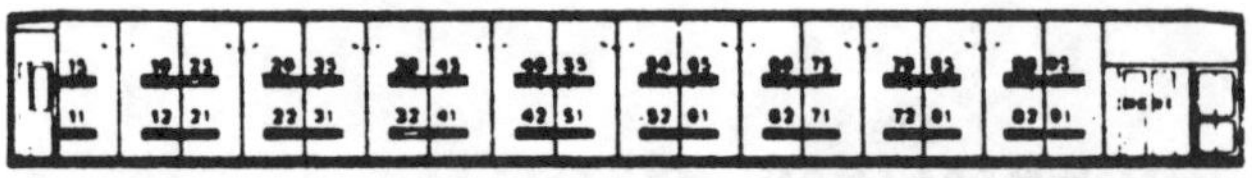

**Type T2S** — Originally built in 1974, updated versions are continuing to be produced. They have 17 compartments on one level, each of which can be used as Special (one berth) or Tourist (two berth). Has exterior door only at one end (as does T2 cars).

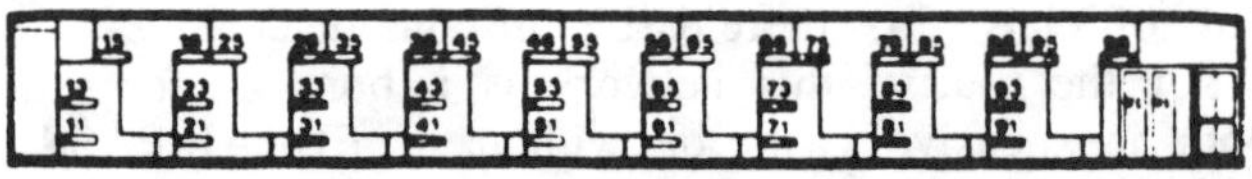

**T2** — 18 compartments arranged in pairs on two levels. Lower compartments used as first class Specials (one berth) or Tourist doubles (superimposed berths); upper compartments are also Tourist with side by side berths. Produced between 1968-1972.

**MU** — Traditional sleepers with 12 compartments, used as either first class Singles/Doubles or as second class Tourist with three berths. First manufactured between 1964-'74 (and a few still being produced), they are used extensively on most TEN and TEE trains.

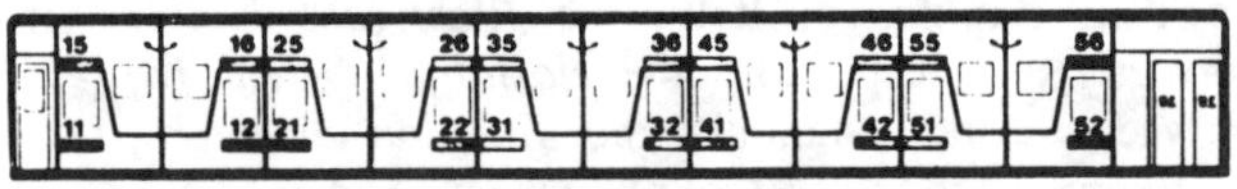

**Type P** — Wagons-Lits version of U.S. duplex roomette car — and only European sleepers with unpainted, stainless steel exteriors. Have 20 small singles on two levels, are used on domestic routes in France (second class), Italy and Spain (first class). Originally built in 1955-56, they're no longer in production — nor are any of the older types except those mentioned above.

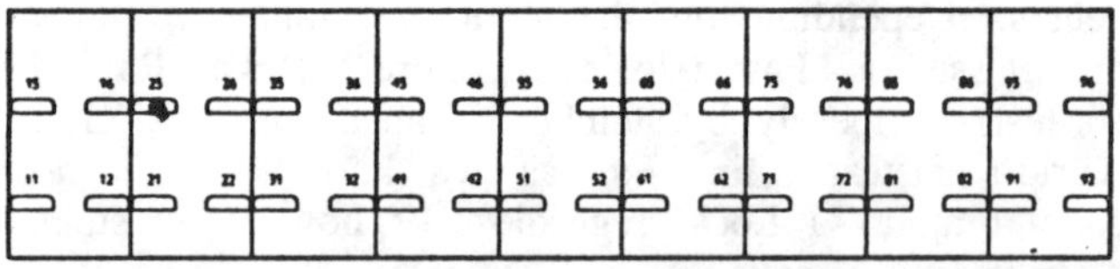

**Couchette Coach** — These airconditioned French cars have 36 couchettes in first class, 60 in second. Two public WCs and two washrooms.

**Below:** Upper double compartment of T2 car.

Wagons Lits Company, and its West German equivalent, German Sleeping & Dining Car Company (DSG) provide staffing, catering, bed linen and servicing in all TEN sleeping cars which have washing facilities and coathangers in each compartment, toilets at one or both ends of the car. An attendant, who travels with each car, has a separate compartment, often with a small kitchen; on journeys of more than overnight, he makes up the compartment for daytime travel.

First class sleeper compartments may be reserved as Singles, Doubles (two berths superimposed) or Special (small bedroom for one passenger). Second class (tourist or economy) usually have three beds (lower, middle, upper); in T2 and T2S cars, there are small two-bed compartments for which a double sleeping car supplement applies. In type TcB cars, second class compartments have four berths. Some cars have doors between bedrooms so that two rooms may be booked as a large bedroom.

In Western Europe, compartments are solely for ladies or men except where married couples or family groups occupy all berths. If you wish exclusive use of a compartment, you must have tickets and sleeping car supplements for unoccupied berths.

In Scandinavia, Portugal, Yugoslavia and other East European countries, the railway also operates the sleepers; one attendant may serve two or more cars.

Besides sleeping car accommodations, there's that European invention, the Couchette — most economical and most popular with the young. A flat fee buys for either boy or girl an open bunk with pillow and blanket — four bunks in first class, six in second class.

Everyone must reserve and pay a supplement[4] for any type of sleeping accommodation, including EURAIL PASS and YOUTHPASS holders. Reservations can be made up to two months in advance. See *Travel Supplement* for additional information.

### European Train Fare Structure

On the Continent, as well as in Great Britain, there are three basic fares: Individual (one way and round trip), Regular Groups of 10-24 or 25 and more (one way only) and Youth Groups in same two categories (also one way only). Tickets are valid for six months from date of validity, are commissionable to travel agents and are available for first or second class.

Persons 21 or more years of age are adults, those under 21 youths. Children 4-11 travel at half fare; those under four and not using a seat ride free when accompanied by an adult. When traveling with a youth group, children 4-11 pay half the youth group fare.

An unlimited number of stopovers is permitted for each ticket category. In Spain, individual travelers must have tickets endorsed before continuing to next destination.

### Circular Trips

These are defined as: a) round trips terminating at starting point but whose return route differs from outbound route; b) round trips to & from different border points (include sea and airports); c) round trips involving same railroad twice but covering different routes (over three or more railroads).

For individual passengers, circular fares are the total of half the RT fare for each segment provided that the lines of the railroads involved are used on both outbound and inbound legs. That formula is applicable for either first or second class travel.

[4] Except children under 10 who share a bed with an adult (but no more than one child per adult).

### DON'T LEAVE HOME WITHOUT IT

No, not American Express but something more valuable to rail travelers: Thomas Cook *Continental Timetable* (for Europe) and a companion volume *Overseas Timetable,* for the rest of the world. With schedules and maps for all rail and connecting ferry / bus routes, these two volumes (revised monthly and bimonthly respectively) allow you to travel anywhere on the globe with confidence that you know where you're going when. They are equally as valuable in trip planning.

Obtainable in North America from Forsyth Travel Library, P.O. Box 2975, Shawnee Mission, Ka. 66201; phone 913-384-0496. *Continental Timetable* is $15.95 (with large Europe Rail Map $21.95) plus $1 postage; phone orders subject to additional $1 charge. *Overseas Timetable* is $20.95 postpaid. MasterCard or Visa accepted.

London Sales Agency is at 45 Berkeley St., London W1A 1EB; phone 01-499-4000.

In other parts of the world, contact nearest Thomas Cook office.

Other important travel aids are *Eurail Timetable* and, especially, *Eurail Official Manual* for travel agents, individuals and groups — available from any Eurail issuing office listed in *Travel Supplement.*

The *Manual* gives ticket prices for individuals, adult and youth groups for all of Europe — plus reservation fees, supplements for TGV, TEE, IC trains and sleeping car accommodations. Also travel times. And special regulations for groups. In a word — invaluable.

Available, too, are voluminous volumes of timetables issued by each national railroad for its domestic and intercountry routes.

Please note that round trip fares (called return fare in England) may be as much as double the one way fares to 20%-30% less (depending on the country involved).

For group circle trips, add the fares for each segment. For group round trips, double the single fare.

Second class individual fares run about 25% to 33% less than first class. Adult group fares may be 20% to 35% less than individual fares. Youth group fares are but a few dollars less than adult group fares.

### Special Regulations for Groups

They must be accompanied by a responsible tour conductor and all members must travel together at all times in first and/or second class.

Free transportation and accommodation is given to one person of a group of 15-50 paying passengers; same applies to each additional 50 payees.

To reserve seats, group organizer must submit his program six weeks before departure.

For special conditions of the various rail lines, consult Eurail's *Official Manual.*

### All About European Stations

Assuming you arrive at the correct station (most major cities have two, three or more), you'll not have too much difficulty finding your way about, despite the crowds, if you pay careful attention to posted pictograms.

**Train Information** — Large printed timetables are posted in the transverse platform beyond the waiting rooms. As a rule, Departures are printed on a yellow background, Arrivals on white. Fast trains are printed in red instead of black. Next to the time, the train name and number appears together with its routing (from origin to final destination) with important in-between stops. At the end is the track/platform (*voie/quai* in French, *gleis* in German, *binario* Italian, *via* Spanish) from which the train arrives/departs. In some major stations there are computerized Arrival/Departure boards.

On track platforms, there's usually a board (*Composition Des Trains* in French) showing the configuration of major express trains (location of cars).

On the outside of each car, there's an identification panel that shows originating city at the top, final destination at the bottom and in between a few important stops enroute. If going to a stop enroute, be sure you know beforehand the train's final destination as your stop may not be listed on the panel. It's also important to realize that some cars of an express train may be switched to different destinations — so make sure you board the car listed on your ticket. Also make sure you're seated in the right class — 1st or 2nd[1] — and desired type — smoking/non-smoking (red/green seats respectively) — each clearly marked on the outside of all cars.

For hassle-free travel, arrive well before scheduled train departures. At stations from which a train starts its journey, you can usually board a half hour or more before departure.

**In The Station** — You'll find every necessary facility as you'll note from the pictograms and, in addition, such things as news, candy, ice cream and snack stands. National or City Tourist Bureaus are there to arrange local hotel reservations — but these offices are normally JAMMED, as is the Currency Exchange.[2]

Taxis are usually in front, or to the side, of the station nearest Tracks 1 and 2. Signs point the way to taxis, buses, trams.

### All About Luggage

The only disadvantage of European train travel is luggage handling, both in the stations and on the trains. For extensive rail travel, a large bag is a LARGE, and often expensive, headache. Take smaller bags *with wheels* or folding garment-hanging type. If possible, plan a circle trip that allows you to leave large luggage at city of departure (either in hotel or station), reclaim it on your return.

Another possibility is to check luggage thru to the next, or even final, destination in the baggage car — but there may not be same day service. Look for the Baggage Room (Left Luggage) sign.[3] In Switzerland, your air ticket allows you to check luggage thru Zurich or Geneva to your home destination.

In major stations, porters are available to take your bags on/off trains.[4] Luggage carts are standard equipment in all stations. However, in other than terminal stations, you must use an underpass to reach Platforms 2, 3, 4 etc., which means climbing up and down a number of stairs. That's when you wish you'd left your large bags at home (which we did on our latest trip).

Some day trains have luggage compartments in which you can place your bags. Otherwise there may be space for same in vestibules between cars, or you can slip larger pieces between forward-facing/backward facing seats. Overhead racks are for smaller pieces.

## Symbols in the stations

[1] First Class cars have a wide yellow stripe under the roof. These provide most comfortable travel as they are far less crowded (except for TGVs), *particularly during summer.*

[2] Main stations in large cities and resorts are centers for tourist information/reservations for day trips and hotels. But because they're so mobbed, especially in summer, best bet for those without advance hotel reservations is to make them thru your current hotel concierge — well worth a tip. Thanks to what amounts to an "old boys club," he always knows which is the best deluxe or first class hotel in other cities, can telephone ahead to secure a reservation for you. But if you do arrive in a city without a reservation, there are usually hotel reservation phones opposite the disembarking platforms. Else try the hotels in the immediate vicinity of the station, at least one of which will be first class, even deluxe.

[3] Best bet as key-type lockers are always filled — and very little less expensive. The manned luggage rooms charge a nominal fee per bag, and usually without time limit.

[4] Per bag charge, which varies from country to country, is posted in the station.

## All About *EURAILPASS*

It entitles holders to unlimited *first class* rail travel thru 16 European countries[1] plus many ferries, boats and buses at reduced fares (up to 50%) or even without extra cost. There are no supplements for TGV, TEE and IC trains but seat reservations, sleeping car and couchette fees are extra.

Passes may be purchased only by those residing outside Europe and North Africa; purchase must be made prior to arrival in Europe. Validity ranges from 7 and 15 days to 3 months (see *Travel Supplement* for costs, ticket-issuing offices).

*Most important: passes must be validated before you board your first train* — at train information windows (*not* regular ticket windows) in any station. At airports with rail connection to city center, passes can be validated there.

In Amsterdam, Barcelona, Brussels, Dusseldorf, Frankfurt, Paris and Zurich, the Pass entitles you to free connecting train service between airport and city center.

*EURAILPASS* is considered a good buy only if traveling by train in two or more countries for a minimum of 1,500 miles within 15 days, 2,000 miles in 21 days, 2,400 miles in a month, and 3,200 or 3,400 miles in 2 or 3 months respectively. Consider, too that you cannot possibly travel by rail every day and still see very much of the cities and towns visited — unless you travel by night, which many young and hardy travelers do.

Another consideration, when rail travel is to be confined to two countries (like France and Switzerland, as an example), is the cost of EURAILPASS versus the combined cost of passes for each country for the same number of days.

As a further assist in determining whether or not you should purchase EURAILPASS, see *Travel Supplement* for one way fares between some principal cities, as well as cost of passes for individual countries.

EURAIL YOUTHPASS, for those under 26 years of age, also provides unlimited travel to the same 16 countries but *only in second class;* supplements for TGV, TEE and IC trains cost extra, as do charges for sleeping accommodations and reservations.

*YOUTHPASS* is valid only for one or two months and must be purchased prior to arrival in Europe.

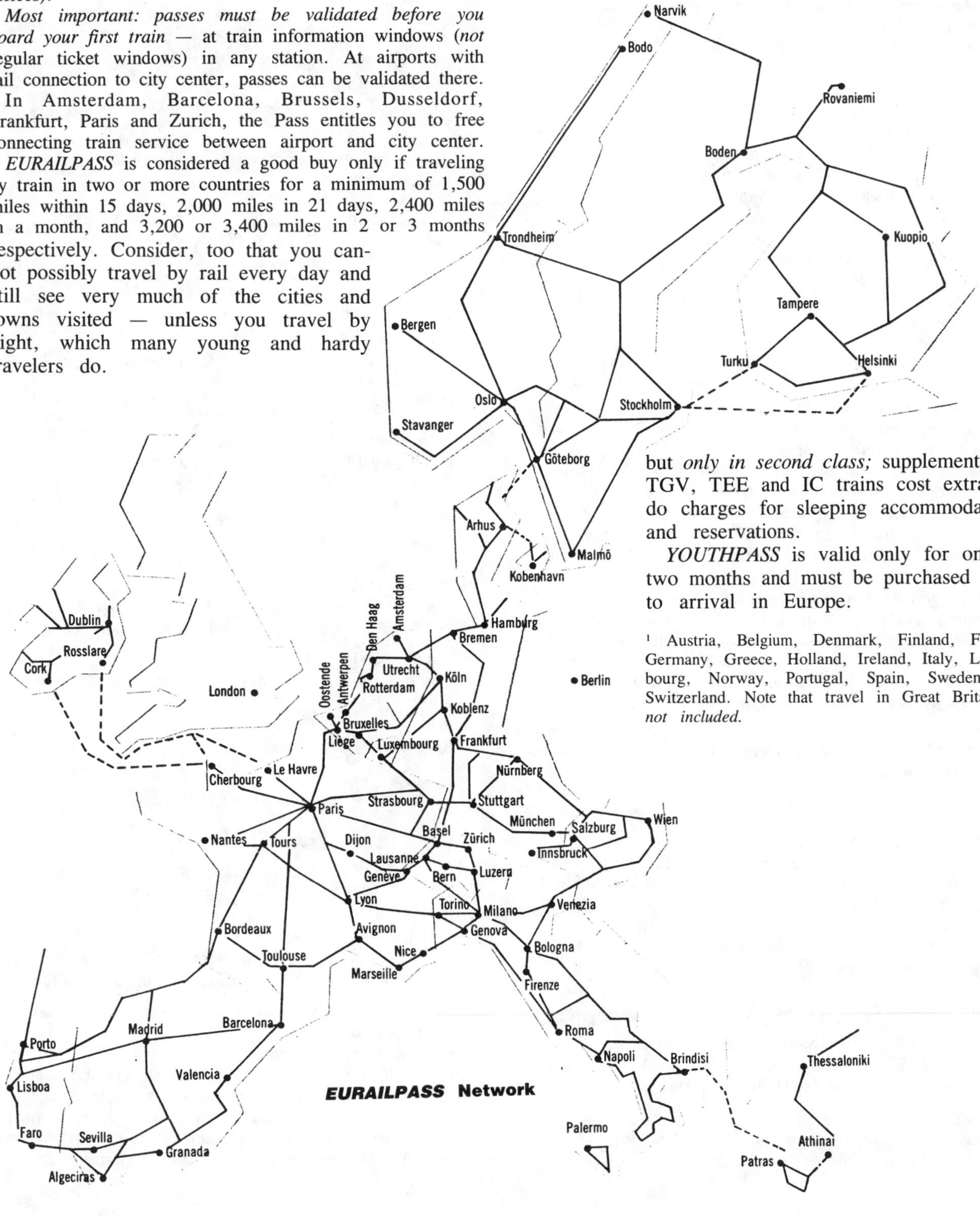

***EURAILPASS* Network**

[1] Austria, Belgium, Denmark, Finland, France, Germany, Greece, Holland, Ireland, Italy, Luxembourg, Norway, Portugal, Spain, Sweden and Switzerland. Note that travel in Great Britain *is not included.*

## GREAT RAIL TRIP ROUTINGS

Although there are many other possible combinations, here are some based on our travels:

1) From London on *Venice Simplon Orient-Express* to Venice, then one of several good express trains to Vienna to catch *Nostalgic Orient Express* to Paris.

2) Either from London or Paris, board *Rheingold Express* in Amsterdam for Basel, Bern and Brig; at latter junction, ride Glacier Express route to Zermatt; on return to Brig or, preferably Andermatt, ride south into Italy or north into France via TGV from either Geneva or Lausanne.

3) From London, cross the Channel to Ostend, then train to Brugge (don't miss stopping there) and Brussels; from there, *Alpina Express* or several day trains run to Switzerland for connections (thru Basel or Zurich) with *Glacier Express.*

4) A special favorite: London to Newcastle on *Flying Scotsman,* ship to Bergen and train to Oslo (see Norway section for other thrilling suggestions). By train or ferry to Copenhagen, then south by *Nord Express* or *Nord-West Express.*

5) Take the TGV from Paris to Avignon and French Riviera, then on to Milan to catch one of the fine TEE trains to Florence, Rome, Naples. And/or over to Venice and train north to Paris or London on *Venice Simplon Orient-Express.*

An alternative to going south from Milan or east to Venice: north to Brig, then Glacier Express route to St. Moritz and on to Innsbruck, Salzburg, Vienna, Munich, Rothenburg, Heidelberg, Frankfurt.

One of the best group rail tours is Olsen-Travelworld's *Fabulous Places and Famous Trains,* a 21-day program in June, July and August. It takes *Venice Simplon Orient-Express* from London to Paris, *TGV* to Geneva, *Glacier Express* from Zermatt to St. Moritz, *Bernina Express* to Chur and standard gauge train to Lucerne. From Zurich to Salzburg, it's *Transalpin Express.* This extensive tour winds up in Vienna.

Another good group rail tour (May, June, July & Sept.) is Osborne Travel's *Great Trains & Grand Hotels* (see *Travel Supplement*) that visits Germany, Switzerland, Italy, Monaco, France (London optional), rides *Rheingold Express, Panoramic Vista Dome, Italy's Vesuvio* and *Colosseo, Overnight Express* to Monte Carlo and TGV to Paris.

Maupintour also has some interesting, well-planned tours. See *Travel Supplement* for prices.

## GREAT DAY TRIPS

Visitors, particularly those on one-and two-week vacations, should take advantage of the easy access by rail from one central city to many of that country's most interesting destinations. Here are some suggestions, all of which can be seen unhurriedly in a day because of the frequency of rail service:

From **London** To
Bath (1 hr., 17 min. OW); Cambridge (1:46); Canterbury (2 hrs.); Oxford (1:10); Salisbury (1:45); Stratford (2:46); Winchester (1:20); Windsor (48 to 60 min.). See Great Britain section for one-day Pullman train trips.

From **Paris** To
Dijon and Lyon for superb dining (2 hrs. to each, OW); Chartres (1 hr.); Reims, Tours (each 2 hrs.); Rouen (1½ hrs.).

## FASTEST ELAPSED TIMES

**From LONDON To**

| | |
|---|---|
| Basel—14:14 | Paris—9:03[2] (via Dieppe) |
| Berlin—20:04 | Paris—5:37[1] |
| Brussels—5:34 | 6:53[2] (via Boulogne) |
| Budapest—25:25 | Paris—6:53[2] (via Calais) |
| Cologne—10:53 | Rome—15:18 |
| Copenhagen—22:29 | Warsaw—31:20 |
| Genoa—23:02 | |
| Hamburg—16:36 | |
| Milan—20:42 | |
| Moscow—51:09 | |

[1] By Hovercraft [2] By Ferry

**From PARIS To**

| | |
|---|---|
| Avignon—3:51 | Lausanne—3:30 |
| Basel—4:42 | Lisbon—12:55 |
| Berlin—15:00 | Lyon—2:00 |
| Bern—4:38 | Madrid—12:55 |
| Bordeaux—4:03 | Marseille—4:53 |
| Brig—8:20 | Milan—10:55 |
| Brussels—2:30 | Moscow—44:00 |
| Cologne—5:38 | Prague—19:41 |
| Copenhagen—16:00 | Rome—14:55 |
| Frankfurt—5:53 | Venice—15:05 |
| Geneva—3:30 | Zurich—5:58 |
| Hamburg—10:06 | |

**From AMSTERDAM To**

| | |
|---|---|
| Basel—7:43 | Frankfurt—5:26 |
| Brussels—2:33 | Milan—13:51 |
| Cologne—2:58 | Vienna—14:41 |

**From GENEVA To**

| | |
|---|---|
| Avignon—4:19 | Hamburg—11:59 |
| Barcelona—10:00 | Lausanne—0:33 |
| Basel—2:24 | Milan—4:20 |
| Brig—2:02 | |

**From MILAN To**

| | |
|---|---|
| Basel—5:28 | Naples—8:15 |
| Florence—3:03 | Nice—4:40 |
| Lyon—6:00 | Rome—5:50 |
| Marseille—7:02 | Zurich—4:01 |

**From MUNICH To**

| | |
|---|---|
| Innsbruck—1:48 | Salzburg—1:36 |
| Milan—7:12 | |

**From VIENNA To**

| | |
|---|---|
| Basel—13:42 | Munich—5:33 |
| Budapest—4:05 | Rome—15:55 |
| Frankfurt—7:57 | Salzburg—3:25 |
| Hamburg—12:12 | Venice—8:58 |
| Innsbruck—7:21 | Zurich—12:33 |
| London—23:00 | |

From **Frankfurt Airport** To
Dusseldorf (3 hrs. OW); Heidelberg and Koblenz (1½ hrs. each); Cologne (2 hrs.), Wiesbaden (1 hr.), Wurzburg (2 hrs.).

**All Over Switzerland**

There are marvelous one-day jaunts out of Zurich and Geneva — in fact, much of Switzerland can be seen in a series of four or five day trips. We were in Andermatt on a morning when the town was socked in by a misty rain — so we hopped a southbound train to Lugano and spent a delightful day in the sun, were back in Andermatt for dinner.

**SOME SUGGESTED LONG DISTANCE ROUTINGS*** **(by TEE or International Inter-City Trains)**

*** In kilometers. To convert to miles, multiply by 0.621. Charts show overall distance and city to city distances.**

**LONDON To ROME — Via Ostend — 1959 km**

London 354 Brussels 252 Luxembourg 332 Basel 372 Milan 150 Genoa 499 Rome

Basel 88 Zurich 118 Chur 125 St. Moritz 42 Innsbruck

**LONDON To ROME — Via Hook of Holland / St. Gotthard Pass — 2123 km**

London 588 Cologne 254 Mannheim 277 Basel 295 Lugano 77 Milan 632 Rome

Cologne–Basel 106 Bern 59 Interlaken 88 Brig 88 Zurich 104 Landquart 50 Davos

**LONDON To ROME (1933 km) & Athens (2879 km) Via Simplon Pass**

London 480 Paris 315 Dijon 203 Lausanne 313 Milan 219 Bologna 413 Rome

Milan 267 Venice 157 Trieste

Bologna 1359 Athens

**LONDON To GENOA — 1752 km**

London 480 Paris 617 Valence 125 Avignon 99 Marseille 225 Nice 184 Genoa

**LONDON To VIENNA (1842 km) Via BASEL**

London 166 Calais 591 Strasbourg 140 Basel 373 Innsbruck 326 Salzburg 246 Vienna

**LONDON To BUDAPEST — Via Ostend — 1843 km**

London 354 Brussels 229 Cologne 333 Frankfurt 238 Nurnberg 516 Vienna 273 Budapest

**LONDON To VIENNA (1622 km) Via Calais & Munich (1223 km)**

London 757 Strasbourg 224 Stuttgart 242 Munich 153 Salzburg 246 Vienna

**LONDON To VIENNA — Via Hook of Holland — 1577 km**

London 588 Cologne 177 Mainz 38 Frankfurt 339 Regensburg 415 Vienna

Mainz 87 Heidelberg 112 Stuttgart 242 Munich

## LONG DISTANCE ROUTING (Continued)

### LONDON To MADRID (1929 km) & Lisbon (2375 km)

London 471 Paris 581 Bordeaux 237 Irun 268 Burgos 372 Madrid

Burgos 818 Lisbon

### LONDON To ISTANBUL — 3360 km

London 310 Hook of Holland 267 Cologne 625 Munich 153 Salzburg 518 Zagreb 416 Belgrade 1071 Istanbul

Belgrade 1277 Athens

### LONDON To WARSAW — 2147 km

London 463 Paris 605 Frankfurt 475 Leipzig 120 Dresdon 584 Warsaw

Frankfurt 573 Berlin

### LONDON To MOSCOW — Via Ostend — 3142 km

London 354 Brussels 905 Berlin 569 Warsaw 1314 Moscow

### LONDON To COPENHAGEN — Via Hook of Holland — 1245 km

London 310 Hook 325 Osnabruck 238 Hamburg 372 Copenhagen

Osnabruck 133 Hannover 306 Berlin 568 Warsaw 1314 Moscow

### LONDON To COPENHAGEN — 1440 km (1365 km from Paris)

London 239 Ostend 115 Brussels 229 Cologne 485 Hamburg 372 Copenhagen

Copenhagen 644 Oslo

Copenhagen 641 Stockholm

### COPENHAGEN To ROME Via St. Gotthard Pass — 2473 km

Copenhagen 372 Hamburg 712 Frankfurt 385 Basel 372 Milan 219 Bologna 97 Florence 316 Rome

### COPENHAGEN To ROME Via Brenner Pass — 2153 km

Copenhagen 372 Hamburg 808 Munich 172 Innsbruck 274 Verona 114 Bologna 413 Rome

Verona 148 Milan

Verona 119 Venice

### COPENHAGEN To VIENNA — (1541 km) & Belgrade (2267 km)

Copenhagen 372 Hamburg 551 Wurzburg 102 Nurnberg 225 Linz 190 Vienna

Wurzburg 257 Munich 153 Salzburg 518 Zagreb 416 Belgrade

### VIENNA To MARSEILLE — 1455 km

Vienna 477 Trieste 53 Venice 267 Milan 149 Genoa 184 Nice 220 Marseille

Venice 589 Rome

## INTERNATIONAL EXPRESSES TO EASTERN EUROPE

From London, there are two routes to Berlin, Warsaw and Moscow: via Ostend *(Ost-West Express)* or Hook of Holland with USSR sleepers.

From Paris, there's a coach train to Prague (called *Zapadni Express* there), a *Simplon Express* to Zagreb and Belgrade and previously mentioned *Orient Express* to Budapest and Bucharest.

*Weiner Walzer* (love that name), Basel to Bucharest, has sleepers only to Vienna, Hungarian dining car from Salzburg to Budapest.

*Chopin* is alive and running — from Vienna to Warsaw (all year) and Moscow (April to December) with first and second class sleepers, coaches. Leaves Vienna at 2220, arrives Warsaw 1140, Moscow 1022 on second day.

From Bern and Basel, there's service to Moscow by way of Frankfurt, West and East Berlin and Warsaw with USSR sleeping cars over the entire route on Tuesdays/ Saturdays (Wed, Sat on return). Leaves Bern at 1545, arrives Moscow 1503 second day.

There's thru service from Hamburg-Vienna to Belgrade; also Venice to Belgrade *(Venezia Express),* the one we took; don't make the same mistake.

Osborne Travel (see *Travel Supplement*) has, as far as we know, the only group (20-25 persons) rail tour of Eastern Europe — a 16-day program visiting West and East Berlin, East Germany, Czechoslovakia, Budapest and Vienna; includes a ride on the *Balt-Orient Express* from Prague to Bratislava. Good way to go as individual travel behind the Curtain is not too inviting.

## CHARTER RAIL TRAVEL

In recent years, national railroads in western Europe have made a strong pitch for convention, business meeting and incentive travel groups with special equipment designed to meet the needs of group planners. By booking whatever cars meet their specific requirements, groups achieve total independence, either on regularly scheduled trains or, if large enough, on a special train of their own.

Although details and equipment differ somewhat country to country, basically they follow similar lines. See **France** for types of cars available for charter.

There are no standard rates; each charter is developed on the basis of numbers of people, cars and types, destinations (whether domestic and/or inter-country), length of the charter and such. Allow plenty of time for advance planning and scheduling.

In addition to the equipment of national and private railroads, *Nostalgic Orient Express* cars are available thru Intraflug.

### Car-Sleeper Trains

Called Trans-Autos-Couchettes (France), Auto-Expreso (Spain), Autoreisezuge (Germany) and Motorail (Britain), by whatever name they're a great way to ride the rails and have your own, or rental, car with you thruout the Continent and across the Channel to England, Scotland and Ireland.

Car sleeper trains are made up of special wagons or vans for the cars, sleepers and/or couchettes for driver and passengers. Continental breakfast is served on these overnight trains except in Britain where Motorail provides coffee/biscuits.

Car-Sleeper Trains from Calais and Boulogne run in connection with cross-Channel ferries.

Consult Thomas Cook *Continental Timetable* for routings and train schedules.

Additionally, cars can be shipped by freight train while passengers travel by regular trains.

One of Europe's crack Trans-Europe Expresses, *Gottardo,* shown here at Fluelen on Lake Lucerne, traverses the highly scenic Zurich to Milan route.

South Eastern Railway_London-Chatam-Dover Railway
CHEMINS DE FER DU NORD & DE L'EST DE FRANCE
LONDRES·PARIS·CONSTANTINOPLE
Départ tous les Jours
De LONDRES & de PARIS pour VIENNE
Les Mercredis
Pour CONSTANTINOPLE
Le Jeudi & le Dimanche
Pour BUKAREST
SERVICE RAPIDE
Sans Changement de Voitures
ET
SANS PASSEPORT
ENTRE
FAST TRAVELLING
Without any Change of Carriages
ET
WITHOUT PASSPORT
BETWEEN
The Trains are Starting
From LONDON & PARIS Every Day For VIENNA
Only on Wednesday
For CONSTANTINOPLE
On Thursdays & Sundays
For BUKAREST
PARIS·MUNICH·VIENNE·BUDAPEST·BELGRADE & CONSTANTINOPLE
& ENTRE
& BETWEEN
PARIS & BUKAREST
ORIENT EXPRESS
LONDRES
LA MANCHE
PARIS
STUTTGARD
MUNICH
VIENNE
BUDAPEST
BELGRADE
BUKAREST
MER NOIRE
CONSTANTINOPLE
SALONIQUE
HIVER 1888-89
WINTER 1888-89
LONDRES-PARIS-VIENNE
Tous les JOURS
PARIS (Gare de l'Est) ..... 7 h 30
MUNICH ..... 1 h 38
VIENNE ..... 10 h 15
Every Day
PARIS-CONSTANTINOPLE
PARIS (Gare de l'Est) ..... 7 h 30
VIENNE ..... 10 h 15
BUDAPEST ..... 5 h 25
BELGRADE ..... 32
CONSTANTINOPLE ..... 6 h 40
PARIS-BUKAREST
PARIS ..... 7 h 30
VIENNE ..... 10 h 15
BUDAPEST ..... 4 h 00
BUKAREST ..... 50
Saturday and Tuesday
Chéret

Without doubt, the world's most glamorous, heralded trains were — and, fortunately, still are — the famed Orient Express or, more precisely, Orient *Expresses* for there were more than one. And thereby hangs a tale.

In the late 1860s, young Georges Nagelmackers (1845-1905), son of an influential Belgian banker, visited America. He was never again quite the same for there he saw the potential for comfortable long distance rail travel, made possible by the patented sleeping cars known as Pullmans.[1] Nagelmackers returned home with a vision: to join the various European rail networks with their disparate tracks and thus form a continuous line across Europe to the gateway of the Near East, Constantinople — or, as the flamboyant Nagelmackers mistakenly but inspiredly called it, the Orient.

After many setbacks but aided by his father's connections and the enthusiastic patronage and influence of King Leopold of Belgium, after traveling all over Europe to cajole and, eventually, finalize operational contracts with state-owned rail systems, his Compagnie Internationale des Wagons-Lits et des Grands Express Europeens inaugurated the first Train d'Orient on June 5, 1883 — an 1800-mile journey (at speeds of up to 60 mph) from Paris to Constantinople (Istanbul) with brief stops in Strasbourg, Stuttgart, Munich and Budapest. At Bucharest, passengers were ferrired across the Danube; in southern Bulgaria horse-drawn carriages had to be used and at Varna on the Black Sea an Austrian Lloyd steamer brought the passengers to Constantinople. But by 1889, tracks were laid all the way to the European side of Constantinople, enabling a newer, longer Orient Express to inaugurate a run from London and Paris by way of Munich, Vienna, Budapest, Belgrade, Bucharest and Sofia entirely by rail — the first train ever to cross a continent uninterruptedly.[2]

Thus it was that the flamboyant Nagelmackers, the P.T. Barnum of railways, set the stage for a new and glittering era. It was he who filled his first Train d'Orient[3] with members of the nobility and high society, leading pundits and journalists who were greeted at every stop by bands, dignitaries and royalty, who were attended with loving care and served the finest of food and wines. And so began the *Belle Epoque* of the Great European Express Trains when everybody who was anybody trained to the capital cities, the leading spas and resorts of the continent where they were met, at first, by coach and four, in later years by chauffeurs in a Delahaye, Bugatti or Daimler and taken to luxury hotels like the Adlon in Berlin, Ritz in Paris, Negresco in Nice.[4] Too, it was an era in which the most beautiful railway cars of all time were built in England and on the continent.

Once started, railroading in the grand manner snowballed. In 1894, the Ostende-Wien-Express (later known as Ostende-Wien-Oriental Express) was inaugurated; the Simplon-Express followed in 1906, then became the Simplon-Orient-Express in 1919 when routed to Constantinople via Athens. In 1924 the Suisse-Arlberg-Vienne-Express (later changed to Arlberg-Orient-Express) was introduced. All were run by the Wagons-Lits company using the tracks and locomotives of the various state-owned railways. There were, of course, other legendary trains of this *Belle Epoque:* Cote d'Azur Pullman Express as well as the Blue Train (Train Bleu) from Paris to the Mediterranean coast of France; Pyrenees-Cote d'Azur Express; Fleche d'Or (Golden Arrow) between Paris and London; Nord Express, Sud Express and other famed names, a few of which are retained to this day though any resemblance to old time luxury is not only remote but lacking.

Except for two: the Orient Express, now known as Nostalgic Istanbul Orient Express, and the Venice Simplon Orient-Express.

The *Belle Epoque* ended with the outbreak of World War II, and though service was resumed on the Arlberg-Orient-Express, Simplon-Orient-Express and *the* Orient Express in 1945 and 1946, the luxury aspects were never the same; instead, they became ordinary international express trains. In 1977, direct sleeping car service between Paris and Istanbul ended on a regularly scheduled basis. A daily Orient Express still runs between Paris, Munich, Vienna, Budapest and Bucharest with first and second class sleeping cars/coaches — only the name is the same.[5] A much paler version, Istanbul Express, runs between Munich, Belgrade, Sofia and Istanbul.[6]

One other train in the current Orient Express family is an East European version: *Balt-Orient Express,* a favorite of business travelers. The complete run of this heavy and well-patronized train, with its red sleeping cars and diners (often one of the latter in front, another to the rear), is from East Berlin to Leipzig, Dresden, Prague, Brno, Bratislava, Budapest, Belgrade and, finally, Bucharest. Departing at midnight, it arrives in Bucharest at 1234 the second day. There are first/second class sleepers and coaches; diners are attached between Prague and Budapest, then a bar car to Bucharest. The return journey leaves Bucharest at 2130.

On the same route, *Pannonia Express* leaves East Berlin at 1102, arrives in Bucharest at 2101 the second night, continues for an 0841 arrival in Sofia. But first class sleepers go only to Budapest from Berlin, or from Prague to Sofia.

[1] Although there were a few rather elementary sleeping cars in service before the Civil War, it was George Mortimer Pullman (1831-1897) who in 1863 built the *Pioneer,* the first of what soon became known as Pullmans. It was he who patented the folding upper berth, the extendable seat cushions for the lower. In 1867, he founded the Pullman Palace Car Company to build sleeping cars for lease to the railroad companies. Pullman also developed a dining car and vestibule car. At Nagelmackers insistance, a Pullman Company was started in England in 1879 to build cars for European service.

[2] With admirable clarity, Nagelmackers advertised his Orient Express as "Fast Travelling Without Any Change of Carriages and Without Passport."

[3] Two sleeping cars, a dining car and two baggage cars formed the first Orient Express. But as the route became established, more cars were added to accommodate an ever-growing passenger list of such distinguished names as Emperor Franz Joseph, King Leopold II and the Maharaja of Rana; Ferdinand and Boris, Kings

## NOSTALGIC

## ISTANBUL

## ORIENT EXPRESS

*The elegance of* Nostalgic Orient Express *is apparent from the moment you're greeted warmly by a smartly liveried attendant.*

*It is further evidenced by the lovely inlaid wood paneling and smart accessories of your compartment — and last, but far from least, the lavish gourmet hors d'oeuvres and meals.*

of Bulgaria; Menelik II and Haile Selassie, Emperors of Ethiopia; King Carol of Romania and his live-in girl friend, Magda Lupescu; Edward, Prince of Wales and, later, his wife, the Duchess of Windsor; also his brother the Duke of York who became King George VI, father of England's current Queen Elizabeth II. A regular (and infamous) passenger was the mysterious Sir Basil Zaharoff, so-called Merchant of Death because of his armament dealings during World War I from which he amassed millions of British pounds. A romantic story concerning his encounter with a young Spanish duchess on the Orient Express is told in the Venice Simplon Orient-Express brochure.

[4] After developing the Great European Express trains, Nagelmackers built luxury hotels in Paris, Lisbon, Monte Carlo, Constantinople and even Beijing to receive his guests — the first concept of a worldwide hotel chain.

[5] One of the longest trains in operation, it has TEN first and second class sleepers (on Mon, Wed, Fri and Sat from Paris to Bucharest; on Tues, Thurs and Sun to Vienna), a Hungarian dining car between Vienna and Budapest. The route is via Strasbourg, Karlsruhe, Stuttgart, Munich and Salzburg. From London, a better bet is to cross the Channel to board the *Ostend-Vienna Express,* a fast and efficient train, reputed to be better than the train from Paris, that arrives in Vienna at 0900 of the second day; *Orient Express* leaves there at 1624 for the ride to Budapest and following day arrival in Bucharest at 1311. There are no sleepers between VIenna-Bucharest.

[6] Runs Sept. 30 to June 1 from Dortmund (October 2-June 1 from Istanbul) thru Munich, Salzburg, Zagreb with first and second class coaches, no diner. Takes two days plus to complete its tortuous run. At Belgrade it splits with some cars becoming the *Hellas-Istanbul Express* bound for Thessaloniki and Athens plus some Yugoslav first and second class sleeping cars which *we do not recommend.* Not having been warned to the contrary, we once took a Yugoslavian first class (so-called) sleeper from Zurich to Zagreb, found maintenance poor, windows so dirty we couldn't see out, no English spoken.

Owned by a Swiss concern, Intraflug Ltd. (and chartered to tour operators), this train represents the most varied collection of *Belle Epoque* railway cars in service today. Included are such celebrities as:

Pullman cars that ran on the great prestige expresses of *Cote d' Azur, Fleche d'Or, Mistral, Gotthard Pullman* and *Sud Express.* Each car seats 28 passengers in comfortable lounge chairs.

*Voiture Presidentielle* No. 3354 (built in 1927). Newly furnished in 1955, it served on every official train for French Presidents Coty, De Gaulle and Pompidou. Many crowned and uncrowned dignitaries were guests aboard this car until acquired by Intraflug in 1976. Both parlours are lined with precious woods and silk drapes. The long state table, seating 18, was used in dining cars of French presidents since 1894. A smaller parlour seats another 12 persons. The original kitchen, with coal-fired stove, dates back to 1927.

Dining car *Sud Express,* built in 1926, was converted from parlour car to diner in 1953, then ran between Irun-Madrid-Lisbon until 1977 when bought by Intraflug at a Monte Carlo art auction. Overhauled and repainted in original colors, it retains its original interior and capacity for 48 persons at tables of four.

There's a bar car (with pianist) from former *Train Bleu,* a shower car (with seven compartments and bath attendant) converted from a *Fleche d'Or* Pullman car.

Finally, and very importantly, there are imposing *Grand Luxe Lx 16, Lx 20* sleeping cars built in 1929 that, because of their lavishness, became a legend in their time — and still are. Most of those in service on the Istanbul Express have a total of 16 beds (four single compartments, six doubles); others have 10 double compartments. Each compartment has a built-in wash basin.

At full capacity (100 passengers), the Nostalgic Istanbul Orient Express consists of nine sleeping cars, two pullmans, dining and bar cars, kitchen and shower cars. There are 33 persons in attendance: a supervisor, two chefs, cook and two kitchen assistants, headwaiter and six waiters and barman make up the Brigade Presidentielle. The train crew has a staff head, travel guide, governess, eight sleeping car porters, shower car steward, doctor, piano player (please not to shoot him), engineer, mechanic and three cleaning hands. Additionally, charter operators have their own staff.

The renaissance of this Orient Express began in 1976 with two trial runs from Milan and Zurich to Istanbul — the first true luxury trains to Istanbul for many years. In 1978, this new train ran from Zurich to Athens; in 1981, Paris to Istanbul via Milan, Trieste and Belgrade — and the next year via Munich, Vienna, Budapest and Bucharest. In 1983, a Jubilee train, *Le Centenaire,* celebrated Nagelmackers' 100th anniversary by retracing the original run (but eliminating the horse-drawn carriages).

## Society Expeditions' Oriental Express

Major operator of Nostalgic Istanbul Orient Express tours from North America is Society Expeditions, an excellent American tour operator with whom we have traveled extensively and who we recommend highly.

Two programs are being offered: Paris to Istanbul and Paris-Vienna.

The Paris to Istanbul 10-day extravaganzas are, to our knowledge, the most lavish ever offered over this route since the days of Nagelmackers. Utilizing the Oriental Express for five days and four nights, the program includes two days in Paris (Trianon Palace Hotel in Versaille), two nights at the Istanbul Hilton (a beautiful hotel and our favorite there), sightseeing in Paris, Reims, Salzburg, Vienna (plus dinner dance in a Viennese palace), Budapest, Brasov, Bucharest and an exhibition of horseback riding in southern Hungary (which we've enjoyed). There's an optional (and excellent) Turkey Archeological Expedition (10 days) that visits Pergamum, Ephesus, Aphrodisias, Kony, lunar-like Cappadocia Valley and Ankara.

The 7-day programs — Paris, Strasbourg, Vienna eastbound; Vienna, Salzburg, Heidelberg to Paris westbound — are equally as elegant. They provide two days and nights in both Paris and Vienna, one night aboard the Orient Express and sightseeing in Strasbourg (eastbound), Salzburg and Heidelberg (westbound).

Additionally, there's a 7-day round trip: Paris, Strasbourg, Vienna, Salzburg, Heidelberg, Paris. There are three nights in Paris, two nights on the train and sightseeing in all cities.

For departure dates and tariffs, see *Travel Supplement*.

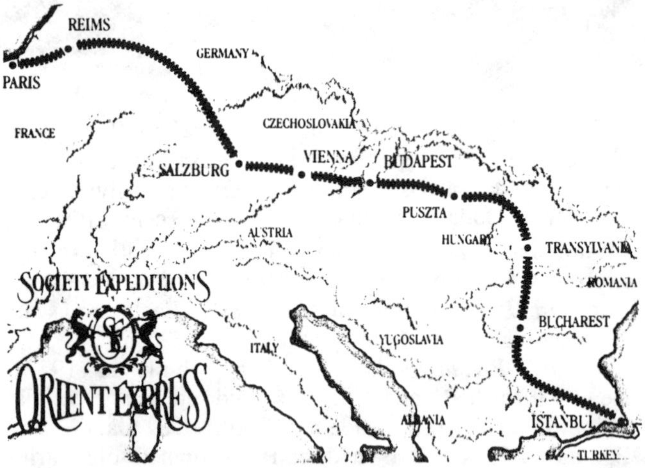


## The Istanbul Train

Operated by Voyages Jules Verne, and not to be confused with previously mentioned Orient Expresses, the Istanbul Train starts from London and closely follows the original 1883 route, including crossing the Black Sea by ship from Varna thru the Bosphorus to Istanbul — a 15-day program that includes two days in Paris, Vienna, Budapest, Bucharest and Istanbul, half-day in Salzburg, two nights in Sinaia, a Bulgarian resort where King Carol received the first Orient Express passengers and overnight on the Istanbul-bound ship. Thus, with the exception of one night, train travel is during the day.

There are single departures in April, May, July and September. Two vintage Pullman cars, for exclusive use by tour passengers, are attached to regularly scheduled trains.

**"I've got another memory I'll never lose . . ."**

**Irvin Farman, veteran newsman and Managing Editor, *Fort Worth Star Telegram,* reports on what it's like to ride back into time on the Nostalgic Orient Express.**

ISTANBUL—The scene in the bar car is something out of Agatha Christie.

The men in dinner jackets, the ladies in long dresses, the conversation multi-lingual. The Grand Marnier, Courvoisier and Dom Perignon are flowing. And, from the upright piano, as if coming straight out of Rick's in Algiers, Otto plays the sentimental tunes from the Forties and Fifties.

A guy with a whisky baritone is harmonizing with a blonde in a white sequin gown . . . "Come to me, my melancholy baby . . . cuddle up and don't feel blue . . ."

The car, furnished with plush red leather armchairs, deep pile carpeting, mahogany paneling, sways gently from time to time. But no one notices.

It's midnight on the Orient Express.

Outside the Balkan landscape, bathed in pale moonlight, rushes by as the fabled King of Trains thunders through the Yugoslavian night.

Perhaps it doesn't make sense to ride a train for three days between Zurich and Istanbul, when you can fly it in two-and-a-half hours. But, fortunately, for the romantics left in the world, the nostalgia business seems to be on the upswing, perhaps as a backlash against the encroachments of fast food emporiums and Preparation H television commercials.

Some 16 hours earlier, the train had departed Track No. 13 in Zurich, Switzerland, 16 cars carrying 80 passengers, Europeans, Japanese, Americans and a group of 12 Texans from Fort Worth.

The old Gothic railroad station seemed ablaze with nostalgia. The departure announcement over the public address system in three languages — German, French and English — added a flow of romance:

"Departing on Track No. 13 the Nostalgic Orient Express for Innsbruck, Belgrade, Sofia and Constantinople . . ."

This was the train of James Bond and the Prince of Wales, King Carol of Romania and Magda Lupescu, of diplomats and couriers, and slinky ladies looking like Marlene Dietrich.

The Orient Express!

The very words drip romance, intrique, and spies coming in from the cold, Mata Haris reclining in plush compartments.

Even the words emblazoned on the outside of the sleek cars added to the mystique: "Compagnie Internationale de Wagon Lits and Des Grandes Express Europeens."

Track 13 is filled with people and anticipation. Some are there to see friends off, some are there merely to watch a bit of history being rerun. For them, I feel a pang of regret, remembering vividly a bittersweet moment from the past when I stood on a dock in New York and watched the Queen Mary cast off on her final voyage, wishing I were one of the fortunates waving back at those of us left behind.

For those of us waiting to board the Orient Express in Zurich this morning, there are only happy thoughts and scenes to delight the eye . . . uniformed porters waiting to load great piles of luggage . . . A grand chef de train with a gigantic handlebar mustache and long silver chain dangling at his side, leather pouch, rakish cap . . . An attendant in full formal morning attire suddenly sitting down at a calliope and pumping out a series of gay tunes . . .

A shrill whistle pierces through the sounds of the station, then you hear the train, steel wheels rolling over steel track, and there she is . . . 15 cars emblazoned with the words that evoke the images that have caused romantics from at least three continents to make the journey to Zurich to ride a train for two nights and three days in an age of jet transportation . . .

We board our sleeping car, then wave from the open windows along the carpeted mahogany-paneled corridor outside our compartments. People on the receding platform wave back, and one of them calls out: "The butler did it."

There will be no murders, however, on this run of the Orient Express . . . Only memorable hours of drinking in the passing landscape, harmonizing at the piano in the bar car, enjoying gourmet meals, experiencing the excitement of living a Great Adventure.

The dining cars feature Lalique inlays done by Renee Lalique back in the 1920s, plush wing easy chairs, oversized, each with a monogrammed linen headrest cover. The arms are freshly covered with linen damask at each sitting. There are fresh flowers on the linen tablecloths.

The meals are black tie affairs served by candlelight, with seven courses, a selection of wines, and consume at least two and-a-half hours.

How many people carry a tuxedo in their luggage on

trips abroad nowadays? But, as someone points out, how many capitalists get an opportunity to eat a black tie dinner while rolling through Yugoslavia and Bulgaria?

The sleeping cars feature mahogany-paneled, carpeted corridors, with clusters of red roses near each entrance. The compartment doors are also mahogany, as are the walls of the compartment itself. The room is carpeted and has a small table with a white linen coverlet and a purple orchid in a white vase. The comfortable seat converts into a bed at night for a single occupant or an upper and lower berth for double occupants. You turn a handle in the wall and a door opens onto a small lavatory with a bottle of fresh water, a glass, soap and a disposable razor. There is no outlet for an electric razor, but you've already been warned about that.

The Swiss countryside is spectacular . . . Mountains, jagged, snow-capped peaks, lush hills and valleys, picturesque farm houses, roaring rivers, broad lakes . . . We are served coffee and croissants in the dining car, and wine and hors d'oeuvres in the bar car, while Otto plays the old songs that remind you of Humphrey Bogart types in trench coats and slinky ladies like Marlene Dietrich . . .

We stop for a passport check at the Austrian border by efficient-looking men in gray military uniforms wearing hats like the doorman at the St. Moritz in New York.

We have lunch in six courses topped off with a glass of Grand Marnier (there was wine with each course) while the magnificence of the Austrian Alps slides past the windows of the dining car . . . Mountain grandeur . . . chalets . . . even a castle built into the mountainside . . . This is the storied Austrian Tyrol . . . Coming up is Innsbruck, site of a past Winter Olympics.

The train stops in Innsbruck for about an hour, giving us time for a short stroll through the picturesque city . . . It seems as if every other shop sells ski equipment . . . The weather is clear and brisk and the first snows are not too far away, but the mountains towering over Innsbruck are already covered with white.

Leaving Innsbruck, we head for Kitzbuhel, the famed ski resort . . . The scenery continues spectacular . . . This may be Austria but it still seems picture postcard Switzerland . . . Quaint towns, each with a white church and a red steeple . . . Huge pine forests flashing by . . . cows graze close to the railroad tracks and you can hear the tinkling of the bells around their necks . . . Dusk is now falling fast in the mountains and the trees are absolutely lovely with colors ranging from deep green to all shades of brown, yellow and rust . . . You see pastoral scenes interspersed with stirring glimpses of soaring white-clad peaks cutting into the horizon . . . Night falls on the Tyrol and you head for the bar car.

We dine by candlelight in black tie and elegant dresses as the Orient Express thunders through the Tauern Tunnel towards the Yugoslavian frontier and Ljubljana-Belgrade . . . The seven course dinner begins at 8 and ends at 11:15 . . . We cross into Yugoslavia in-between courses.

I awake around 6:30 and raise the window blind in my compartment. The train is passing through a town called Vincovic and I'm struck by the change in appearance of the people . . . Slavic faces, drab clothes, women all wearing babushkas, white stockings and shapeless black dresses . . . The houses are rundown and need paint . . . This is a vast agricultural area . . . Yugoslavia seems like a giant field of maize, mile after mile of it, the land flat as West Texas, few trees . . . We've left "The Sound of Music" and entered "March Slav."

After breakfast, we arrive late in Belgrade, so there will be no city tour as scheduled . . . Just enough time for a stroll through the station and a few streets outside . . . Belgrade seems drab and depressing.

After lunch, however, Yugoslavia begins to look a lot better . . . Mountains, streams, more prosperous-appearing farms and villages . . . These must be the mountains that Tito and the partisans fought in and hid from the Germans . . . We take on an old-fashioned steam locomotive for this part of the run . . . The sounds are romantic, the steam whistle nostalgic, but the air is blackened by smoke and there is the smell of burning coal coming through the closed windows.

Sights to remember: Teams of oxen pulling carts filled with maize . . . Vineyards growing up to the train tracks . . . Three old men squatting and smoking, holding their cigarettes European-style, looking like a page out of the National Geographic . . .

We near the Bulgarian border and are warned by the train staff not to take photographs of the frontier or the train station . . . It is also suggested that we not try to take pictures while touring Sofia . . . The train slips by a farm family going home after a day's labor in the fields, leading an old, tired horse pulling a wagon.

We cross into Bulgaria during dinner . . . Another passport and visa check (you need a visa to enter the country) . . . And while waiting for dessert and coffee, we roll into Sofia . . . A band is playing in the station and there are folk dancers in native costumes . . . Bulgaria has decided it wants more tourist dollars, so the red carpet is rolled out for us . . . We board buses for a tour of the city.

Sofia is very impressive by night, expecially the government buildings and the new cultural palace brilliantly illuminated . . . There are wide boulevards, the widest named for Karl Marx . . . The parts of Sofia we see are very modern, except for the old churches and mosques . . . But somehow I doubt if it will ever replace Paris or Rome as a tourist attraction for Americans . . . We have a post-midnight dessert and coffee and after dinner drinks in the bar car, as the train continues its journey south.

I awake to a bright Sunday morning in Bulgaria . . . And then, suddenly, we are in Turkey and another passport check . . . At Edirne, we are greeted by a 3-man band in native garb, two trumpets and a drummer, and board buses for a visit to a famous mosque . . . Turkey is 99 percent Moslem.

From Edirne, the rest of the trip to Istanbul is very captivating . . . People bathing in the Sea of Marmara . . . fields of swaying tobacco, shepherds, black buffalo, blue-domed churches and minarets . . . Abject poverty . . . A family living in a lean-to on the edge of a stream . . . Affluence in the form of expensive high-rise apartments by the sea . . . Then we're in Istanbul, where the East meets the West, the gateway to the Orient . . . People wave at us from crowded tenements . . . Cars crowd the narrow, winding streets and broad thoroughfares.

We are greeted at the railroad depot by bands, native dancers, sword dancers, signs welcoming us . . . The operators of the Orient Express know how to put on a show . . . We walk like conquering heros through crowds of applauding people to the buses that will take us to the Istanbul Hilton Hotel overlooking the Bosphorus.

From my hotel room, I look out over the Bosphorus . . . Asia lies just across the expanse of water . . . and The Great Adventure has come to a glowing end in a gorgeous Turkish sunset.

Perhaps there is no longer room for anachronisms like the Orient Express, nor the 20th Century Limited and Super-Chief which once carried the kings and queens of celluloid between Broadway and Hollywood . . . yet I've got another memory I'll never lose.

## VENICE TO LONDON ON THE *ORIENT EXPRESS*

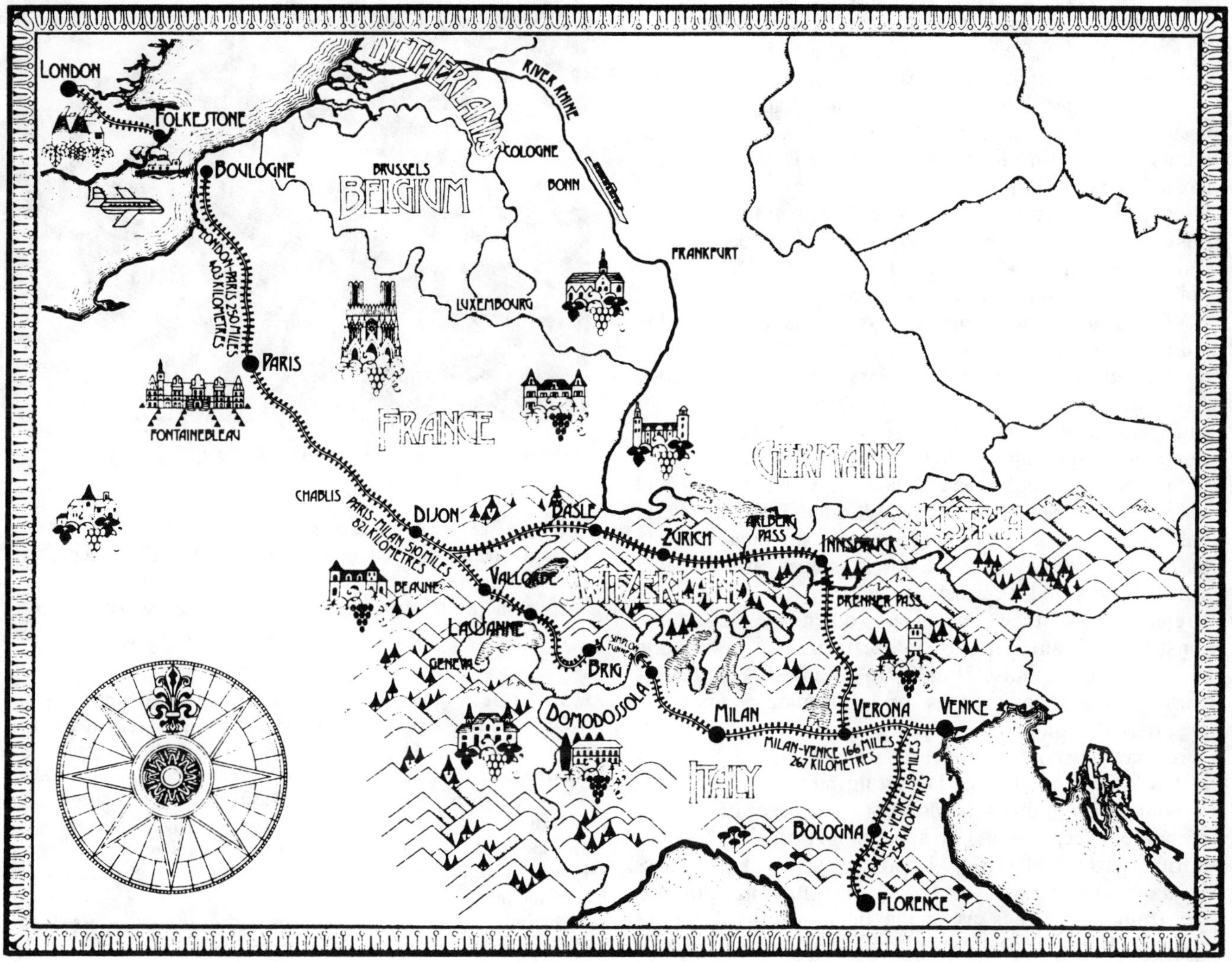


*It's been said that Shangri-La is not a place but a state of mind.*

*Much the same might be said of the* Orient Express.

*. . . France's high speed TGVs, at 160 mph (or more) the world's fastest train, provides a smoother ride.*

*. . . Amtrak's deluxe bedrooms are more spacious and comfortable than the old Wagons-Lits compartments.*

*. . . There are some routes where the scenery is even more dramatic.*

*Yet on what other trains do you ride with history, intrigue and the ghosts of the famous and infamous?*

*Where else such lavish sleeping cars paneled with inlaid woods, Pullmans (lounge cars) equipped with commodious wing back armchairs?*

*Where else art deco restaurant cars, tables set with gleaming silverware, delicate crystal and crisp napery and decorated with flowers and rose-shaded lamps — just as they were in bygone years?*

*On what other trains do women (and men) dress so elegantly for dinner, ÷ enjoy gourmet-type meals served so deftly and with such eclat?*

*And where else cocktails and dancing in a Gay Twenties bar car to the piano tunes of the '20s, '30s and '40s?*

*So, remember. When you board the* Venice Simplon Orient-Express, *you're not London- or Venice-bound. You're enroute to Shangri-La.*

Long before the long line of blue cars with their gold crests pulled out of the Venice station at 9:58 am on September, 1 1984, an electric air of anticipation enveloped it. Passengers of all ages lined up early on the red carpet leading to the check-in desks where tickets were examined, luggage checked with red-jacketed porters. No last minute rush to claim a seat — sleeping accommodations had been pre-assigned. Yet everyone, all smiles and gaiety, was anxious to begin the beguin; after all, this was the storied Orient Express ''and we simply *had* to do it once.'' Car attendants in blue 1920s uniforms were busy posing for photos with boarding passengers. Finally a shrill whistle blast from the handsomely uniformed conductor. Hurrah, we're off!

Verona to Zurich, and vice-versa, is a fascinating ride across Italy, Austria, Liechtenstein and Switzerland over the Brenner Pass, thru 6½-mile long Arlberg Tunnel and along the Zurich See. One of Europe's most scenic, it's replete with rocky heights, dramatic gorges and valleys, mountain pastures dotted with grazing cattle and quaint farmhouses — all played to the Sound of Music. Around Bolzano, Italy, the grandiose limestone Dolomites surround us; in the spring, we're told, the lower slopes are carpeted with vari-colored flowers. Up and up we climb over Brenner Pass, then down and down we slide into Innsbruck. From here to Switzerland is a succession of ski resorts amidst 10,000- to 13,000-ft. mountains with glimpses of castles and farmhouses perched precariously on their slopes.

In the morning we awake to rural France or, if a late riser, to Paris. Departing at 8:58, the next 3 hours, 42 minutes across flat, northern France is, with the exception of an appetizing brunch, the only boring part of the trip. Upon arrival in Folkestone, England, by ferry, we board the stunning Pullman car train that awaits us at the dock for the 1½-hour run to Victoria Station, London, where we arrive exactly 32 hours and five minutes after leaving Venice.

Should this sound too idyllic, we hasten to affirm that there are many who would find it so. It's an expensive trip. The upper and lower berth compartments are cramped and without a toilet though with a wash basin; nice public toilets are at each end of the car.

The ride itself, at up to 70 mph, can be a wild one in these aged cars. Although Babette (and a number of others) slept soundly most of the night, Charles (as well as many others) awakened at 2 am to the sounds of a groaning, clanking steed rushing headlong into the fury of the night. Tossed to and fro, he thought wildly of the Valkyries, those mythological Norse maidens hovering over the field of battle to choose those to be slain, those to be flown to Valhalla as heroes — and wondered for the next few hours just where he'd wind up.

So what's our conclusion? Should you or should you not?

*Fun and songs in the bar car.*

If you're a romantic and adventurer, or if young enough never to have known the Railroad Age, an Orient Express trip is not to be missed.

If you're a pragmatist, forget the whole thing. As for us, Babette wants to do it again.

**More About *Venice Simplon Orient-Express***

On the first day, lunch and dinner are served in the restaurant car (two sittings). On the second morning, a continental breakfast is brought to your compartment, followed by brunch (9:30 to 11:30) in the restaurant car. On the English side of the Channel, light refreshments are beautifully served by liveried attendants in elegant English Pullman cars. All meals, but not wines and liquor, are included in the tariff.

On our trip, all the women wore dressy dresses for dinner, a few quite elaborately so, and about 50% of the men wore tuxedos, the rest dark suits. No question, a gala evening enhanced by subdued lighting and the subtle distinction of doing something different.

Besides sleeping cars, four of which are airconditioned, there's a club car, Pullman lounge car, restaurant car with tables for two and four (two sittings) and two service cars where luggage not needed in your compartment is checked thru to your final destination. There are 40 crew members to pamper a maximum of 175 passengers.

During 1984, the Brenner Pass summer routing proved so attractive to passengers because of its superb scenery that as of 1985, the Simplon Pass route was eliminated. Though retaining the *Venice Simplon* name, the train now runs from London to Venice via Innsbruck and Brenner Pass. From March 15 thru November 17, leaves London on Thursdays and Sundays at 1144, arrives in Venice next evening at 1943; departs Venice on Wednesdays and Saturdays at 0958.

Just as the original *Orient Express* was privately owned and operated, so too *Venice Simplon Orient-Express* — as a division of Sea Containers Group, an American firm listed on the New York Stock Exchange. See *Travel Supplement* for fares, reservation offices.

Elegant dining and haute cuisine are trademarks of the *Venice Simplon Orient-Express.*

According to Babette, "It was a thrilling experience . . . took me back to the glamorous days when I rode the *20th Century Limited* between Chicago and New York."

MENU

**LE DINER**

**Le Gratin de Crustacés à la Thermidor**
*Sea food Thermidor*

* * *

**Le Filet de Boeuf poêlé "Hercule Poirot"**
*Fillet of beef tossed in butter served with a Bordeaux sauce*

**Meli - Melo de Tomates-Aubergines**
*Tomatoes and aubergines Orient-Express style*

**Gâteau de Carottes**
*Creamed Carrots*

* * *

**La Sélection du Maître Fromager**
*A selection of fine chesees*

* * *

**Le Miroir aux Fraises servi avec un Coulis de Framboise**
*Strawberry mousse with raspberry sauce*

## THE TRANS-SIBERIAN RAILWAY

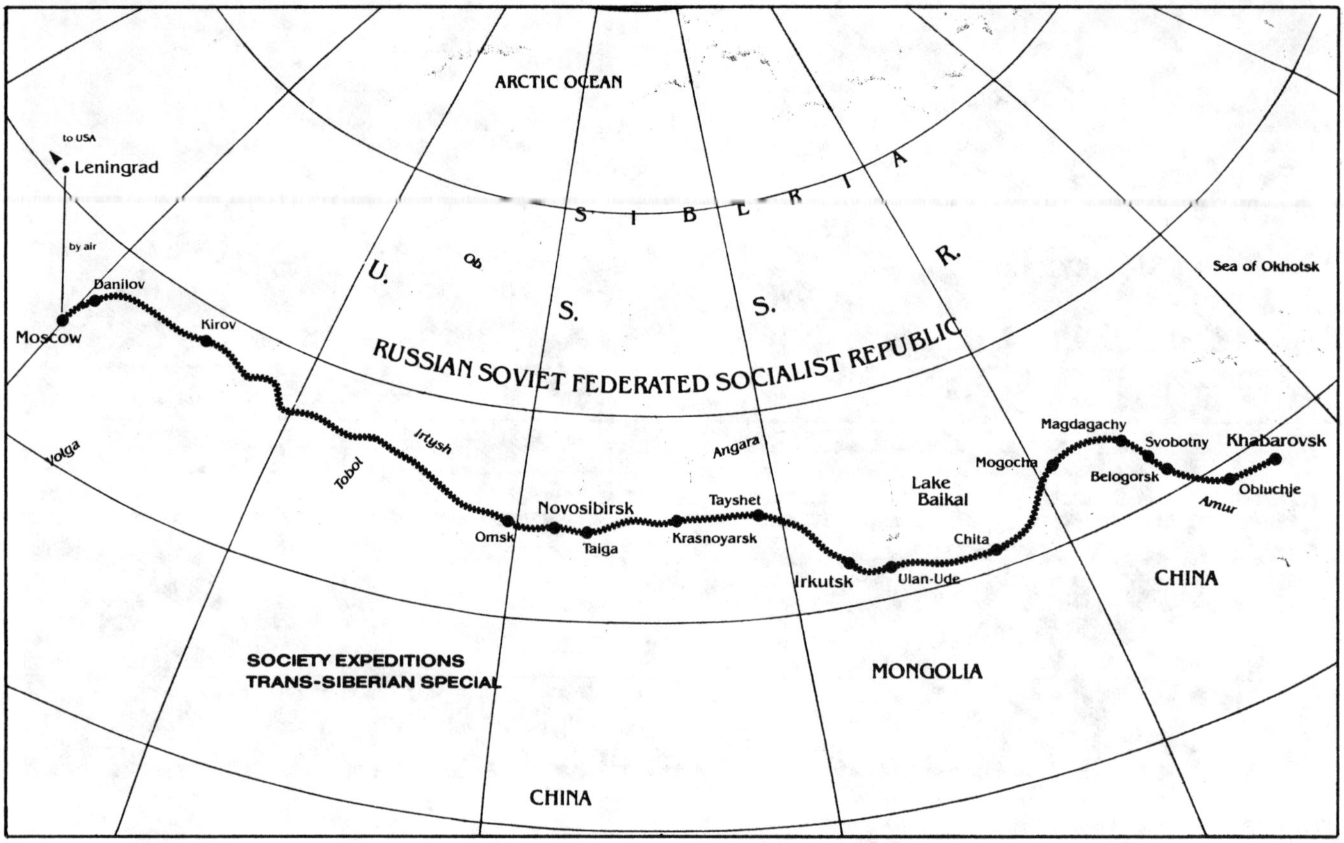


Just as transcontinental railroads made possible the Winning of the West in both the United States and Canada, so has the Trans-Siberian contributed to the settlement and industrial development of Siberia in the USSR. Today, it contributes the major portion of the longest continuous stretch of rail tracks in the world: 5,973 miles from Leningrad in the northwest to Vladivostok on the Pacific to the southeast — or 6,528 miles to Nakhodka at the southeastern tip of Russia on the Sea of Japan.

It all began on May 12, 1891 under Czar Nicholas I. Work progressed at about 375 miles of completed track per year, including a total of 30 miles of bridges. Up to 70,000 laborers were used at two separate points: Vladivostok northward and eastward from Chelyabinsk in the Urals. The going was incredibly difficult; in the west there was a lack of drinking water and construction materials while in the east temperatures dropped as low as −40°C in winter, and in the summer hordes of gnats and mosquitoes were a menace.

Although the all-Russian route was not completed until 1917, by December 1899, tracks reached from Moscow to the Manchurian border where they connected with those of the eastern Chinese Railroad[1].

[1] Again our old friend, Compagnie Internationale des Wagons-Lits, appears on the scene when it signed a contract with the Russians to run a luxury train similar to the Orient Express on this Trans-Asian line and then negotiated with the Eastern Chinese line to extend this first class service into China, one that continues to this day.

By June of 1901, nine trains per month ran between Moscow and Irkutsk in eight days, including a ferry crossing of Lake Baikal. After blasting 38 tunnels thru the mountains along the south shore of the lake, the rail network from European Russia to Manchuria was completed in 1903.

Originally single tracked, a second track was laid in the 1930s and electrification undertaken afterwards. Today, this is one of the most heavily utilized of the world's rail lines. And certainly one of the most legendary for travelers.

### The Trans-Siberian Rail Trip

There are two ways to go:

By the regularly scheduled daily train, **Rossiya** (Russia) that runs from Moscow to Vladivostok (5,308 miles) or Nakhodka (5,863 miles) — or by a deluxe charter train, *Trans-Siberian Special.*

If a lower price and a desire to "meet the Russians" are considerations, opt for the former. But if you want comfort, good food, interesting lectures and excursions, you're better off with the Special — an East German version of a typical European train operated by Russians and chartered from time to time by various train tour operators. Society Expeditions is, to our knowledge, the only American outfit with regularly scheduled tour departures.

*Trans-Siberian Special* consists of seven sleeping cars, each with its own shower compartment, two dining cars and a bar/lounge car for lectures, socializ-

ing and dancing. Double compartments (eight to a car) are comfortable, have vanity and washbasin with hot/cold water. 80 passengers are cared for by a combined Russian/Society Expeditions staff of 45 that includes specialists on Russian history, culture and language who lecture informally enroute. Six skilled chefs prepare regional specialties (accompanied by caviar and vodka); dining and sleeping car stewards provide 24-hour service.

We've heard from those who have booked this 5,300-mile Moscow to Khabarovsk run into the remoteness of Siberia that the train is certainly first class, food good, the excursions at Novosibirsk, Irkutsk, Lake Baikal and Khabarovsk extremely interesting.

Including flights between New York/Moscow (and one way by air to or from Khabarovsk), these are 16-day programs that run from May into October, late December and early January. Altogether there are seven days aboard the train, three overnights in Moscow, two nights in an Irkutsk hotel and one in Khabarovsk — an excellent mix designed to eliminate the boredom of the usual train trip across Siberia, yet with sufficient time to observe the village and rural scenes enroute. Too, there's a three-day Leningrad option, a splendid idea as one should not miss this attractive city and its marvelous Hermitage Museum.

Globetrotter Tours of New Zealand has an excellent, escorted *Grand Tour of the USSR,* Tokyo to London in 33 days, that includes the *Rossiya* from Khabarovsk to Irkutsk — plus Samarkand, Tashkent, Moscow, Leningrad and other Russian cities by air and train, then by overnight train to Tallinn, capital of the Estonian Republic, and by ferry to Helsinki and Stockholm. April departure.

Voyages of Discovery's *Round The World* tour (unescorted except in USSR by Intourist) is quite unique: San Francisco-Tokyo by air, Yokohama to Nakhodka by ship, then the *Rossiya* to Moscow with overnight in an Irkutsk hotel. Overnight to Leningrad on the *Red Arrow Express* and day of sightseeing before taking day train to Helsinki. Itinerary flexible from here on as included in tour price is a two-week Eurailpass, an open air ticket on British Caledonian Airways to Los Angeles. Covers 35 days in all. Departures from April thru October.

A 15-day *Trans Siberian Express* version departs any Sunday from New York by air to Moscow and back from Leningrad. Includes four days on *Rossiya* to Irkutsk.

*Rossiya,* the Big Red Train, makes the Moscow-Irkutsk-Khabarovsk-Vladivostok run in seven days. Departs daily in both directions with airconditioned, European-type sleeping cars and a restaurant car. Soft class (1st) sleepers have two-berth compartments, hard class (2nd) four-berth.[2]

If you wish, this train trip can become the second leg of an Around the World trek by arranging with Intourist, the Russian tourist bureau, to either fly from Khabarovsk to Niigata, Japan and then by bullet train to Tokyo, or from Khabarovsk to Nakhodka by train, then by ferry to Yokohama, Japan.[3]

Should you wish to take the ferry to Japan, it's necessary to lay over in Khabarovsk for a night, board the following evening train (with sleeping cars)[4] that connects next morning with the ferry.

[2] Space for foreign travelers is allocated by Intourist. Be sure your accommodation is a two-berth compartment in a 1st class, European-type sleeping car. Chinese trains, on the other hand, have four-berth compartments (two lowers, two uppers).

[3] Motor vessels *Felix Dzerjinsky* and *Khabarovsk* (4,722 tons; Far East Shipping, a Russian company) sail to/from Yokahama four times monthly May thru August, twice during April and October, three times in September. This 1180-mile voyage takes 52 hours. At the end of July, there's a continuation to Hong Kong (4 days) and a return sailing. Check current schedule with Intourist.

[4] Unlike the *Rossiya,* this boat train, the *Vostok,* has a certain bourgeois finery since it's run solely for the benefit of decadent capitalists bearing hard currency. Cars are filled with mahogany, brass and cutglass, floors covered with thick Turkish carpeting; bathrooms are decorated in art-nouveau. And unlike *Rossiya,* the *Vostok's* dining car has plenty of everything.

## Diary Of A Tour Leader*

"After 1600 kms of very pleasant journeying (from Beijing), find Ulan Bator an ugly place with buildings practical enough, no doubt, but often unattractive, set along half-formed or neglected paths along which ladies pick their way, often in high heeled shoes. Seemingly, once a building is erected, little is done to maintain it . . . a dreary unkempt town of 450,000 but undoubtedly superior to anything else in Mongolia. Hot water heating system goes into all buildings thru huge, above ground pipes from power station. A brilliant idea but not beautiful.

"Hotel arrival with one lift out of action, the other perverse — gave us a laugh albeit a little hollow for tiredness descends quickly after a long journey and baths and beds dominate minds. No bath plug but tightly stuffed toilet paper did the trick (I'd forgotten the 'universal plug' I'd carefully reminded others to pack).

"Museum visit a delight for a student of natural sciences. Great variety of stuffed birds and animals. The giant Tarbosaurus is unique; of the 12 skeletons ever found, eight were in Mongolia. Not nice to meet on a dark night. Interesting mockups of previous nomadic life."

Aboard the train for Irkutsk, the group found there was no dining car and that their supposedly "very good seats" were terrible. "The depth of the group's experience in world travel surfaced for there wasn't a moan — just acceptance that things like this are part of journeying in remote areas. That night we told yarns, swapped lies about our respective (and marvelous) homelands and munched pretty awful biscuits (cookies) as if they were cordon bleu. We had a ball and really got down to knowing each other.

"No trouble at Mongolian border, no cameras opened. Oh so different at the Russian entry. As we pulled into the station, soldiers lined both sides of the tracks (to make sure no one jumped off, no doubt). The patrol took our passports, then insisted on checking cabins to see if we were hiding anyone. Even the corridor carpet was lifted and a torch (flashlight) flashed into storage bays underneath. Tension rose considerably when another team asked to see books and maps. Then for over 15 minutes, five of them pored over a *Newsweek* I'd been reading. It had the story of the Korean plane incident (with diagrams). Finally, off went the Chief to headquarters to get this vital piece of literature checked out. Strangely, other cabins were not then checked for 'western propaganda.' My *Newsweek* was later returned, with a bit of a grin, and off we went — and to sleep at 1 a.m. Breakfast at 9:30: three fried eggs, bread and jam but no butter or coffee. A chocolate bar to top it off cost equivalent of $3 US.

"Soviet trains do little to reflect the depth of culture portrayed elsewhere in Russia. They are dirty and smell after awhile like the rear end of a camel train. An Amtrak car attendant would have a thousand fits. Barbara took a Polaroid photo of a Russian family and they were delighted. In a tiny way we did our bit for friendship; one dad responded by giving me three boiled pine cones which, when opened, provided dozens of little hard shelled nuts (very popular eating in Siberia). We found them rather tasteless but appreciated the gesture."

After a beautiful run along the shores of Lake Baikal, the group arrived in Irkutsk, found it a "stately city of 450,000 with interesting wooden buildings. We visited an 'active' church — beautiful singing by a small congregation and five youngish priests. Later a beautiful recital by local trio in the hotel bar — very moving. A brandy and soft drink cost equivalent of $4 US."

Regarding the Intourist guide, Alexie, who met the group in Irkutsk to accompany it to Leningrad, Simpson describes him as "refined, well-educated and good company, but oh boy, is he conditioned! Very anti-American, so much as to be completely sure the Soviets are right and everyone else is wrong. As he can't escape from the system, I suppose there's little point in taking a balanced view through wanting to know and understand more of the outside world. Only overseas newspaper available to us in English is the *London Daily Worker,* a completely communist production."

Later, when the tour left Leningrad for Helsinki, "we gave Alexie a pair of pants and a coat — Jeans, the unobtainable. We bought them from Ross (a tour member) and although the pants were far too big — 'My wife is expert, she will make them small' — Alexie said he was very, very excited, overwhelmed. University graduate, teacher, fluent in three languages, excellent with the guitar, witty when in the mood, proud citizen of the USSR — this talented young man, a father at 24 years of age, just could NOT BELIEVE he had at last a *set of jeans!* It was our turn to get emotional.

"Just before the train left, he said to us, 'You are all leaving and I will be here all alone.' Then he cried. Maybe, temporarily, our friendly influence had weakened the crust of his convictions — maybe he was just sorry that he wasn't going to be spoilt so much now. I'll remember him as a nice lad who evinced no interest in our way of life and who had an inferior general knowledge that condemned discussion to statement making, then to oblivion. As a national guide, he was poor, making too many careless mistakes when advising on timetabling or programming. He didn't do his homework well enough; this in small ways tended to confuse and could have upset a less experienced group.

"Right to the end he got it wrong. 'No dining car to Helsinki, Alan' — so I bought bags of food from the hotel kitchen. Only to find a dining car attached to the train. It was time that Alexie and I parted.

"At the border, Soviet customs came aboard and made a cursory inspection so there was little tension. They seemed more interested in counting heads and looking under bunks for escapers from paradise than in checking our bags. I took my carrybag out of the cabin and deliberately placed it in the corridor near the door on the assumption that if it wasn't inside, it didn't exist — and sure enough, no one gave it a second glance."

Back in Irkutsk, apples cost the equivalent of $1 US each, "shops had so little in them it was pathetic. New refrigerators of appalling design, even worse manufacture; color TVs at $1000 US, pianos so poorly finished that top, sides and front rippled, poor standard of arts and crafts, inferior looking sports gear and oh, what dreadful shoes. No one bought anything — so different from China.

"Flight from Irkutsk to Tashkent, some 3500 km, took over six hours as we stopped at Alma Ata; most fortunate otherwise 160 bladders might have burst for there was no toilet working on the plane! All we could do was bear with it for there was no way we could cross our legs — not on Soviet planes. It never ceases to amaze me how Soviets can keep a plane in the air yet invariably, even in new hotels, can't get plumbing to work properly."

From Tashkent, the group flew to Samarkand. "This time, like all good Soviets, we visited toilets just before departure. Again not only did the plane's toilets not work, the seat belts were ready for a museum.

*By Alan Simpson, Tour Director of Globetrotter Tours, New Zealand. These excerpts cover some of the Mongolian-Russian segments of a Globetrotter tour in late '83.

"They play secrets here a lot. Always wanting passports, even at remote hotels. On arrival, we are stripped of them and left feeling remarkably naked and pained until conditioning sets in and we meekly hand over these precious documents without comment. All workers carry ID cards here."

After a fascinating three-night stay in Samarkand, they returned to Tashkent and "our fine hotel. Well, it looks fine. Quentin brushed against the washbasin in his room and it came off the wall and smashed. Seems the basin had been disconnected and management hadn't quite gotten around to connect it. Actually, much of hotel life here is below what we'd even faintly put up with in homeland hotels. Somehow, like their trains, things eventually operate and quite efficiently but are too repeatedly below standard for us to be impressed by bureaucratic control."

On the three-hour flight to Tbilisi (a very beautiful city), the surprise of the trip: "the toilet worked, though a terribly poor setup. Flies pestered us as we dozed. Plane was cold, seats bony, cabin stinking it was so dirty. From wakeup at 4:45 a.m. til 11:15 arrival at hotel, all that was offered us was a small cup of luke warm mineral water (which only the brave drank)."

The hotel in Tbilisi, capital of Georgia, served the best food they'd had in Russia. Yet the display and packaging of merchandise in the shops were "more like the 1920s in a back country New Zealand town — years and years behind what we take for granted today. Prices seem high, too.

"But a wonderful concert by Georgian Dancers in a fine auditorium was a great treat. Apart from the outstandingly rich and lovely singing of a 32-man choir and the incredible feats of dancing, often magnificently graceful, by eight women and 16 men, it was the beauty of costuming that took our breath away in each of the seven changes. A brilliant mass of whirling colors completely fascinated us. How lucky we are to be here."

In what they thought was a top grade sleeping car, two to a cabin and clean, the train ride to Sochi on the Black Sea turned out to be "easily the worst I've experienced anywhere. Apart from the noise and the milk delivery speed of our temporary tomb, we had no dining car on a ride that finally lasted 18 hours. Passengers are of little concern — it's freight that matters.

"It's the system that keeps Soviet citizens and ourselves apart. Naira, our Tbilisi guide, couldn't accept my lunchtime homily on some of the true facts of living other than in the USSR. Nicholai, the local Sochi guide, is outright RED — determined to haul down the USA flag. A charming, deeply educated man of 67 with a heavy accent but outstanding English. Knew every tree in the park by its common and Latin name. Complete tirade against the United States. On another day, he gave a talk on conservation which was alright until he got onto Soviet supremacy in all things bright and beautiful. An outright attack on the West got Bebe to her feet protesting. By now Ross is 'real upset' and maybe that's a good thing as it's about time people realize the Soviets are in deadly earnest when they say the world should be rid of the capitalist menace. Nicholai said it loud and clear. Message received?"

For lack of space, we have skipped most of Mr. Simpson's descriptions of their destinations, majority of which were enjoyable. Moscow, and particularly the Bolshoi Ballet, was *the* Russian highlight. So we'll close this account with some final Simpson observations:

"Do people here put their litter in bins, refrain from desecrating with graffiti, drive cars at reasonable speeds and quietly because of their sense of pride or out of fear of the law? I think it could be the former for Moscow, with trees in leaf, is very beautiful, neat and clean. The extraordinary circus we went to this evening, so exceptional in its diverse program, sound and light and costume effects and absolute perfection of timing and expertise, was another example of how well Soviets do things when they have 'priority.' So much seen in other cities varied in quality, but Moscow, center of Soviet tourism, is the showplace that must reluctantly impress even the most hardened of those who believe in our way of life — and give great encouragement to those who, within the western world, work to destroy us.

"We are impressed with the care taken to beautify the cities we've seen. Over a long period there has been, obviously, no vandalism, official or otherwise, except that statues of Stalin have disappeared and Lenin now dominates. Although new apartment buildings are ugly and dehumanizing, there is great civic pride in Moscow, though the city can't compare to the beauty of Paris or Rome or —. It's just that with the verbal hatred of the West constantly disseminated, it's surprising to see so much positive effort to retain the old and to beautify. It's a relief.

"Tonight a 'farewell to the USSR' with everyone in high spirits — like cattle smelling water, we can 'feel' approaching Helsinki and for the first time there's impatience in the air to shrug off the constriction, to leave the Communist unknowns, to reach for our knowns now just across the border.

"After three weeks in the USSR, we certainly aren't as squeamish about Russian food as on arrival at Irkutsk. I can now drink the soup with my eyes open! No wonder the Soviets held out against the Nazis in Leningrad for three years — they can eat anything.

"As we crossed into Finland, we cheered as five weeks of feeling under surveillance suddenly evaporated. 'Isn't the air fresh,'' said Isabel — a statement, not a question. I knew what she meant. Without being in a Communist Society for awhile, one just cannot appreciate what it's like to get away from it all."

**More About The Trans-Siberian Rail Trip**

From sources other than the two diaries, we glean these opinions of the daily Big Red Train:

A sometimes arduous but nonetheless an unforgettable ride.

Mattresses are thin, bunks uncomfortable, table d'hote meals barely edible or inedible, the scenery monotonous. Taped pop songs blare from loudspeakers. "Frustrations build up with the relentlessness of the clacking wheels."

Dining cars do not serve alcohol, yet drunkenness seems as much a problem aboard as it is elsewhere in the country.

Train authorities frown upon fraternization with Westerners. A compartment occupied by an American woman became so popular with Soviet passengers that they were forced to leave, while later on two Soviets left when they learned she was an American.

*Rossiya's* clocks are kept on Moscow time, meaning you may have breakfast at teatime, go to bed at daybreak back in Moscow.

The worst comment we've read was written by a Sarasota, Florida man. "Compartments were small, sometimes having an upper and lower berth, sometimes two lowers. Sometimes we had washing facilities (cold water only), sometimes not. There were a few washrooms shared by two adjoining compartments. Cars had a toilet at each end — universally filthy and only used out of dire necessity."

On the positive side, one gets an indelible impression

of the vastness of the USSR — and reminders of Stalin's purges of the 1930s in the cities of the Gulag Archipelago along the route. At station stops, village women hawk a wide variety of food and flowers, wrapped in cornucopias of old newspapers. Passengers pile out to restock on food. Scenes that aren't seen in Moscow or Leningrad.

From west to east, you cross the mighty Volga River, boundary between Europe and Asia, the Ural Mountains, the swift Angara River, beautiful Lake Baikal and much of the vastness of Siberia.

The name derives from two Tatar words: *sib* to sleep and *ir*, land — the mysterious sleeping land of limitless space until its comparatively recent development into an industrial powerhouse. Here are 53,000 rivers, more than a million lakes, giant forests with huge trees (including trans-Ural pines whose yellow trunks make them look like enormous candles).

### More About Soviet Trains

There are single- and double-berth compartments in most first class sleeping cars, four-berth in second class. All are supposed to be airconditioned/heated and though not spacious are fairly comfortable, have picture windows.

Transit passengers may stopover enroute providing they exit the country in 10 days or less and prior arrangements for same have been made thru Intourist.

Tourists arriving by train from the west enter the USSR thru Brest, from Vienna and the Balkans at the border stations of Chop or Ugeny. From Brest to Moscow, you cross Byelorussia (capital Minsk) and on to Smolensk. The Chop route crosses the Soviet Ukraine, winding along the picturesque slopes of the Carpathian Mountains to Lvov and then to Kiev on the banks of the Dnieper River. From Ugeny the train goes to Kishinev, capital of Soviet Moldavia, and then crosses the Dniester River and the Ukranian steppes to Vinnitsa.

### USSR TRIP PLANNING

Individual and group travel arrangement and payments must be cleared thru INTOURIST (official Soviet travel organization) in U.S. or Canada.* For tours with stopovers in the USSR, a tourist visa is needed. For transiting the country overland, a transit visa is required.

**Tourist Visa** — Requires submission of valid passport (or pages 2 and 3 of U.S. passport), four black/white passport photos (1¾ × 1½"), one completed application form, typed and signed, INTOURIST confirmation number, travel agency voucher number. Date of departure from North America and complete travel itinerary (with dates) in USSR must be noted on application. Visas are valid only for duration of tour, only for cities listed in the itinerary. Tourists can enter/leave the country thru any border points open for passenger traffic. Though "tourist visa is granted free of charge in the form of an enclosure without stamping the passport," INTOURIST hastens to add (with a straight face?), "To cover postage and telegraphic expenses, a charge of $10 (in Canada, $6 Canadian) is requested for each visa application." As usual, stick it to the Americans.

**Transit Visa** — All that's needed for a Trans-Siberian rail trip. Valid for 10 days. Require INTOURIST confirmation, reservations and vouchers.

Transiting the USSR by air, without stopovers, does *not* require a visa — merely a valid passport, entry visa (if needed) to destination country and air ticket with confirmed onward flight date within 24 hours from airport of entry.

***Important** — A recent U.S. Dept. of State travel advisory warns of instances of harassment, even arrest, of U.S. tourists by the KGB on trumped up charges of espionage, etc.*

### USSR TRAVEL-FACTS

**Arrival/Departure** — Upon arrival, pass thru Passport & Visa Control, then fill out Customs Declaration form, for which you receive a Customs Certificate; this must be presented each time you exchange money. The form entitles you to exchange unspent roubles for dollars.

After clearing Customs, proceed to Intourist Desk for transport to your assigned hotel. Groups are met by an official guide.

At least five hours before departure, FITs should order transfer car from hotel to airport from Intourist, which has a desk in all hotels. Turn in unspent roubles and, in Customs area, the Customs Certificate (your baggage may be inspected); proceed thru Passport & Visa Control to departure lounge.

Incoming passengers must declare fur pieces, precious metals, stones and pearls (and jewelry containing same); they must be taken out of the country with you.

**Climate/Clothing** — From May to September, it's warm in most areas; summer can be hot. Okay to wear bikinis and short shorts at the beaches but *never* on city streets. Leningrad has mild summers when twilight lingers 'til midnight; Moscow and central Russia are usually hot in summer, moderately cold in winter. During late fall, winter and early spring, you'll need warm clothing.

**Currency** — Rouble (made up of 100 kopecks) is the monetary unit. Bills come in denominations of 1, 3, 5, 10, 25, 50 and 100 roubles; coins are 1, 2, 3, 5, 10, 15, 20, 50 kopecks and one rouble.

Exchange rate was pegged (by USSR) in 1984 at R79 = $1.00 US — or one rouble = $1.26. Import/export of roubles is against the law, as are foreign currency transactions with anyone except the State Bank, branches of which are at all border crossings, hotels, international airports and seaports. Most are open from 0800 to 2000/2100; if arriving late at night, best to exchange foreign currency at airport as hotel exchange desks are normally closed then.

**Credit Cards/Travel Checks** — Tourist services are chargeable on major credit cards. You can cash dollar travel checks issued by Americna Express, Barclay's Bank, Citibank, Thomas Cook, Perera Express and Republic National Bank of Dallas. English pound, Swiss franc travel checks also accepted.

**Electric Current** — 220v, AC 50c; European plugs or adapters required. (Some tourist hotels have 127v current).

**Entertainment** — Groups can reserve tickets in advance for ballet, opera, circus or concerts. FITs should reserve thru their hotel Service Desk. September thru May is theater season; performances usually start at 1900 or 1930. Dress is optional.

**Hotels** — All Intourist hotels for foreign tourists have Service Bureaus for all types of bookings, sightseeing, restaurant reservations, place long distance phone calls; open from 0900 to 2200. Hotel checkout time: noon.

**Insurance** — All-inclusive coverage, both personal and car, can be arranged prior to departure thru American International Group, 70 Pine St., New York 10270; maintains full claim facilities within USSR.

**Mail** — Airmail letter rate is 16 kopecks (about 25¢), airmail postcards 14 kopecks. Surface rates are 6 and 4 kopecks.

**Medical Care** — Free to tourists if hospitalization is not involved. Doctors can be called to hotel rooms.

**Photography** — No restrictions except no picture-taking of military installations, border posts.

**Restaurants/Bars** — You can pay for a la carte meals in Intourist restaurants with foreign currency. At specialty bars (and also shops) that sell foreign as well as domestic liquors, you pay only in foreign currencies. Tourist restaurant menus are in Russian and foreign languages.

**Shopping Hours** — Some department stores from 0800 to 2000, specialty shops 1100 to 2000, food stores 0800 to 2000. Stores (except food) closed on Sundays. Best selections are in the hard currency stores.

**Time Zones** — Russia (Moscow, Leningrad): GMT+3; Caucasus: +4; Central Asia: +5 or 6; Siberia: +6-9. Daylight saving in effect from March 31 to midnight of Sept. 30.

**Transportation** — Metro and bus fares are 5 kopecks, trolleybus 4 kopecks and tram fare only 3 kopecks. Cab flag drop is 20 kopecks plus 20 kopecks per kilometer.

## Via Trans-Mongolian Railway to Beijing

This weekly service runs over the Moscow-Irkutsk line, at which point it turns south to Ulan Bator, capital of Mongolia, and to Beijing, 4,822 miles in all. There are 1st and 2nd class sleeping cars, a restaurant car.

Again it's Society Expeditions for the plush way to go. Its overland *Paris to Peking Express* (a 24-day program) visits Paris, Warsaw, Moscow, Novosibirsk, Irkutsk, Lake Baikal, Ulan Bator and, finally, Beijing. There are sightseeing excursions at all stops plus a two-day expedition into the Mongolian steppe for overnight in a comfortable yurt (tent) and a visit to Karakorum, Ghenghis Khan's ancient city. An optional extension is available aboard the *Imperial Peking Express;* see China Train Travel section for details.

*Paris to Peking Express* operates in May, August and September. Paris-Moscow segment provides first class rail accommodations and dining car attached to regularly scheduled trains. From Moscow to Ulan Bator, there are eight nights aboard the *Trans-Siberian Special,* two nights on *Imperial Peking Express* between Ulan Bator and Beijing.

One of the longest, most exhaustive overland rail trips is *Central Kingdom Express* from London to Hong Kong (and vice-versa) — 39 days enroute plus two in Hong Kong. Conducted by Voyages Jules Verne, the program utilizes pre-booked, first class (two-berth) compartments on European and Russian trains, four-berth on Chinese, first class hotels. Each tour is staff escorted with guided sightseeing excursions at all stops. In Europe, there are overnights in Paris, Berlin (West and East), Warsaw and Moscow. The Trans-Siberian segment to Irkutsk and Lake Baikal comes next followed by Ulan Bator, Datong and Beijing, after which Xian, Luoyang, Nanjing, Shanghai and Guangzhou are visited before reaching Hong Kong.

There are one to three monthly departures, April thru September, from London, single departures in April, July and September from Hong Kong — all with Hong Kong-London air return (or vice-versa). From North America, this becomes a Round The World Trip.

*Red Arrow Express,* also conducted by Voyages Jules Verne, is a 21-day version of the foregoing with monthly westbound departures April thru October, single eastbound departures in May and June, twice monthly in July, August and September.

A third version, 24-day *Tian an Men Express,* flies from London to Leningrad, goes by train to Moscow, flies to Irkutsk and then continues by rail to Beijing before flying to Hong Kong. Flights from the U.S.to London and back from Hong Kong provide another Round The World tour.

Globetrotter Tours has two escorted Hong Kong to London tours via China, Mongolia and USSR. *Fast Track* is 28 days (May) that includes riding the rails from Guangzhou to Beijing, Ulan Bator and Irkutsk. *Grand Tour of China, Mongolia, Soviet Union* (38 days) is very comprehensive. 14 days in China, then by train from Beijing to Ulan Bator and Irkutsk for 14 days in USSR, followed by train to Helsinki, ferry to Stockholm and ferry and train to London. Departures in May and September. Escorted; four-berth train compartment to Irkutsk (two-berth on ferries).

An interesting London-Hong Kong routing by air/rail/ship (18 nights) visits Leningrad, Moscow and Irkutsk by air, the Trans-Siberian Express to Nakhodka where a 650-passenger Russian liner is boarded for a five-day cruise to Yokahama and Hong Kong. Departures May-September in both directions. U.S. agent is International Cruise Center.

Citizen Exchange Council, a non-profit organization, has a summer and early fall program (three weeks) from New York to Leningrad/Moscow to Khabarovsk, then by Trans-Siberian Express to Mongolia and an excursion into the Gobi Desert. An experienced Russian-speaking American leads both groups.

### MONGOLIA TRAVEL-FACTS

**Area** — 604,103 square miles; slightly smaller than Arizona, New Mexico, Texas and Louisiana combined. Almost 90% is pastureland or Gobi Desert wasteland; 10% forested. North and west of the Gobi are mountains (up to 14,350 ft.)

**Capital** — Ulaanbaatar (correct spelling); pop. 485,000.

**Climate** — Long, cold winters (Oct.-April), short summers. Monthly mean temperatures: −17°F in January to 64°F in July. Annual rainfall averages 10″. Has some of world's highest barometric pressures.

**Currency** — Approx. 3.5 tugriks = $1 US.

**Economy** — Heavily agricultural (90% of exports); also exports coal.

**Education** — 7 years compulsory in cities; minimum of four elsewhere.

**Government** — Communist. Modeled (and dependent) on Soviet system. U.S. does not recognize the Mongolian People's Republic, has no diplomatic relations with it. Mongolia is represented by a mission to the United Nations in New York. Only political party is MPRP (Mongolian Peoples Revolutionary Party). There's universal suffrage for adults 18 years and older. Elections held every four years.

**Language** — 90% Khalkah Mongolian. Cyrilic alphabet introduced in 1946.

**Life Expectancy** — 63-65 years.

**Literacy** — About 80%.

**Military Alignment** — With USSR. More than 40 Soviet divisions are stationed along the Mongolian-Chinese border; there are some 35,000 Soviet advisors in the country.

**National Flag** — Three vertical bands (red, skyblue, red); on left red band, there's a golden 5-pointed star under which the golden soyombo (yellow symbols) are arranged.

**National Holidays** — Workers' Day, May 1; People's Revolution Day, July 11.

**Population** — 1.77 million, predominately Mongolian (75% Khalka). Annual growth rate is 2.75%. Rural pop. is about 49%.

**Religion** — Formerly, Tibetan Buddhist Lamaism was predominate. Currently, religious activity is mostly restricted; only a few showcase monasteries remain open.

**First Hand Report On The Central Kingdom Express***

"We are delighted with our airconditioned car. A 2-bed compartment for each couple. Window has white cottage curtains, a 2′ × 4′ table is covered with a white damask cloth; atop it is a vase of fresh flowers. Bathrooms are at both ends of the car. A large samovar of hot water is provided. Two cute Russian girls in bright blue uniforms are our conductor and porter. I'm told they are students."

Before breakfast of Day 2, "Our porter comes by and offers tea. We ask for coffee. None, so she brings a pot of hot water and we make our own with coffee from home." On Day 3, "Our little porter takes off her jacket and assumes maid duty. Every day she comes in with an Electrolux-type vacuum and sweeps our compartment, goes down the corridor washing the window sills and railings."

About the food, they are less enthusiastic. "Food is ample but strange. Lots of thick white bread, butter and jelly," they write about breakfast, "plus a plate of salami and cheese. Then the main course: a boiled chicken leg and red cabbage. Meals are served at 9 am, 2 and 7 pm. Our group goes together to the dining car, about five cars ahead, and we occupy the entire car for our time. The routine is easy and pleasant, but the food leaves a little to be desired. Always potatoes, cabbage, heavy thick bread, soup, weak coffee and a bottle of colored water. No wine or beer and almost no meat (usually pork or chicken) nor fresh vegetables/fruit."

On the fourth day, they note that "the food is getting worse — still plenty of bread and butter, very little meat or vegetables. Good soup but no wine or beer." Too, we discover that "the bathrooms are out of toilet tissue and towels, but the train is still comfortable."

Day after day they played bridge, read and watched the Russian countryside roll by. "Many groups of little houses, all run-down shanties with outhouses. Little garden plots, mostly potatoes. Land is very flat. Warm and sunny now but must be terribly bleak in winter. At every stop, if time permits, we jump off and run up and down the platform, take pictures.

"As we move east the time advances one or two hours daily; much daylight along latitude 55. The endless *taiga*[5] is just that with occasional breaks for villages and factories. Since the land is fairly flat, without mountains, only one electric engine is needed." But on Day 4, the train enters Siberia. "The countryside is more hilly and many more trees. Cities look about the same but settlements are very dilapidated. Villages are numerous — about six to 10 miles apart — and fairly large towns are being constructed about every 30 to 40 miles. In fact, our trip seems to be thru an endless construction camp of hi-rise buildings. The Russian people seem, in most instances, to be depressed and glum. Turned inwardly, it would seem."

On Day 5, they arrive in Irkutsk in time for lunch at the Intourist Hotel, then leave for Lake Baikal. "The Baikal Hotel is quite new but already pretty shabby with very old-fashioned bathrooms. But we have plenty of hot water and all enjoy our first shower in five days.

"The lake is beautiful and one of the largest in the world; in fact, it contains 20% of all the fresh water on earth, averages 5,000 feet in depth, is over 400 miles long and 120 miles wide, has over 100 rivers flowing in and even one, the Angara, flowing out. Nearly two-thirds of documented fauna are found nowhere else — even including one herd of seals."

On Day 7, "the train follows the eastern edge of Lake Baikal for over 100 miles, then turns southeast for Ulan Bator. At midnight we reach the border, are held up for three hours while the Russians search for whatever it is they search for with the usual visa, passport and currency checks (we are not allowed to take any roubles out of the country). We then move into Mongolia and stop again for the Mongolian routine (about 1½ hours). Everyone remains frozen — no loud talk, no getting into bed — such is the reputation of these border guards. This is truly an armed frontier. We have been warned to hide cameras and under no circumstances take any pictures of the border, stations, police or military installations."

Enroute to Ulan Bator on Day 8, "the train moves along thru rolling hills, nearly treeless, with endless meadows of graying land. We see many horsemen on small Mongolian ponies, numerous yurts, singly and in villages, very few trucks — and a number of very large radar and military installations (all looking south to China)." Upon arrival at 10:30 in Ulan Bator, there's a City Tour. "Our guide is a young Mongolian named Sharof who speaks fairly good English. He is very proud of the progress made by his country since it became a republic in 1921. From illiterate, nomadic tribes living in tents, they now have a modern city with hi-rise apartments. However, most of the older people still live in yurts, wear Russian or Chinese type clothing; the young people wear jeans and other western garb. Sharof claims a 99% literacy rate (probably nearer 85%).

"Mongolia is fast emerging from a herdsmen to socialist economy as dictated by the Russians. There's a low population density; over 40% of the people are 16 years and under, so large families are encouraged. Education is emphasized.

"Compared to the grim Russians, these people are a great relief with their relaxed and friendly ways. Also somewhat casual and irresponsible, which carries over into their unpredictable train schedules. Regardless of your ticket, you are never sure of getting aboard on a particular day nor into your assigned compartment."

On day 9 "we luck out and board the train at noon for China. We are now in a Chinese car; all compartments have four beds. There are two smiling Chinese attendants; one brings us a large thermos of boiling water to make tea and coffee. The car is very clean, including the windows — but no dining car. We buy a large sausage — that is the group's lunch and dinner, also our breakfast next morning."

Day 10 starts at 6 am with customs and passport inspection at the Mongolian-Chinese border. "We hide all cameras/film as they might be confiscated. After four hours, hand over our Mongolian visas and move into China where the bogies[6] are changed to accommodate the narrow gauge Chinese tracks. Here we are permitted to alight and take pictures, after which we sit down to our first full meal in nearly 28 hours — a nine-course Chinese dinner complete with chopsticks. Every plate and platter was cleaned."

*These excerpts from the diary of Mr./Mrs. Diven Meredith of Palm Desert, Ca. on their trip from London to Hong Kong in the summer of 1982 present vivid vignettes of what life on a Big Red Train is like. Many of the Merediths' comments, we hasten to add, should not be considered indicative of life aboard the Trans-Siberian Special.

[5] *Taiga* is swampy, coniferous forest land that covers much of Siberia, begins where the northern *tundra* ends. Latter is a level or undulating treeless plain with permanently frozen subsoil.

[6] Swiveling trucks or axles with wheels used on locomotives and rail cars. These can be changed to adapt to standard or narrow gauge rails.

# MORE GREAT RAIL TRIPS

*This poster, originally in four colors, was printed about 1910 when the Bernina Railway was opened. In 1943, the line was incorporated as part of the Rhatische Bahn route — as scenically captivating as shown by the artist, Marcel Lebrun.*

# SWITZERLAND

Glacier Express, *on its run from St. Moritz to Zermatt, not only passes thru spectacular mountain scenery but also quaint villages like Niederwald, birthplace of Caesar Ritz, famed hotelier.*

## GLACIER EXPRESS/RHONE RHEIN EXPRESS

All of Switzerland is a Great Rail Trip. For this is an incredibly beautiful country, particularly in the central Alpine regions. Which is our reason for nominating the Zermatt to St. Moritz rail line as the most scenic 291 km (141½ miles) in Europe — and, as far as we know, in the world. No other train trip can match it in its splendid mountain panoramas — from expansive vistas of pastoral valleys and pine-clad slopes to towering, jagged cliffs and glistening snowfields and glaciers that dazzle the eye. There's no way words can adequately describe this prolificacy of beauty — you must see it to become a believer.

We became true believers these past two summers when we traveled for over a month thruout Switzerland on that magic carpet known as Schweizer Ferienkarte — Swiss Holiday Pass. We'll never forget the pleasures, the superb scenery, the many hours of exaltation it brought us. What a rare bargain!

The ease and rapidity of rail travel in this small but varied country cannot be over-emphasized. Trains run frequently, mostly with the precision of a Swiss watch, to every city and resort — usually in one or two hours (or less) from one destination to another. In fact, you can travel the north-south length of Switzerland in four hours, 55 minutes.

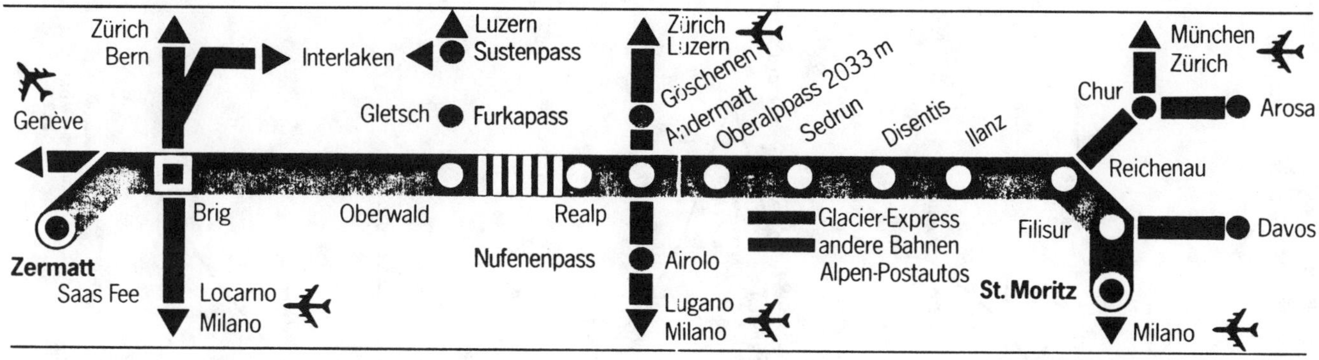


**The Number 1 Swiss Rail Trip**

Due to less than factual newspaper and magazine articles, it's erroneously believed that only the *Glacier Express* runs between St. Moritz and Zermatt. Actually, there are six daily trains in each direction over this narrow gauge line, a joint operation by three private railways (BVZ-Furka Overalp-Rhatische Bahn), of which *Glacier Express*[1] and *Rhone-Rhein Express* are the only name trains — and the only ones with a restaurant car.[2]

As we've said, words cannot fully describe the scenic wonders you'll encounter, so we'll leave it to you to gasp over their beauty and variety. What we can do, however, is to describe the routing potentials, suggest how to fit them into your travel plans and give you some idea of the glories that await you.

As illustrated, there are three segments to the so-called Glacier Express route. Brig to Zermatt is the most spectacular; however, it requires a return over the same line since Zermatt has no other rail access. That, we hasten to add, is hardly a hardship (as we well know) considering the scenery and the fact that Zermatt-Brig is but an hour and 24-minute run.

The next segment, Brig-Andermatt (1:47) is equally as pleasing. Finally, there's the Andermatt-Disentis-Chur segment that, enroute to Disentis over the line's highest elevation, presents marvelous vistas crowned by distant snow-capped mountains: however, much of the run east of Disentis is, comparatively speaking, anti-climactic.

Both Brig and Andermatt are the keys to this Great Swiss Rail Trip, for they can be reached from north or south, enable you to continue your journey in either direction or even to the east or west. If time's a factor, take the Andermatt-Zermatt segment, using Andermatt as entry point from north or south (even from Zurich to the northeast), Brig the departure point (upon returning from Zermatt) for continuing your journey in any direction.

We trained north from Milan to Brig, the Simplon Pass route, overnighted there. Next day to Zermatt and several days later back to Brig and on to Andermatt via the *Glacier Express.*

If you're expecting an unusually deluxe train, you are in for a disappointment; the bright red cars, both first and second class, are the same as those on other trains except for a thru car to St. Moritz; on other trains, including *Rhone-Rhein Express,* you must change at Chur to a connecting train. This comment, however, in no way downgrades these regular cars which have comfortable seats (particularly in first class), wide view windows, smoking and non-smoking (Raucher, Nicht Raucher) sections.

---

As currently scheduled, *Glacier Express* leaves St. Moritz daily at 0855, Chur at 1053, Disentis 1209, Andermatt 1327 and Brig 1523 to arrive in Zermatt at 1643; leaves Zermatt at 1010, Brig at 1140, Andermatt at 1329, Disentis at 1450 to arrive in Chur at 1603, St. Moritz at 1752. *Rhone-Rhein Express* leaves Chur at 0853, Disentis at 1012, Andermatt at 1118, Brig at 1312 for 1443 arrival in Zermatt; leaves latter at 1210 for 1804 arrival in Chur where there are good connections for St. Moritz, Zurich, Klosters/Davos.

---

We strongly recommend an Andermatt-Groschenen[3] stopover in whatever direction you're traveling in order to see by PostAuto bus (PTT) some of the world's most magnificent mountain passes: St. Gotthard, Nufennen, Furka and Susten — *none of which can be seen by train* since both east-west and north-south rail lines tunnel *under* this gorgeous area.[4]

Here's what we wrote about two of the most exhilarating days of our lives:

August 12th, Andermatt — "Today was the day that was. Highlight of the summer — a three-pass (St. Gotthard, Nufenen, Furka) PostAuto tour (four hours, 13 min.) that surpasses any mountain drive we've ever taken. Superb — sensational — magnificent — awe-inspiring — incredible and breathtaking. It was all those plus whatever other adjectives one can think of to connote utter sublimity.

*'I'm sitting on top of the world,*
*Just singing a song . . .'*

[1] Only Swiss train for which seat reservations are required. On all other trains, reservations are neither required nor available.

[2] During the summer tourist season, this is a dubious distinction since table d'hote meals (no a la carte) are mediocre, service is rush-rush and the dining car can be very hot. We'd been warned but some fellow passengers had not and complained bitterly at the waste of money, abject food and poor service. Best to bring sandwiches or box lunch, buy beer, wine or soft drinks in the restaurant car.

[3] Andermatt is the narrow gauge east-west rail station, Groschenen that of the standard gauge north-south international line. They're just 15 minutes apart by connecting narrow-gauge train or PostAuto bus, a stunning ride thru a rocky gorge.

[4] If not stopping over in Andermatt, you can (through proper scheduling) arrange to take a Post Auto bus from Groschenen or Andermatt to Airolo (or vice-versa) when traveling north-south in order to ride *over* St. Gotthard Pass instead of tunneling thru it.

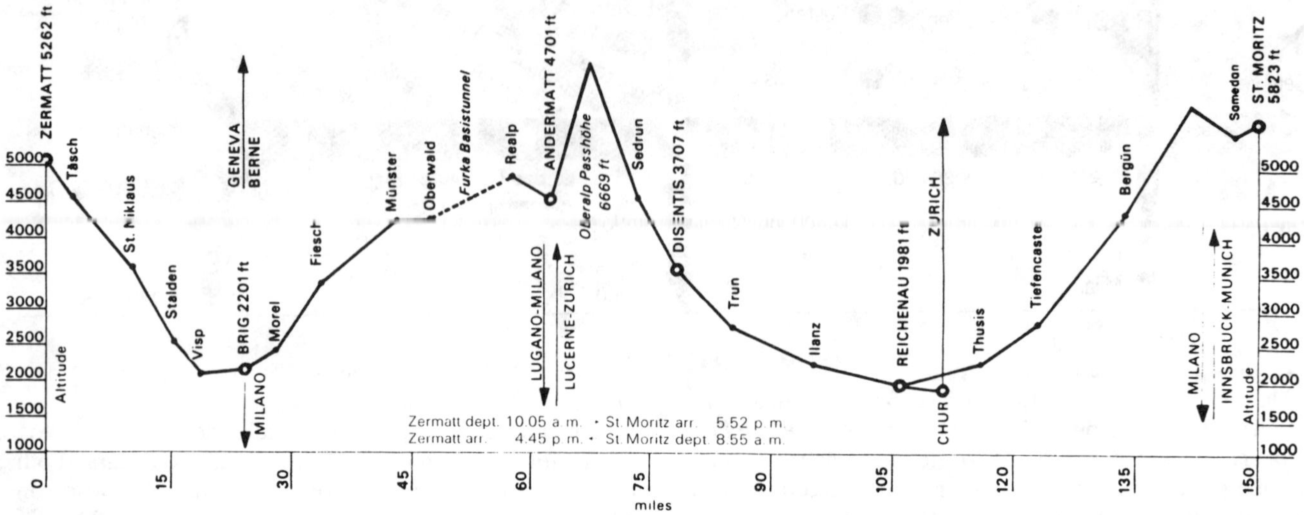


"And feeling that so much beauty is more than one can expect.

"Alternately the road hairpins from valley floor to passes, from which one looks out on forever, then spirals down over U and S curves — sometimes as many as six to 10 can be seen below — once again to the bottom — then up, then down and again up, this time to the aquamarine Rhone glacier followed, finally, by the last downward spiral.

"Such beauty and other-worldliness reinforce our opinion that Switzerland telescopes more scenery within its small area than any other country in Europe.

"Although some stretches of road are narrow, all are beautifully engineered, including curves that actually extend out over the slopes by means of supporting pylons."

---

Here's the PostAuto schedule: Lv. Andermatt @ 1015, ar. Gotthardpass 1040. Descend to Airolo (ar. 1115), then up to Nufenpass @ 1200. Ar. Oberwald @ 1300, Rhonegletscher @ 1330. Finally back via Furkapass for 1428 arrival in Andermatt.

---

August 13th — "How do you top the tops? Never did we believe that could be done, yet today the impossible became a reality — a PostAuto drive from Andermatt to Meiringen via Susten Pass. Yesterday we saw vast panoramas of mountains and valleys and pasturelands — ahead and behind, above and below. Today we drove *thru and into* the mountains, often at the upper levels of craggy, snowy peaks — so close we could, figuratively, touch 'em. Yesterday was majestic, today imposing — another version of this incredibly beautiful country.

"And then came still another topper. After an hour's layover in Meiringen, we took PostAuto to Schwarzwaldalp for a connecting bus to Grindelwald — thru and over another stunning mountain range on a single track road (with pullouts for passing); on blind curves we closed our eyes as the horn sounded its three-chord blast and the front of the bus seemed to hang out over the void. Needless to say, we're returning to Meiringen by rail — once is enough."

What more can we say except to emphasize: Don't miss this Great Swiss Rail Trip!

**Number 2 Swiss Rail Trip**

It's *Bernina Express,* world's steepest non-cogwheel train (70% gradient) and Europe's highest Alpine crossing railway — another scenic spectacular that stretches from St. Moritz to Montebello (for an exciting view of Morteratsch Glacier) and then a stop at Alp Grum where there's a magnificent panorama of ice and snow. It all winds down at Tirano, Italy, after a two-hour plus run through frigid to sub-tropical zones.

In the summer, this run can be made in the *Bernina Express'* Panorama (open air) cars. Actually, there are seven daily trains between St. Moritz and Tirano (and vice-versa), of which the *Bernina Express,* with dining car, is the only name train.*

We have ridden from Chur and Klosters to St. Moritz (both routes very scenic) but time ran out on us before we could return to Italy via Tirano. But we have the word of those who've taken it that this is well worth

*Southbound, the train actually departs from Pontresina, 11 minutes south of St. Moritz, arrives in Tirano at 1254 after eight stops. Northbound departure is 1500 with 1711 arrival in St. Moritz.

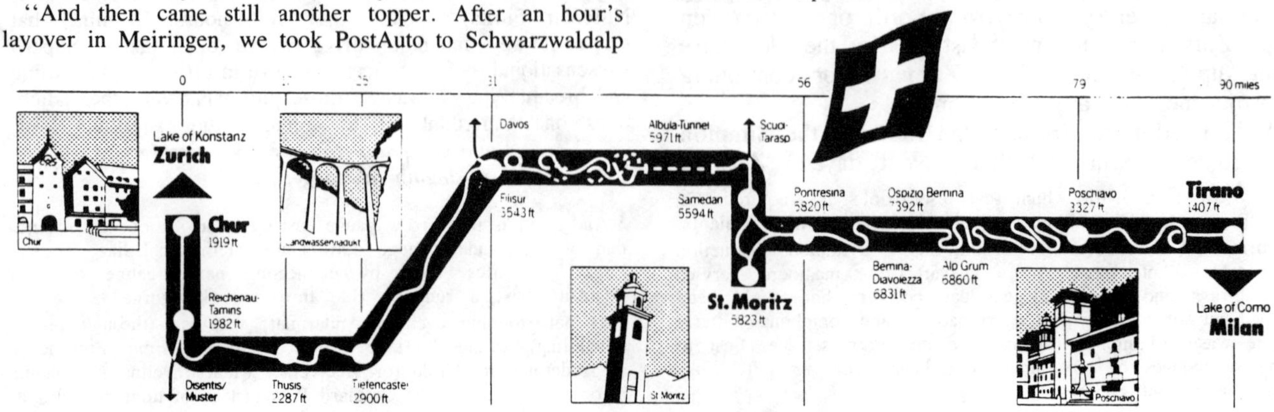

doing between Switzerland and Italy (or vice-versa). Obviously, a *Bernina Express/Glacier Express* combination out of St. Moritz is an enticing one.

Still another narrow gauge spectacular runs from Montreux to Zweisimmen, an hour, forty-minute run via famed ski resort of Gstaad, on the *Panoramic Express,* an observation train with bar. From Zweisimmen, there are frequent connections to Interlaken, an hour's run.

Actually, there are hourly departures from Montreux to Zweisimmen by other trains, all with 1st and 2nd class cars.

### More About Swiss Trains

Swiss Federal Railways (SBB) as well as inter-connecting private railways form a commuter network that's a miracle of precision timing. Trains arrive in main depots about 15 minutes before return departures on an hourly shuttle basis (or less) between cities.

All seats in domestic trains, except for *Glacier Express,* are unreserved. There are overhead racks for small and medium size luggage; large pieces must be stored in the aisles or between seats, a good reason for not taking them. Luggage carts are usually plentiful at all main stations. Zurich, Luzern and Basel stations are on one level, Bern has easily negotiated ramps from train platforms, Lausanne stairs (though not steep). However, at resorts and smaller towns, unless train arrival is on Track (Geis) 1 you must carry your bags down the stairs to the underpass, then up to the main station.

Standard gauge 1st and 2nd class cars are normally divided into Smoking (Raucher/Fumeur) and Non-Smoking (Nicht Raucher/Non-Fumeur) halves; former with red seats, latter green. Seating, on both sides of a center aisle, is a pair of seats facing another pair. Some 1st class cars provide a roomier arrangement: two seats on one side of the aisle, a single on the other side, usually with luggage space as you enter or else between car doors. Some cars have both 1st and 2nd class sections.

Dining in standard gauge Swiss restaurant cars is, we're told, a pleasant experience: a 23-page menu of soup to cheese specialties and a large selection of wines are served by starch-jacketed waiters on tables set with crisp linens, gleaming flatware and glistening crystal.

Four prototypes of a new restaurant car, WRIV, are already in service with 20 or more to follow. 48 passengers are seated in smoking/non-smoking sections; one side has eight tables of four, the other eight tables for two.

Ease of travel with a Swiss Holiday Card is inestimable — and it's valid on private Swiss lines (*Glacier Express,* for example) *whereas EURAILPASS is not.* See *Travel Supplement* for details and prices of this and other special fares.

Airline passengers flying out of Zurich or Geneva with confirmed reservations can check their baggage at any Swiss rail or postal bus station directly to their final destination. Conversely, airline passengers flying into Zurich may check their luggage at the airport to any Swiss destination. In Geneva, they must go to the train station to do that. Very inexpensive, too.

As of 1985, American Express, Diner's, MasterCard and Visa credit cards can be used to purchase rail tickets at all stations.

Cars as well as bicycles can be rented or reserved from Hertz at any of SBBs 600+ stations (from 6 am to 11 pm) by phone or in person; rentals are returnable to any SBB station. Most trains have bike racks in the baggage cars.

### Recommended Stopovers & Hotels Along the Glacier Express Route

**Andermatt** — A plain yet appealing village surrounded by pine-clad, snowy-crested mountains and bisected, as most Swiss towns are, by a turbulent, rock-strewn stream. Though far less cosmopolitan and picturesque than big name resorts, it is unsurpassed as a touring center into a spectacularly scenic area.

*Drei Konig* (3-star), center of town and a short walk from the station, is a very pleasant, family-run hotel with a fairly good restaurant and comfortable rooms with good bath facilities; best rooms have Alpine decor, 1½-story ceiling and balcony. There are six other 3-star hotels (highest rating here), of which we also recommend the *Krone;* its restaurant is tops.

**Brig** — An unpretentious small town but an important rail transit center with great views of the Alps, both to the north and south.

Though not listed in Swiss Hotel Guide, *Schloss Hotel* was recommended as the best in town. For overnight, its small rooms are adequate; if possible, get one facing the imposing Schloss (castle) and mountain peaks beyond.

We had an extremely pleasant dinner on the terrace of the *Schloss Kellar,* a nearby restaurant not connected with our hotel.

**Grindelwald** — Though not on the Glacier Express route (but accessible from Andermatt as previously noted), we can't resist listing what is, possibly, the most stunning panorama of snow-clad mountains, including mighty Jungfrau and slightly less mighty Jungfraujoch, to be found outside the Himalayas. As an important ski and climbing center, it attracts snow lovers from around the world — particularly Japan; we saw more Japanese here than we do in Little Tokyo in Los Angeles. With the main strasse jammed with shops, restaurants and visitors, with the two-car trains shuttling between town and Kleine Scheidegg[5] crammed with passengers, this is indeed an exciting resort.

There are, of course, no lack of hotels: one five-star (the posh, continental-style *Regina;* no credit cards accepted), seven four-stars and 13 three-stars. We nominate four-star *Belvedere* as one of the most gracious in Switzerland with a super-dramatic, unobstructed mountainscape view. And a beautiful indoor pool. We'd love to spend a week here; unfortunately, without advance reservations, we had to settle on *Weisses Kreuz* (supposedly four-star, we'd award it a minimal one).

We saw a number of attractive restaurants, had an excellent dinner (with attentive service) at the four-star *Spinne,* another hotel we'd recommend. Same applies to *Schweizerhof.*[5] But *Belvdere* remains our No. 1 choice.

From Interlaken, it's a 14.6-mile run to Grindelwald (3,393 ft.) by Bernese Oberland friction rack train. Change here for the cogwheel train to Kleine Scheidegg (6,762 ft.), then again for the leg to Jungfraujoch, at 11,333 ft. the highest rail station in Europe. From here there are magnificent views of the Jungfrau (13,642 ft.) and a number of glaciers, including, to the south, mighty Aletsch, the largest river of ice (13.7 miles) on the continent.

Interlaken to Grindelwald takes 41 minutes; after changing trains, it's another 35 min. to Kl. Scheidegg. The final leg, via Eigergletscher takes 51 min. A return from Kl. Scheidegg to Interlaken can be made via Wengen-Lauterbrunnen in an hour and 19 min., thus completing a circle trip of great beauty and variety — on a clear day.

[5] Though this (Swiss Inn) is the most common hotel name in the country, it is not the name of a chain — each hotel is individually owned, usually by members of the founding family. Same applies to various Post hotels.

# Map of Switzerland

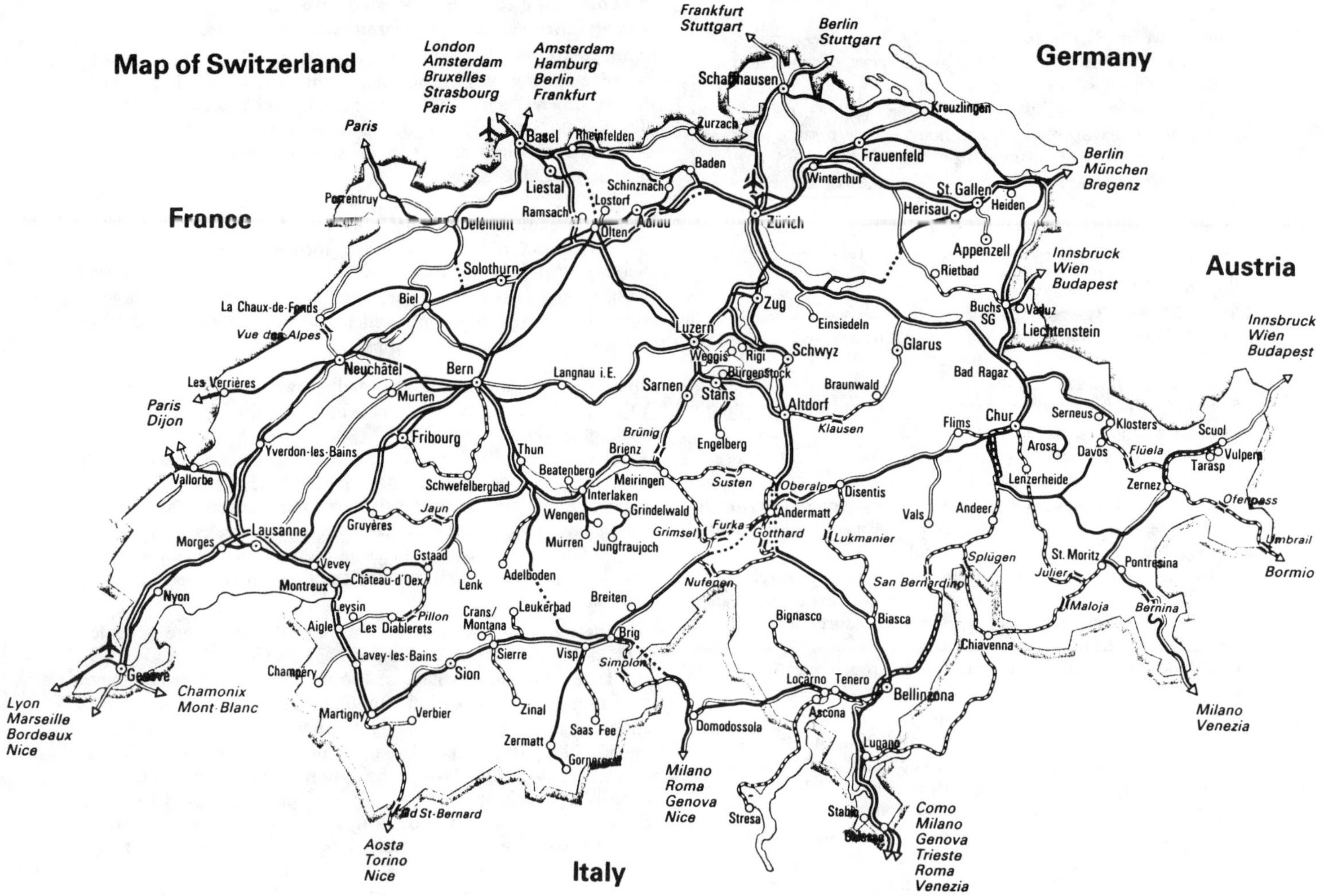

Super Highways

Highways

Highways with postal bus service

Railway lines

⊙ State capitals

∘ Towns

≍ Mountain passes

✈ International airports

**GLACIER EXPRESS**
Zermatt – Brig – Andermatt – Disentis/M. –
**St. Moritz**

| | Zürich | Zug | Schaffhausen | St. Moritz | St. Gallen | Porrentruy | Olten | Montreux | Luzern | Lugano | Locarno | Lausanne | Kreuzlingen | Interlaken | Genève | Fribourg | Chur | Chiasso | Chaux-de-Fonds, La | Buchs/SG | Brig | Bern | Basel |
|---|---|---|---|---|---|---|---|---|---|---|---|---|---|---|---|---|---|---|---|---|---|---|---|
| Andermatt | 117 | 78 | 170 | 162 | 155 | 204 | 125 | 200 | 75 | 111 | 102 | 234 | 164 | 93 | 296 | 186 | 92 | 135 | 220 | 133 | 78 | 154 | 169 |
| Basel | 85 | 113 | 93 | 291 | 166 | 68 | 41 | 182 | 94 | 267 | 258 | 198 | 139 | 147 | 264 | 127 | 196 | 291 | 98 | 188 | 236 | 91 | |
| Bern | 123 | 117 | 170 | 315 | 206 | 114 | 69 | 86 | 91 | 262 | 253 | 106 | 187 | 60 | 165 | 31 | 238 | 286 | 69 | 230 | 177 | | |
| Brig | 195 | 156 | 247 | 240 | 228 | 306 | 190 | 123 | 153 | 146 | 113 | 153 | 242 | 117 | 215 | 180 | 170 | 170 | 244 | 211 | | | |
| Buchs/SG | 111 | 107 | 124 | 129 | 52 | 251 | 172 | 316 | 130 | 187 | 178 | 333 | 85 | 194 | 395 | 261 | 42 | 211 | 265 | | | | |
| Chaux-de-Fonds, La | 158 | 164 | 206 | 360 | 239 | 62 | 101 | 122 | 160 | 316 | 307 | 98 | 225 | 129 | 142 | 68 | 273 | 340 | | | | | |
| Chiasso | 239 | 200 | 294 | 131 | 272 | 326 | 248 | 297 | 197 | 26 | 61 | 327 | 286 | 215 | 389 | 304 | 170 | | | | | | |
| Chur | 119 | 115 | 171 | 77 | 94 | 257 | 180 | 324 | 138 | 146 | 137 | 341 | 125 | 185 | 403 | 266 | | | | | | | |
| Fribourg | 151 | 157 | 200 | 333 | 232 | 125 | 96 | 58 | 123 | 278 | 269 | 63 | 218 | 78 | 137 | | | | | | | | |
| Genève | 288 | 295 | 334 | 424 | 366 | 204 | 234 | 93 | 262 | 361 | 324 | 62 | 352 | 215 | | | | | | | | | |
| Interlaken | 118 | 88 | 144 | 255 | 182 | 168 | 123 | 136 | 64 | 191 | 182 | 153 | 195 | | | | | | | | | | |
| Kreuzlingen | 71 | 101 | 46 | 212 | 34 | 207 | 139 | 273 | 132 | 262 | 253 | 290 | | | | | | | | | | | |
| Lausanne | 226 | 232 | 272 | 378 | 304 | 157 | 172 | 26 | 200 | 299 | 262 | | | | | | | | | | | | |
| Locarno | 206 | 167 | 258 | 163 | 252 | 293 | 215 | 246 | 164 | 37 | | | | | | | | | | | | | |
| Lugano | 215 | 176 | 267 | 126 | 261 | 302 | 224 | 283 | 173 | | | | | | | | | | | | | | |
| Luzern | 55 | 25 | 107 | 237 | 118 | 130 | 52 | 183 | | | | | | | | | | | | | | | |
| Montreux | 189 | 215 | 255 | 363 | 287 | 183 | 155 | | | | | | | | | | | | | | | | |
| Olten | 61 | 66 | 106 | 262 | 136 | 88 | | | | | | | | | | | | | | | | | |
| Porrentruy | 144 | 150 | 158 | 346 | 222 | | | | | | | | | | | | | | | | | | |
| St. Gallen | 85 | 95 | 80 | 190 | | | | | | | | | | | | | | | | | | | |
| St. Moritz | 206 | 202 | 258 | | | | | | | | | | | | | | | | | | | | |
| Schaffhausen | 53 | 82 | | | | | | | | | | | | | | | | | | | | | |
| Zug | 30 | | | | | | | | | | | | | | | | | | | | | | |

Distances in kilometres

**St. Moritz** — This famous resort overlooks a small lake within a mountainous bowl, a lovely setting and, no doubt, doubly so in winter when the mountains are snow-clad. But with tennis, riding, golfing, windsurfing, ice skating and, especially, hiking — four cable cars climb into the upper reaches from where you can hike forever — it is also an outstanding summer resort.

The town, built hillside well above the lake (St. Moritz See), is essentially disappointing, though there are some excellent shops and confisseries.

Of the five-star hotels, the *Carlton's* understated elegance and majestic view high up above the town is unquestionably the best — far better than the gloomy *Kulm* and that baroque monstrosity, *Badrutt's Palace.* Four-star *Neues Post,* centrally located, is an adequate choice, has nice restaurant. Same applies to *Schweizerhof.* Three-star *Waldhaus,* near the station and beautifully sited at one end of the lake, is the resort's best value.

Whichever hotel you opt for, always reserve a room with lake view — worth the extra cost.

**Zermatt** — Dominated by the white-clad Matterhorn, this extremely attractive resort, perhaps the country's most colorful, lies at the bottom and along the sides of a mountain valley thru which the inevitable tumultous stream tumbles. Innumerable window boxes filled with vari-colored geraniums (a hallmark of most Swiss towns) decorate the facades of rustic-style buildings. Here, too, the streets and the slopes are jammed with visitors[7] for there's excellent shopping and entertainment, lots of attractive restaurants, tearooms and confisseries, many horse-drawn carriages, cable cars, cogwheel trains and ski lifts, good hiking, skiing and mountain viewing.

We stayed at the *Pollux* (four-star), loved its friendly service, large rooms; those on top floor are 1½-story, cheerfully furnished in Swiss rustic (blonde knotty pine), have well-equipped bath, a balcony. Hotel's *Avenstube* is an excellent, attractive restaurant. Here, as all around town, there's nightly live music, entertainment.

*Schweizerhof* (four-star) is equally attractive though a larger, more contemporary type with several restaurants, indoor pool, nightly entertainment. Both hotels are on the main street, not far from the Bahnhof.

There are dozens of other hotels and gasthauses, headed by two rather austere five-stars. In fact, the number of listed hotels indicates that Zermatt is the most popular resort in Switzerland.

**Klosters** — Although not on the Glacier Express route, it's not too far from St. Moritz — and since it's our very favorite Swiss resort, we simply had to tell you about it in the hope that you, too, will enjoy it as much as we did for five delightful days.

Here is a pleasing, friendly, refreshing, unpolluted and untainted small town in which you'd want to raise your children. Though not nearly as dramatic a site as Grindelwald, the overall effect of the subdued, varied greens of the valley and its softly rounded mountains is, somehow, fullfilling. And hikes into the countryside, with houses and slim, graceful church spires perched way up, are so satisfying and rewarding. We were sad when we left, can't wait to return.

No. 1 hotel is the lovely, gracious continental-style *Pardenn* (five-star) with a great view across the valley, particularly from the balcony of a sitting/bedroom accommodation. Has Grill, Tavern and dining room and terrace dining, indoor pool/health club. Had an excellent dinner in the Grill — in fact, we dined well at the *Alpina, Vereina, Steinbock* and *Walserhof,* all excellent four-star hotels.

*Walserhof,* where we stayed, is an outstanding small hotel with beautifully appointed bed/sitting rooms, marble tiled baths, verandas with flower boxes. Only drawback: being on main highway, noisy during the day — but we were rarely in the room then. Hotel's Swiss rustic Stube, paneled in pseudo-antique pine, is stunning.

While there we trained to Davos *(Dah-VOHS)* and St. Moritz (our second visit to the latter). We found Davos disappointingly commercial and, comparatively, drab despite its reputation as a big time ski resort.

From Chur, you reach Klosters via Landquart (change trains) in a little over an hour. From St. Moritz to Klosters, it's a 2:26 run including changes at Filisur and Davos. Either way, Klosters is well worth the detour.

[7] Except for mini-cars used by hotels to transport guests and baggage or mini-trucks of suppliers, there is no auto traffic in or around Zermatt; tourists arriving by car must park them in Tasch, about 13 minutes away by shuttle train.

# SCANDINAVIA

This is one of the most attractive rail touring areas in Europe, one in which tourists can enjoyably spend an entire vacation . . . and one that's an ideal prelude to a Trans-Siberian trip.

Trains are modern, clean and efficient — and many of the routes are highly scenic, particularly those we've described in Norway.

See *Travel Supplement* for information on Scandinavian rail passes and fares.

Blossom Time and Winter are especially fine times to see Fjord Country in all its spectacular beauty.

## NORWAY

The rugged, dramatic beauty of western Norway's mountains and fjords is rivaled only by that of South Island, New Zealand — except in Norway there's more of it. If grandly overpowering panoramas of ice, snow and towering forests are your thing, you'll revel in this scenic wonderland stretching from Stavenger and Bergen in the south past the Arctic Circle to the North Cape, the northernmost tip of Europe where Norway, Sweden, Finland and Russia meet.

By train and boat, the ways to go, fjord country is a succession of tall granite cliffs serrated by cascading waterfalls and studded with masses of evergreens. Beyond are quiet, green valleys with quaint houses. In the sunlight, the mountain-bound fjords with their deep blue waters come alive, leave their brooding somberness behind — and leave you feeling so beautiful inside.

It is here in the Land of the Midnight Sun that you have the opportunity to enjoy two of the world's most exciting train rides. We've taken both — we urge you to do the same.

## OSLO TO ANDALSNES *(Oon-DOLLS-ness)*

This is a seven-hour trip northwest across Norway with a number of stops enroute. The route along Lake Mjosa and the Lagen River is both lovely and picturesque with many vignettes of farm houses and pine-clad hills looking for all the world like paintings we'd just seen in Oslo's National Gallery. The scenery was particularly noteworthy after leaving the town of Hamar; at times the tracks were at river level, then suddenly rose until we were looking down at rushing waters. Nonetheless, as pretty as it was, this part of the ride did not warrant a "don't miss" rating. But after leaving Dombas,[1] the picture changed to the dramatic; the terrain became mountainous (the eastward slopes of the western coastal range that runs the length of Norway) while thousands and thousands of pines ran up to the sky as the train ascended westward thru the Rauma River gorge. At 4:05 we left Bjorli and started the truly spectacular leg that climbed to 633 meters (about 2057 ft.). Twenty minutes later, at Flatmark, mist threw diaphanous veils over green mountain tops, innumerable waterfalls tumbled down their sides; at the one called Bridal Veil, we counted six different falls even though the snowpacks were sparse at this time of year (early Fall). From Marstein onward, the gorge narrows and tall, perpendicular walls of black granite towering on both sides enclose the train in a crushing, breathlessly hypnotic embrace; along the banks of the richly green river, farmhouses appear like toys against the giant cliffs which reach a height of 3,000 feet.[2] This spectacular requires rubberneck virtuosity for wherever you look, forward, backward and upward, right and left, you see masses of granite magnificence that's nothing short of overwhelming. For sheer dramatic beauty, this outperforms any other train trip we've taken — and that includes Cuzco to Machu Picchu and Garmisch to Innsbruck.

Andalsnes, surrounded as it is by snow-clad, jagged peaks often obscured by mists and clouds, is as strikingly situated as any sea level village in the world. Tidy streets are lined with attractive, well-kempt, prosperous-looking houses and gardens that, on a Sunday morning, seem to doze in contentment. Older houses, two-story with basement and attic, are mostly frame construction though there are some of brick, part stone or concrete, and also stucco. But most newer houses are Norwegian ranch style: one-story with V sloped roofs and an insulating basement that includes a garage, storage space and family room. There are some two-story apartment buildings.

[1] At Dombas, part of the train runs north to Trondheim (Dovre Line), the other (Raume Line) continues west to Andalsnes.

[2] This is Trollveggen (Troll's Wall), highest vertical granite cliff in northern Europe. Nearby Ramsdalshorn Mountain, not far from Andalsnes, rivals Matterhorn as a climber's challenge.

## OSLO TO BERGEN

This 8½-hour ride is certainly *not* the "indisputably finest one-day train trip in Europe" as one author states. It does, however, have some great scenic stretches though none as spectacularly dramatic as the one previously described. Nonetheless, this run to Bergen does provide a final 3½ hours, from Haugensted to Myrdal and on to Voss and Bergen, that in anyone's book provides panoramas of unusual beauty at track elevations up to 1300 meters — and you're still looking upwards at jagged, snow-covered peaks despite a particularly dry summer; in the winter, the snowfields and, behind them, glaciers must be awesome.

Much of the route lies along rivers and lakes, runs thru green valleys rising steeply to pine-studded hills. On sunshiny days, it's a brightly tinted picture of rural tranquility, though one wonders about the compensations for living in such isolation during long winter months when there's little or no sun. Yet it must have its moments, just as it does for train passengers who, after a less than ecstatic 5-hour run are suddenly jolted upright by the rugged, rocky, snowy terrain and, beyond, a glacier that heralded our arrival at Finse, headquarters (at 1222 meters) for a battalion of men who, nine months a year, fight to keep the tracks, and snowsheds covering them, clear of mountains of snow — a forsaken land in which to wage such an essential battle but an enchanting one to onlookers. At Halingskied (1300 meters), the train winds downhill thru tunnels and snowsheds[3] to Myrdal,[4] where there's a startling glimpse of a gorgeous, deep blue crater lake. Between here and Voss it's all downhill; in the distance the tall, snowy coastal range hovers high above. Here the mountains are less rocky and harshly rugged, more pine clad and soothing. After Voss, famed for its myriad waterfalls, the tracks follow the flowing beauty of green fjords encased by walls of granite that would be startling were it not for the super spectacle encountered out of Andalsnes.

Unquestionably, this is an unusually beautiful trip — one best taken Oslo to Bergen; if done vice-versa, the final five hours would prove a tedious letdown.[5] Whether or not both Oslo-Bergen and Oslo-Andalsnes trips should be taken is a matter of how much time you allot to your Norwegian vacation and how it is routed. However, Oslo-Andalsnes is unquestionably the most spectacular.

[3] Between Oslo and Bergen (300 miles), there are about 200 tunnels, 300 bridges and 18 miles of snowsheds. Line was opened in 1909, electrified in 1964.

[4] If not taking one of the day trips out of Bergen to Sognefjord, Flam and Stalheim, then a detour from Myrdal to Flam by a connecting 12½-mile rail link (Flam Line) is in order. After overnight in Flam, take the early morning boat to Gudvangen in Sognefjord, then bus to Stalheim for lunch, then by bus to Voss and train to Bergen. Of course, the reverse routing is in order if going to Oslo from Bergen. However, the detour in either direction eliminates the most beautiful segment of the trip.

[5] Same applies to the Andalsnes-Oslo rail trip. We returned from Andalsnes on the night sleeper train (very comfortable), arrived in Oslo early in the morning with plenty of time to board the 10:05 am train for Bergen.

## All About Norwegian Trains

There's first and second class cars; some trains, like the one we took to Andalsnes, are all second class and, strangely enough, preferable to first class as many of the second class cars are newer; though far from luxurious, the cars are clean, have comfortable airplane type seats with pull-down table tops, fresh linen headrests and the wide windows provide excellent viewing. Our train had a cafeteria car plus a food vendor selling hot coffee, tea and sandwiches.

Wagon-Lits style sleeping cars have double (some triple) compartments that are small but adequate and very efficiently arranged with wash basin (and potty for men). As in the day trains, there are toilets at both ends of each car.

There are multi-daily departures on the Oslo-Andalsnes, Oslo-Trondheim, Oslo-Bergen (direct or via Myrdal-Voss) lines. However, best to take the forenoon departures.

Express trains *(Ekspresstog)* have reserved seats only; passengers without same must pay a reservation fee to the conductor. Best also to reserve seats on Fast trains *(Hurtigtog)* either at Norwegian State Railways (NSB) office or thru a travel agency.[6] Same applies to sleeping car compartments operated by NSB within Norway and to Denmark via Sweden. For journeys between Norway and Sweden, sleeping cars are run by Swedish State Railways.

*Special Note:* State Railways' newest cars, B7s, tilt on curves and when pulled by NSBs newest electric locomotives, EL17s, provide sustained runs of up to 100 mph.

These aluminum B7s, five to six tons lighter than steel cars, have disc brakes, an air-filled rubber cushion that insulates against track noise and vibrations. They come in three types: second class, combined first/second class, service cars; latter have nursery and handicapped passenger compartments.

In every respect — seating, climate control, closed toilet system, protective window shades, enclosed passages between cars, automatic doors, et all — these B7s compare favorably with anything else on rails.

## Norwegian Trip Planning

Besides at least one of the two train trips, you *must* spend several days in Oslo and Bergen — plus time to explore fjord country by boat and train out of Bergen. If not visiting countries farther east, arrive in Oslo then journey west to Bergen.

Although not a beautiful city, Oslo is an interesting one with some great attractions. We loved the spacious, airy Munch *(Monk)* Museum filled with the works of Edvard Munch, the great Norwegian expressionist painter, a distrubed genius who died at the age of 46. More of his and other Norwegian paintings are at the National Gallery; many are of great vigor, power and sturdiness that give a vivid account of Norway of the past. But Oslos' greatest highlights are the Folk Center, Viking Museum, Kon Tiki Museum and, above all, the utterly dazzling Vigeland Sculpture Park and Museum; the latter are two of Europe's standout cultural attractions. To stroll thru this land of super-large sculptures, their impact as colossal as their size, is an experience quite unmatched elsewhere in Europe.

Bergen, a lovely, lovely port city, is simply a pure delight. Its downtown dock area is a picturesque Nordic dream with colorful houses climbing the surrounding hills. Great sightseeing: Edvard Grieg's home, Hill of the Trolls, stunning Stave Church, interesting Hanseatic Museum, good collections of Munch and other top Norwegian artists at the two art museums.

Two or three days in each city are none too much.

Depending on your overall itinerary, you can arrive in Oslo (our preference) and depart from Bergen — or vice-versa. The rail trip to Andalsnes should be taken out of Oslo, in which case you must return by rail to Oslo or else take one of the daily mail boats from Aalesund, a short bus ride from Andalsnes, to Bergen (morning departure, 2 pm arrival).

By rail, bus and steamer, Bergen is *the* center for day tours to the fjords and mountains of the southern west coast. Particularly outstanding are the tours to Sognefjord-Stalheim and Sognefjord-Flam Valley. At least another day for one of those should be added to your stay in Bergen.

### GETTING TO NORWAY

The fast way is by air to Oslo and Bergen, the pleasant way by sea. We've done both and if an extra day is not a factor, we opt for the ferry route, particularly since it's much less expensive.

The ferries connecting Norway with continental Europe are *not* car-carrying tugboats but beautiful ocean liners capable of transporting cars. At least those of Danish Seaways (DFDS) that we took from Newcastle, England to Oslo and back from Bergen were — and as far as we know, so are those of the Fred Olsen Bergen Line.

Both ships we took — *England* (8,500 tons) to Oslo, *Venus* (10,000 tons) from Bergen — were completely air-conditioned, had excellent facilities: attractive, large dining room; lounge with two bars; cafeteria and nightclub; two duty free shops with large, well-priced selection of liquors, cigarettes and perfumes. Accommodations range from two deluxe suites to double and single cabins with or without toilet/shower. There are public toilets and tiled shower rooms for those with dormitory accommodations (extendible airplane-type lounge seats). Best cabins with private facilities are those on A deck — but be sure to get an outside one as those inside, though large, are very dark. B deck cabins are passable; do not recommend those on C deck. Crossing between Newcastle and Oslo takes 27 hours, to Bergen about 21 hours. Rates are reasonable (even for A deck);[7] dormitory accommodations inexpensive.

[6] For extremely efficient service, we recommend Winge Reisebureau in Oslo (Karl Johansgate 33), Bergen (Strandgaten 5), London (20 Pall Mall) or Paris (10 rue Auber). They have Pleasant Scandinavia Tours, overland and by mail boat, that are outstanding.

[7] With a EurailPass, you get a 20% discount on published fares. However, we do not recommend booking thru Bergen Line, the DFDS agent, in New York as dollar fares were 15% to 40% higher in the U.S. than fares quoted in pounds for Great Britain. Furthermore, we were booked in a cabin without toilet/shower (none available according to New York) only to find plenty available when we reconfirmed in England. We suggest booking thru Winge (see footnote 6) or DFDS, Latham House, 16 Minories, London EC 3N 1AM, England.

The Newcastle-Bergen or Newcastle-Stavanger-Bergen runs (and vice-versa) are equally as satisfactory; in fact, *Venus* was a bit more elaborate than *England.* Fares are less than those to Oslo, particularly in Low Season (Aug. 24 - Oct. 18); High Season begins May 22 when the ships begin Spring-Summer crossings three times weekly. Car ferrying rates are inexpensive (free if there are four paying passengers in one party).

From Amsterdam, Fred Olsen-Bergen Line uses *Venus* and *Jupiter* twice weekly for overnight crossings to Stavanger-Bergen and return, once weekly to Kristiansand and return. Between Copenhagen-Oslo, there's daily year round overnight service by DFDS.

There's direct rail service to Oslo from Stockholm (6½ hours) and Copenhagen (via Goteborg, Sweden). From Hamburg, it's a 5¼-hour run to Copenhagen by express train.

**NORWEGIAN COASTAL VOYAGES**

Year 'round, four Norwegian shipping firms combine to offer *daily* sailings from Bergen to Kirkenes — 11-day round trip voyages on 12 small steamers, or mail boats as they're generally called. This unique service, only one of its kind, carries mail and supplies to 32 coastal villages, furnishes transportation to their inhabitants and provides an enchanting cruise for tourists willing to forego the amenities of luxury liners. And in conjunction with Norwegian and Swedish railways, this is a great way to circle around Norway or both Norway and Sweden. Here are two suggested routings:

1) Oslo-Andalsnes rail trip (one day), bus to Molde and board the mail boat bound for Bodo (three days). Return to Oslo by rail via Trondheim, then by rail to Bergen.

2) Instead of disembarking in Bodo, continue to the North Cape and Kirkenes (three more days), then return to Narvik by bus. From there, one can train across Lapland and descend south to Stockholm, or else bus from Narvik to the train for Trondheim.

Of course, one can sail up to Kirkenes and back but ports of call are the same both north and southbound. SAS serves many of these ports so a fast return can be made if desired.

In July and August, there are two voyages to Spitzbergen each month, one in August, of 12 days; three days are spent exploring the channels and islands of this huge archipelago — a magnificent experience that we enjoyed on a *World Discoverer* cruise a few years ago.

We had booked passage for the 11-day voyage for September of '82, but the weather in Bergen had been so rainy that we cancelled. However, we did inspect the *King Olaf* and *Harald Jarl,* the newest and largest of the fleet. Each has two staterooms with private toilet/shower; balance are not as large though adequate but without private facilities. The lounge and dining room are comfortable (no bar, no liquor service) and we hear the food is wholesomely good. There was a promenade deck and covered aft viewing deck. Friends of ours took and enjoyed the round trip, particularly the three (optional) shore excursions.[8]

*Important:* Because of their popularity, all 12 ships are usually sold out way in advance — a year or more for the few cabins with private facilities. Winge Reisebureau is, we're sure, your best bet for reservations. Incidentally, they have tours that include three or four days of coastal cruising.

The winter rate (Oct.1 - March 31) is almost half that for May 23 - August 31, the peak season. Rates are lower for the three other periods: May 1-22; Sept. 1-20; Sept. 21-30. Passengers 67 years and over get a special rate except for May 23 - Aug. 31 period.

**DINING & DRINKING The Norsk Way**

Our most vivid recollection of our last trip around Norway, other than the fantastic scenery, is that of hotel breakfast and luncheon *koldtbords,* literally groaning boards of food and not all cold; no way did we eat one meal *and* the other. Varying somewhat from hotel to hotel, breakfast *koldtbord* includes fruit, canned fruit juices, stewed prunes, cereals, cheese (Norwegians eat LARGE amounts of cheese), cold cuts, herring (*sild,* prepared in numerous ways) and all sorts of pickled things (prominently beets), hard boiled eggs (hidden in a basket to keep warm) and often scrambled as well, hashed brown potatoes, variety of breads, jams and coffee cakes (they don't know what you mean by "a Danish"), coffee, tea, chocolate or milk. Lunch is similar except cereals and juices are eliminated (but not the herring and other pickled things) and several hot dishes and desserts added.

The average Norwegian eats more sensibly: a big breakfast, sandwich at noon and main meal *(middag)* around 5 pm and, perhaps, a sandwich or two before retiring.

Although their specialties are good, pleasant and nicely prepared, Norwegian chefs lack the nuances and brilliance of their Danish counterparts, although fish and seafood are delicious (and very fresh): tiny crayfish *(kreps),* shrimp *(reker),* crab, salmon *(laks),* cod *(torsk)* and trout *(orret)*; fish may be poached *(kokt),* sauteed or smoked. You may also have a chance to try elk and reindeer steaks, some of the unusual types of arctic berries. Top hotels also serve the usual run of continental dishes.

*Akevitt* is the national drink; best brand is *Linje* (or *Linie,* line, in reference to the custom of shipping it across the equator to mellow). In Norway, it's coupled with, usually, an Export beer (to prevent a red nose, they say). Besides Export (strong), there's Pilsner (lager), Big (very light) and Bokkel (dark). St. Halvard is a pleasant liqueur similar in taste to Benedictine. Imported wines and liquors are VERY expensive, and liquor laws very stringent, complex and confusing — yet we don't recall not being able to enjoy a drink at any normal hour in tourist hotels.

At cocktail time in Oslo, we heartily recommend the half-hour train ride to Holmenkollen Hill for drinks and/or dinner at the restaurant while watching the sun play over the fjord — or continue all the way to Frognerseteren where the view is even better and the restaurant serves Norwegian specialties. Liveliest spot in Bergen is the Hotel Norge.

**SHOPPING Is Interesting**

Though not offering as extensive a range as in Denmark, there's still some excellent buys. Outstanding, we felt, were hand knit or hand loomed sweaters, caps, socks, scarves in traditional, colorful Norwegian patterns; if going to Bergen, buy 'em there. Other buys are items of enameled silver, another Norwegian specialty, and beautifully styled pewter; David-Andersen, a fine Oslo store, is *the* place for both. Hand blown glass and other craft goods are both attractive and reasonably priced, as are Viking design reproductions in jewelry. Merchants deduct the 17% tax providing purchases are mailed to your home; we received ours in a relatively short time (about two months) via surface mail.

[8] From Molde, there's an overland bus/ferry trip to connect with ship at Kristiansund. At Trondheim, there's a visit to the Ringve Museum. And weather permitting after June 1, there's a grand North Cape bus excursion into the interior.

It should be noted that these mail boats *do not* cruise into the fjords as do luxury liners. Entering the fjords is a highlight that shouldn't be missed; be sure to do this out of Bergen if you haven't previously enjoyed the tremendous beauty of these inland waterways.

# DENMARK

Although not nearly as scenically spectacular as Norway, Denmark's rail trips can be rewarding. For here is a country comprising 500 islands and a peninsula whose railroads are connected by swift, ultramodern ferries unlike any others for they have four tracks capable of carrying 18 passenger rail cars at speeds up to 20 mph.

Danish State Railways (DSB), whose main lines are electrified, connects Scandinavia with the rest of Europe. According to one writer, "The high standard of comfort aboard these trains is based on Danish design and furniture making. Throughout Europe, the red Danish passenger coaches are enthusiastically admired by travelers."

But the most delightful part of Danish train travel is, if time's a factor, the possibility of seeing a goodly portion of this country, often referred to as Fairyland, in a whirlwind, one-day rail tour.

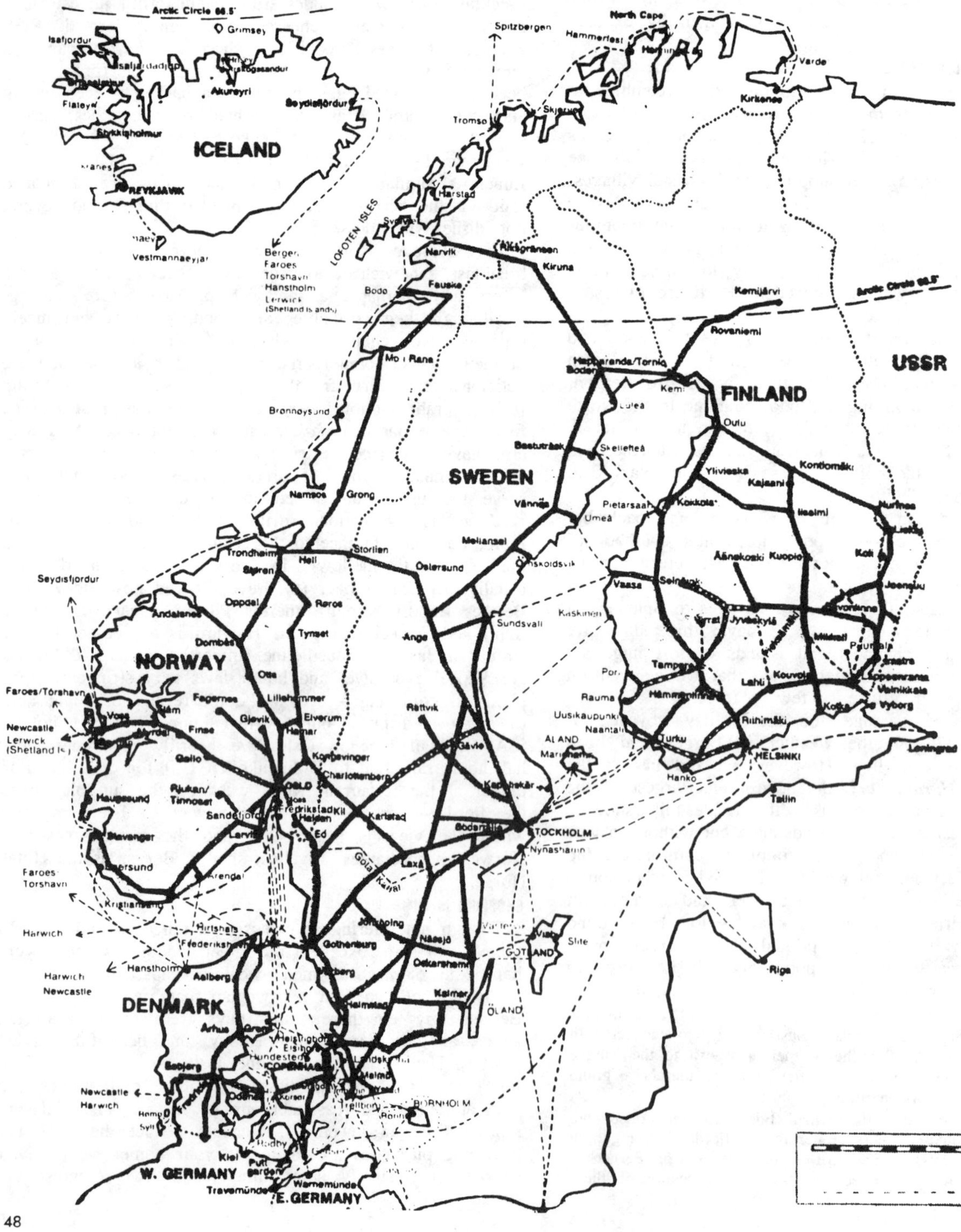

Denmark's complex of trains, ferries and ferry terminals amazes all visitors by its inter-meshed accuracy. As a result, riding the rails here is a new experience.

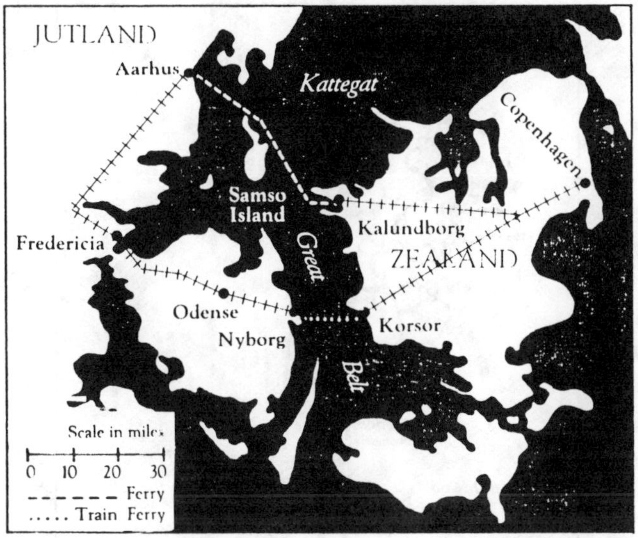


**Recommended Circle Trip**

It begins and ends in Copenhagen's Central Station, a great arched building that resembles a mammoth Viking hall yet is one of the world's most hospitable rail terminals with every type of amenity and facility.

Board one of the morning trains for Kalundborg, a port on the west coast of Zealand, for an hour and a half ramble past whitewashed, red-roofed houses and across fertile green and yellow fields dotted with large stands of trees. At Kalundborg rail and ferry terminal, walk onto the large, impressive Aarhus-bound ferry that has many cruise ship facilities, including cabins if you wish to rest during the three-hour crossing of the Great Belt.

Founded by Vikings, Aarhus is Denmark's second largest city (250,000 pop.) — a pleasant mix of lovely, medieval-looking churches and modern provincial buildings. Here in the pedestrian malls (*Stroget* or walking streets) shopping is both delightful and extensive. Nearby, in a portion of the Botanical Gardens, is Old Town, an open air museum of 60 half-timbered houses and stores dating from 1600 to 1860 — moved here from various parts of Denmark.

Return in the afternoon on the *Limfjorden,* an articulated, limited-stop express (advance seat reservations needed) that runs effortlessly over ribbon-smooth rails. At Odense, Hans Christian Andersen's boyhood home is now a delightful museum, while the DSB rail museum, just behind the station, contains historic engines, cars and model trains.

At Nyborg, the train is broken into two sections and run onto the deck of an 8,000-ton, 499-ft. ferry operated exclusively for rail passengers — the last word in late 20th century ferry design.

In an hour, train and passengers are disembarked at Korsor and quickly on their way to Copenhagen.

Other DSB circle trips, including one to Sweden, are detailed in a special folder obtainable at Central Station.

**Scandinavian Tourist Bureau**

New York 10017 — 655 Third Ave. (212-949-2333)

Information/schedules only for each of the Scandinavian countries. However, tickets and Railpasses can be purchased in the U.S. thru Crown Line Tours, 3300 S. Gessmer, Houston, Tx 77063 (800-722-6737). *Note:* Scandinavian Railpass can be sold only as part of a travel package.

# Finland To Russia

Possibly the best approach to the East from the West (and vice-versa) is along the Gulf of Finland from Helsinki to Leningrad or Moscow, primarily because of the excellent, combined VR (Finnish State Railways) and SZD (Soviet State Railways) express train service.

*Repin,* named after Soviet artist Ilya Repin, leaves Helsinki daily June 3 - Sept. 29 (daily except Saturdays balance of year) at noon, arrives Leningrad (289 miles) at 2005. Russian locomotive and staff are substituted at Vainikkala. Day coaches are hard class (plastic or leather seats) but soft class cars with two berth compartments are also available (and recommended). Return journey leaves Leningrad at 1100, arrives Helsinki at 1700.

*Tolstoi,* with both soft and hard class sleepers, leaves Helsinki at 1700, arrives Moscow at 0922 (does not stop in Leningrad). Leaves at 2200, arrives Helsinki (692 miles) at 1230.*

Both trains have, we're told, elegant Soviet restaurant cars in which formally dressed waiters serve Russian meals which, on this run at least, include such delicacies as caviar, sturgeon, steak and ham. Tastefully wood paneled, the cars have picture windows gaily curtained, tables set with china, crystal and flatware on white linen cloths, decorated with a vase of fresh flowers.

Finnish section of the trip is covered by EURAILPASS but not on Soviet portion; arrange latter with Intourist. Sleeping car accommodations and soft class day compartments cost extra.

* Moscow time is one hour ahead of Helsinki's.

# ENGLAND / SCOTLAND

In September of 1825, the 20-mile long Stockton & Darlington Railway became the world's first publicly owned railroad. From 1837, one of the first regular passenger services ran between Birmingham and Euston. In 1938, the *Mallard* was rocketing along at 126 mph. Today, Great Britain has the highest density passenger service in Europe with 16,000 daily trains serving over 2,000 stations thruout the nation. And although this network is primarily city to city commuter oriented, it still encompasses a fascinating and extensive Great Rail Trip. To illustrate it, we have chosen Voyages Jules Verne's superbly designed

### *The Flying Scotsman*

Not to be confused with British Rail's crack train between London and Edinburgh, this 16-day program, with one departure in May and another in September, is a model for anyone wishing to see much of the best of Britain's scenic and historic highlights. It should be mentioned, however, that though you can easily follow this model on your own, you'll miss doing so on the vintage Pullman train used on the tour.[1]

The itinerary is classic: London to York, Edinburgh, Inverness, Kyle of Localsh and Isle of Skye, Mallaig and Ft. Williams to famed Gleneagles, then the beautiful Lake District, fascinating Chester and back to London via Oxford. This entire area, which we have explored in depth, is one of our most favorite — and the itinerary, within the framework of 16 days, cannot be improved upon. We highly recommend it.

Aside from the London-Edinburgh run, we have not ridden the rails in this area but we have driven all thru it — and found it strikingly rugged. The coastline north of Kyle of Localsh we described as "alternating seascapes and mountain panoramas, pine forests and granite cliffs and peaks, long arches and tunnels of leafy trees, placid lakes and boiling trout streams, pastoral grazing lands, dotted with sheep — not to be missed by anyone loving the dramatic, majestic and beautiful."

Individual travelers can traverse the same route on their own: Britrail's *Flying Scotsman* to Edinburgh (4½ hours) — or else an overnight sleeper — followed by one of three daily (except Sunday) trains to Inverness (3½ hours),[2] then on to Kyle of Localash (2:50). From Mallaig (reached by ferry from Kyle of Localsh *but only in summer)* to Fort William and Crianlarich (for Gleneagles) is a four-hour run.

From Perth to Glasgow to Oxenholme (for Lake District) requires consulting *Continental Timetable* for workable connections. Oxenholme to Crewe is a 1:38 run; Crewe to Chester 42 min. by another train. But you can return direct to London from Chester in 4:21; Oxford should be visited as a side trip from London.[3]

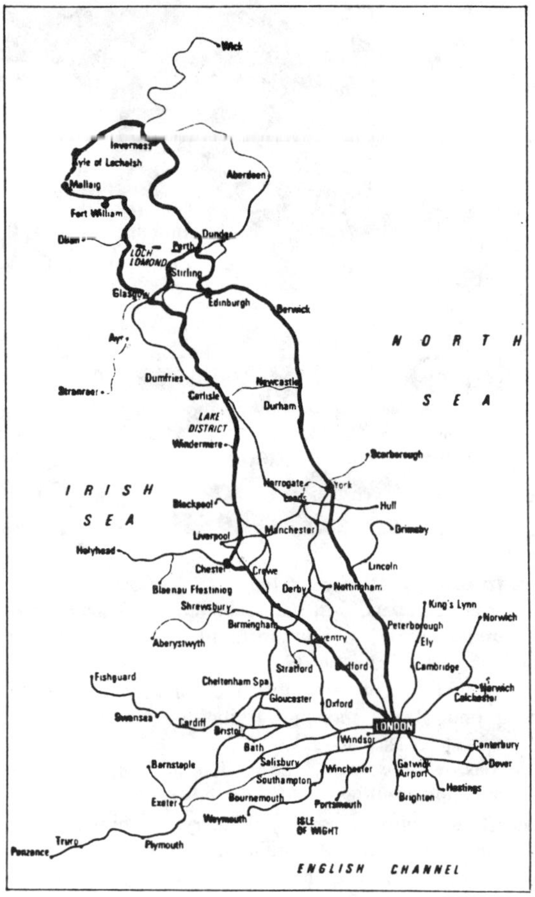


Route of *Flying Scotsman* and *Highlands Fling* (shown in heavy black)

### *A Highlands Fling*

A much shorter version can be booked thru British Rail.[4] During the summer, a vintage saloon (lounge) car is attached to the train making the 40-mile run from Fort William to Mallaig over the West Highland Line (which starts in Glasgow). Then there's a 1930 Great Western observation car, described as elegant and nostalgic, that's attached to the rear of the 1710 train from Kyle of Localsh to Inverness[5]. The gap between Mallaig and Kyle (Strait) of Localsh up the Sound of Sleat is covered in two hours by a spartan passenger/freight ferry.

[1] Overnight accommodations are in deluxe or first class hotels.

[2] One is a night train, Monday to Friday, with first and second class sleepers; although it arrives at 0450, you can sleep-in until a reasonable hour.

[3] *Destination: England* tells you how — along with much more valuable trip planning for all of England.

[4] Because of its popularity, this summer *Fling* should be booked well in advance thru Britrail.

[5] This line, the 83-mile Dingwald and Skye Railway, took four years to complete (in 1897) at a record cost for its day since 29 bridges and 31 rock cuttings were required. Doors of the station hotel in Achnasheen, built in 1870, open directly onto the platform.

According to a British Rail brochure, the saloon car used on the Mallaig run "conveyed rail general managers, ministers of transport, members of Parliament, royalty, dignitaries and show business personalities to all parts of the British Rail system." Actually, there are two such cars, *Loch Eil* and *Lochober,* attached to both ends of the train (because there's no turning facility at Mallaig) but only the rear one, westbound or eastbound, is used. Each has a public address system for providing running commentary.

"As we left Fort William, we could see, towering in the distance, monumental, 4,406-ft. Ben Nevis, highest peak in the British Isles. After running along Loch Eil, we crossed Glenfinnan Viaduct — a curved, 1,000-ft. long structure both beautiful and revolutionary, the latter because it was built of concrete — first such use in railway engineering.

"A kaleidoscope of water and mountain views followed as we touched Lochs Eilt, Ailort, Dubh and nam Uamh. Soon water vistas changed from fresh to salt as the little train skirted the Sound of Sleat before coming to a stop at Mallaig."[6]

To do this abbreviated *Fling* quickly and painlessly from London, board a sleeper to Fort William at 2100 from Euston Station for a 0950 arrival in Fort William; the saloon car is attached to the 1205 train to Mallaig. From Inverness, *The Royal Highlander* departs at 1930, arrives London at 0647.

[6] As reported by Karl Zimmerman, Dobbs Ferry, N.Y., in *International Railway Traveler.*

Eilean Donan Castle in the Highlands.

## Highlights of Britain's *Great Rail Trip*

### The English Lakes

There is a grandeur and solitude here that, to the extent of our wanderings in England and Scotland, make this the most beautiful and awe-inspiring segment of the British Isles. Rockies, Alps and Andes are far more overwhelming, yet none conveys the harmonious sense of tranquility one feels here. Though not very tall, the mountains loom benignly over the valleys which are narrow and lie close to the protecting green flanks — and the rich and varied shades of firs, pines and other trees and shrubs are as sparkling and refreshing as a tall glass of spring water.

### Chester, A Walled City

One of England's most attractive cities. The downtown walled section, parts dating to Roman times, has a small town, medieval attractiveness mixed with the cosmopolitan smartness of its many and varied shops. Malls, lined with old or reconstructed buildings of bygone days, are crowded with people. To top it off, two miles of walkable, fortified walls completely surround the inner city. And would you believe a town crier, bedecked in colorful knee britches and tunic, who "Hear Ye's, Hear Ye's" at high noon? In all, an overwhelmingly pleasant feeling that past epochs are alive and thriving in the late 20th century.

### The Roman & Medieval City of York

Like Chester, an utterly fascinating and superbly walkable city. And when you talk of being steeped in history and tradition, that's York (from which New York derived its name). Romans arrived in 71 AD, made it a permanent fortress and capital, called Eboracum. It was here that Constantine the Great, later to found Constantinople, was crowned Emperor of Western Rome. In King Arthur's days, Saxon York was Eoforwic; in 867 it became the Viking port of Jorvik. Norman and Medieval York became the second city of England; the stone walls and gates were built in the 13th century.

The glory of York is the triple-spired Minster, largest Gothic church in England, which dominates the skyline with imposing splendor, particularly at night when brilliantly floodlighted. Beyond that, there's much to see in the still quaint streets and buildings, along the city walls and in the Castle Museum that recreates the York of yesteryear. And for rail fans, there's an outstanding National Railway Museum with its nostalgic collection of locomotives and coaches (those of royalty are eyepoppingly sumptuous).

### Edinburgh, Capital of Scotland

Although not a city of overwhelming beauty (and on dull days rather grim looking), it's one that has proven singularly attractive to tourists. The central section, dominated by the imposing bulk of Edinburgh Castle looming over it, provides an invigorating atmosphere, especially along bustling Princes Street that's flanked by blocks of spacious, colorful gardens which include the world's oldest floral clock and a soaring Gothic monument to Sir Walter Scott. On your extremely interesting city tour you'll not only walk thru the immensity of the Castle but also visit the old Palace of Holyroodhouse, official residence of the Queen when she's in Scotland, and medieval-looking Old Town that surrounds it.

Edinburgh is the center from which tours visit many of Scotland's most memorable historical sites: the Trossachs (Gaelic for "bristly country") and its Lochs Katrine and Achray, lovely setting for Scott's *Lady of the Lake* and *Rob Roy;* Melrose Abbey where the heart of Scotland's hero, Robert the Bruce, is supposed to be buried; Abbotsford House on the River Tween where Scott lived and Dryburgh Abbey where he's buried; imposing Scone Palace and charming Glamis Castle — and many, many more.

Elegant dining is the keynote of British Pullman Car travel. Afternoon (Ceylon) Tea consists of Finger Sandwiches, Country Scones with Clotted Cream and Strawberry Jam, Norfolk Fruit Cake and Coffee Kisses.

**British Pullman Day Excursions**

Special day tours thru the English countryside on a vintage train are presented by the Venice Simplon Orient-Express company from April into November.

This train is comprised of eight Pullman carriages, once part of the famous trains of the 1920s, such as the *Brighton Belle* and *Golden Arrow* — all beautifully restored and, as we know from our Folkestone to London ride, extremely elegant.

On Thursdays and Sundays, as well as alternate Wednesdays, five trips are available, three round trip by train, the other two by executive coach and train: Canterbury, Leeds Castle, Hever Castle, Folkestone and Bath/Bristol, the latter with brunch outbound, supper while returning to London — but all with at least one elegant serving aboard. Detailed itineraries are available from Venice Simplon Orient-Express in New York and London.

---

*Two coaches, each literally a museum piece, take just six favoured passengers on a tour of Scotland in the lap of ultimate luxury. Ensconsed in the elegance of the Observation Saloon, our travellers can watch the rugged beauty of the Highlands unfold or, forsaking this spacious comfort, they can wander out on to the Open Verandah — the only one on the railways of Britain — to breathe the mountain air, scented with the tang of peat and heather. Then, when hunger calls, the polished mahogany splendours of the Dining Saloon are the scene of sumptuous six-course meals, prepared on board from the finest ingredients by some of the most talented cooks in Britain.*

*And, as night falls, in the stillness of a quiet siding, passengers retire to the supreme comfort of the Sleeping Coach, which once formed part of a Royal Train. The two bathrooms permit occupants to wallow in large and steaming baths — an extremely rare experience aboard a train.*

*If this is extravagance, so be it! It is also hugely enjoyable —* ***and*** *practical, for the twisting mountain roads of Scotland can be tiring and sometimes crowded and the hotels are frequently austere.*

*The little-used railways of the West Highlands are a delight in themselves, affording dramatic panoramas that we and many others believe have no equal elsewhere in the world.*

*Places of special interest; the exceptional garden, castle or island inaccessible by rail will be reached in the accompanying vehicle. Its driver, who is most knowledgeable about the region, is always ready to whisk passengers to the place of their choice — a choice that is bewildering in the richness of its diversity.*

*For the* ***cognoscenti****, well-versed in the art of civilised travel, the HIGHLAND BELLE, with its friendly and individual service, sets a new standard of excellence.*

**Highland Belle**

The brochure from which the above was excerpted is as provocative as any we've ever read. But before you rush to sign up for "The Grand Tour of the Highlands of Scotland, over 1,000 miles long," we must remind you that "the six favoured passengers" cannot book individually since *Highland Belle* is available only as a complete charter, for one or two weeks, from Glasgow to Fort William and Mallaig, Kyle of Localsh and Inverness though exact routing differs from those previously described. Included are personally escorted picnics, sightseeing, and visits to famous castles by private car or motor launch.

See *Travel Supplement* for charter rates, agents.

## More About British Rail Trains

Faster and more expensive than buses, even in economy (2nd) class, trains provide an alternative to air travel that's particularly attractive if you wish to see some of the countryside, though train routes are usually less scenic than the roads.

First class daytime cars (on all but commuter trains) have a row of single seats facing each other with table in between and, across the aisle, another row of two seats abreast with table between the facing seats, all adjustable. First class is indicated by a yellow strip above the windows on the outside. There is a luggage compartment at one end of the car. Fares are about 50% higher than economy class. Seats in both classes can be reserved in advance, mandatory on trains like *Flying Scotsman* to Edinburgh.

Economy cars have two seats facing another two on both sides of the center aisle. There are overhead luggage racks (as in 1st class) but otherwise little or no place to store large wardrobe-type pieces except in vestibules between cars which, when cars are crowded, become jammed with luggage. However, the last car on the train usually has a large luggage compartment; since it's a 2nd class car, try to get seated there if traveling with large pieces.

Most Inter-City 125 trains, traveling at speeds up to 125 mph, have a Restaurant Car (or Buffet Car for snacks, drinks on other trains.)[1]

Best buys from London to Glasgow, Edinburgh-Aberdeen and the English West Coast are *Nightriders* — airconditioned, reduced fare trains with reclining seats, bar service and video-showing Leisure Coaches.[2] First class fare is about one-half the usual economy daytime fare. Seats must be reserved.

When it comes to overnight sleeping accommodations, Mark III sleepers, newest in Europe (1981-82), are supposedly superior and lower-priced than continental sleepers. Night trains feature first class only, single or twin berth cabins, 12 or 13 to a car. All have chemical toilet and wash basin, wall to wall carpeting; bottled drinking water is furnished. Coffee or tea is served upon awakening.

If possible, avoid weekend train (and bus) travel — stations, cars and buses are jammed, particularly during the summer.

Porters are available at stations, as are trolleys (luggage carts). If you don't have seat reservations, by all means use a porter — he'll see that you get best available seating, and fast.

Left luggage facilities (baggage room) and, usually, automatic lockers are available in practically all stations.

## Cross-Channel Ferries

Most travelers, when planning trips from England to the Continent, or vice-versa, fail to consider that it's often less expensive and more convenient to cross by rail/sea than by air — particularly when making the ferry crossing at night, thus saving a day of sightseeing, even a night's accommodation. They also permit a post-rush-hour exit from London, provide a comfortable floating hotel and arrival in Paris, Brussels or Amsterdam before 1000 the next day.

Services run throughout the year, can be booked virtually up to the time of departure, and are considerably more reliable than air travel, particularly in the winter.

Best bet for Paris is a first class seat on the 1935 evening train from Waterloo Station; just 70 minutes later you are met at Southampton by a courtesy car that takes you to the P & O Ferries terminal and your cabin — or, if you prefer, the bar and spacious lounge aboard the *Leopard.* Unlike airports, this is hassle-free. You have a drink, walk around deck and go to bed when you wish. You wake up in France and, after a short trip to Le Havre rail station, have a continental breakfast aboard one of SNCF's better trains, *Parisienne,* arriving in Paris at 1000. From Paris, it's an 1830 departure, 0900 arrival at Waterloo.

Entire cost for two is less than accommodations in a good London or Paris hotel.

Another favorite route — and the most elegant — is from London's Liverpool Street Station to Hook of Holland via Harwich on the *St. Nicholas,* a luxury floating hotel with a wide range of cabin accommodations, first class and economy, a casino, nightclub, disco, cinema and duty free supermarket[3]. There's a 1940 train departure from London (or earlier ones if you want more time to enjoy the ferry's amenities) as well as connections from Glasgow and other cities. Arrival at the Hook is shortly after 0600, but you can enjoy a leisurely breakfast aboard and be in Amsterdam shortly after 0900. However, you must get up earlier to make the Brussels train which arrives there at 0950.

Surprisingly, you can also be in Cologne and Dusseldorf before 1100, Frankfurt or Hamburg by lunchtime.

From the Continent over the same route, evening train departures bring you into London by 0915.

Another excellent way to go is by Dover to Ostend jetfoil, a seagoing jumbo jet carrying about the same number of people on two decks; actual Channel crossing (which we thoroughly enjoyed) takes an hour and 10 minutes. Direct connecting trains leave Victoria Station in London both morning and afternoon, the last one at 1600 (1700 Continental time) with Ostend arrival at 2030, Brussels 2210, Antwerp at 2315.

There are, of course, a variety of other ferry and hovercraft services across the Channel but those mentioned are considered top choices by England's *Executive Travel,* a magazine that does an excellent job of advising businessmen.

For individual passengers, seat reservation is compulsory on boat trains from Victoria and Liverpool St. stations.

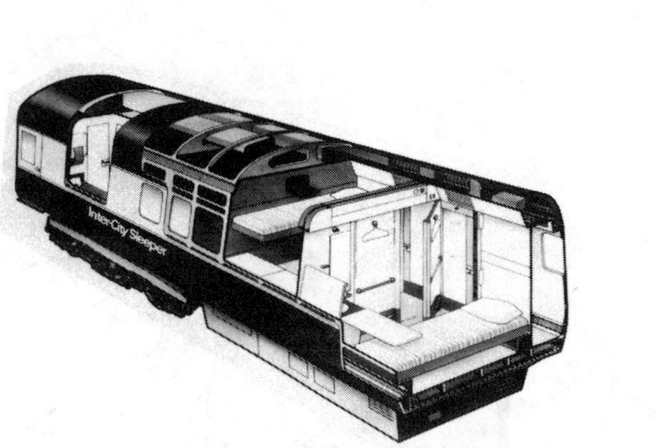


**SLE** and **SLEP** (Mark 3) airconditioned sleepers, inaugurated in 1981, are the only type being built in Britain. All others (SLF, SLS, SLC) have been withdrawn from service.

[1] Although it's said that meals on British trains could be better (as is the case with most railroad dining), we remember the meal we had on the *Flying Scotsman* as perfectly satisfactory. However, the English don't take chances; they bring self-catered meals — for their dogs.

[2] These are former first class cars fitted with four TV screens and 40 seats; latter are unreserved but available only to those with reserved seat ticketing.

[3] Even meeting rooms with audio-visual and video equipment for groups of up to 70 people. On Sealink, Townsend Thoresen and DFDS ferries, you can book accommodations in a special business class with extra percs — for an extra fare.

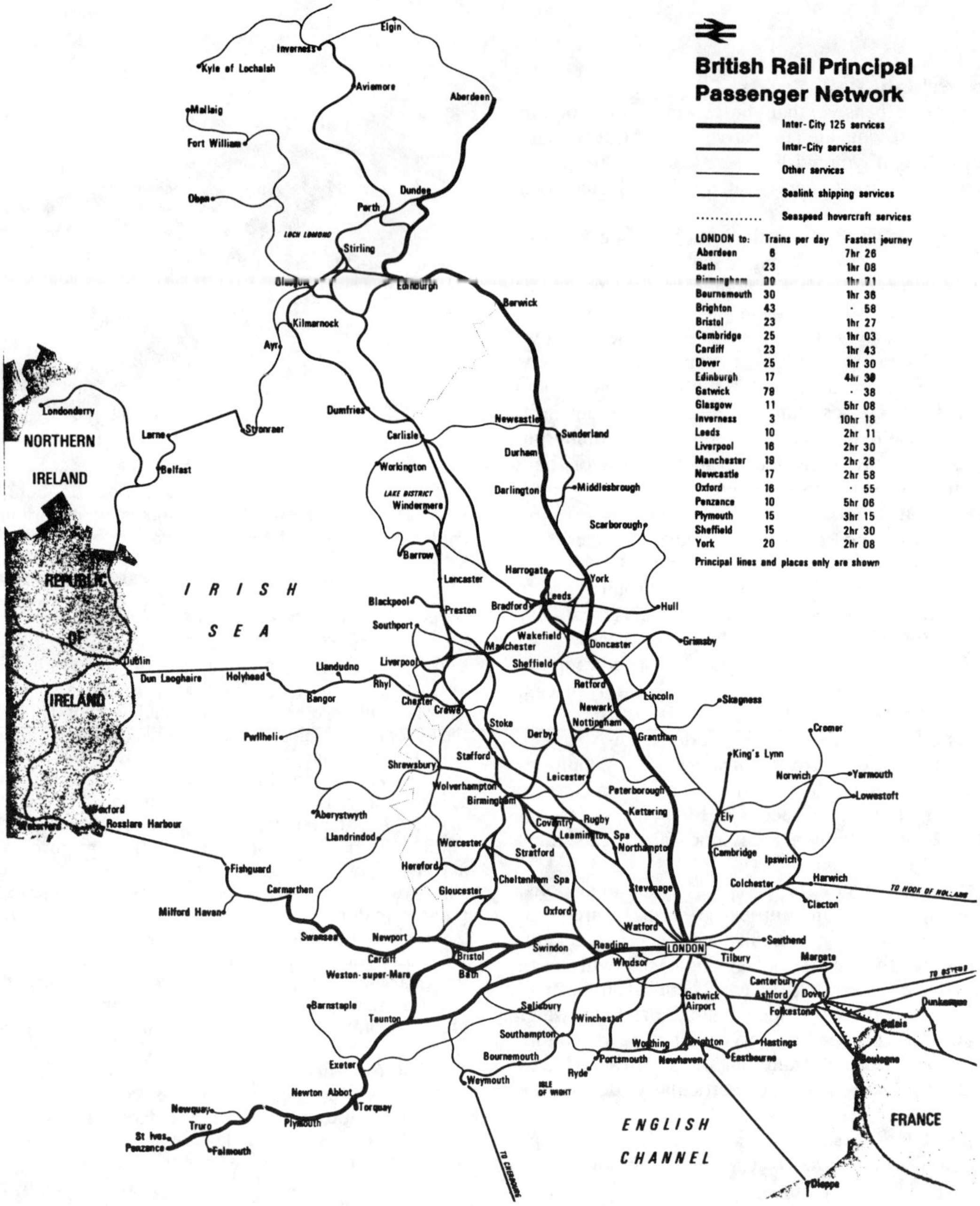


Matter of fact, best to reserve seats on all British trains.

Seat reservations for groups is compulsory on all cross-Channel services.

**Motorail**

If traveling by car, you and your car can embark on the same train on some 50 routes to all parts of Britain. Several start from ferry ports — and some do not operate thruout the year.

***Britrail Pass***

Provides unlimited train travel for 7, 14, 21 consecutive days, as well as one month, thruout England, Scotland and Wales — plus Sealink ships to / from Isle of Wight and pleasure steamers on Lake Windemere.

There are First Class, Economy and Youth (16-25) and Senior Citizen Passes. *Must be purchased before arrival in Great Britain.* Passes are open-dated for use within a year; validity starts when date-stamped at the British Rail station from which first trip is taken.

Senior Citizen Passes permit first class travel at Economy Pass rate. Children 5-15 pay half fare.

Travel agents may issue Britrail Passes on British Airways ticket vouchers.

***Britrail Seapass***

Enables *Britrail Pass* holders to travel from London to the continent, or to Ireland, at special one way or round trip fares.

***Scottish Highlands & Island Travelpass***

Unlimited travel for five or 10 days on all trains (Economy class) and many bus and ship lines in Scotland's North and Northwest.

See *Travel Supplement* for current costs of these Passes.

You can purchase a Rail / Drive package that combines a Britrail Pass with unlimited mileage car rental from any British Rail station.

Available, too, is a RailSailDrive package to Ireland (and SailRailDrive *from* Ireland) that includes Britrail Passes. Costs depend on type of car, time of year and number of passengers per car.

There are British Rail desks in each of Heathrow's terminals as well as at Gatwick Airport.

**The World's Greatest Stationary Rail Trip**

For lavish Pomp and Circumstance, make the short rail or bus trip from London to Windsor Station. For here is the most marvelous re-creation we have ever seen: the arrival of Queen Victoria's Royal Train at Windsor on June 19, 1897. So wonderfully lifelike and imposing, you can't believe you're not witnessing the actual reenactment of the event. Yet Madame Tussaud's *Royalty and Empire Exhibition* is actually an assemblage of over 100 wax figures that immortalizes a moment in Victorian history that epitomizes the glory of the Empire.

Transported back to June 19, 1897, you witness the arrival of the Royal Train[1] bearing Queen Victoria's eldest daughter, Empress Frederic of Prussia, Prince Henry of Prussia, Grand Duke Serge of Russia and his wife, the Grand Duchess Elizabeth. Greeting them on the platform are Lord Emlyn, chairman of Great Western Railway, and the Station Master. And in the cab of the locomotive, *The Queen,* are the driver and fireman.

Awaiting the guests in the Royal Waiting Room[2] are Her Majesty Queen Victoria, the Prince and Princess of Wales (soon to be King Edward VII and Queen Alexandra); they have driven from Windsor Castle to greet the guests.

After climbing the stairs to a long, eliptical viewing stand, you see the royal party emerging from the station before which stands an Ascot Landau with four Windsor greys and postilion outriders. Greeting the Queen and her royal guests are the Prime Minister, Lord Salisbury, and other dignitaries. The Guard of Honor (by our count 76 soldiers and officers) gives the Royal Salute, the Regimental Band plays *God Save The Queen* and a short selection of music played for Queen Victoria in 1897. Chills run up and down your spine.

This exciting adventure concludes with an audio-visual showing in an adjoining theater of "Sixty Glorious Years" that shows how England, during Queen Victoria's reign, grew from a small rural country to the most dominant empire since Roman times. When the Queen met the Tsar of Russia in 1896, they owned over half the world between them.[3]

[1] Attached to the locomotive are two cars: the Queen's personal Royal Day Saloon (which contains two original items, a footstool and a cushion cover embroidered with V.R. and Order of the Garter) and Royal Saloon No. 9002, one of two carriages that bracketed the Queen's Day Saloon in 1897. This was the first Royal Train to have a corridor connection between cars.

[2] The original station on this site was opened on October 8, 1849. Shortly after, Queen Victoria and her court used it when traveling to Paddington; for nearly 50 years, this elegant timber structure served the court and the town. But in 1897, Great Western Railway obtained permission to build a new station to commemorate the Queen's Diamond Jubilee. It is that very building, restored to its original splendor, thru which you stroll today. While doing so, don't fail to visit the rest rooms — if for no other reason than to see and use The Original Automatic Toweless Hand Dryer — 1896.

[3] At the 1897 Spithead Review, as part of the Diamond Jubilee celebration, 165 ships, manned by 40,000 officers and men, covered a combined line 30 miles long — achieved without taking a single vessel from the fleets in the Mediterranean, China Seas, India, Australia and North America.

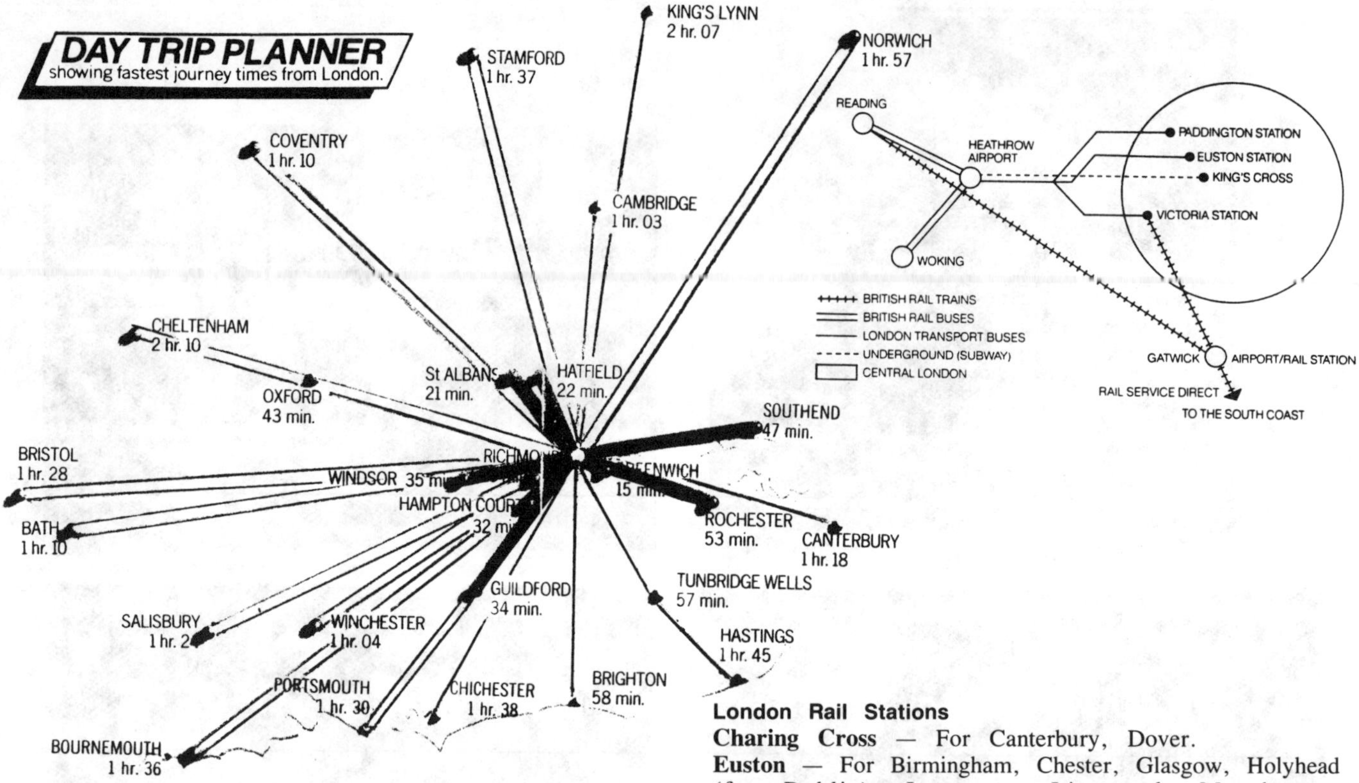


**London Rail Stations**

**Charing Cross** — For Canterbury, Dover.

**Euston** — For Birmingham, Chester, Glasgow, Holyhead (for Dublin), Inverness, Liverpool, Manchester, Windermere.

**Kings Cross** — Aberdeen, Dundee, Edinburgh, Hull, Leeds, Newcastle, York.

**Liverpool** — Cambridge, Harwich, Ipswich, Norwich, Southend, Tilbury (Docks).

**Paddington** — Bath, Bristol, Cardiff, Cheltenham, Exeter, Gloucester, Newport, Oxford, Penzance, Plymouth, Stratford, Swansea, Tounton, Torquay.

**St. Pancras** — Bedford, Leicester, Luton, Nottingham, Sheffield.

**Victoria** — Brighton, Canterbury, Dover, Eastbourne, Gatwick.

**Waterloo** — Bournemouth, Portsmouth, Salisbury, Southampton, Weymouth.

***Triple Ticket* From London**

A great bargain that permits you to take three day trips from (and back to) London on any train over a period of six months from date of purchase. Only restriction is that one trip must be made in each of three groups of destinations outlined in Britrail's brochure, *Day Trips From London By Train* — 27 attractive destinations in all, including Bristol, Salisbury and Winchester in Group 3; Cambridge, Canterbury and Oxford in Group 2; Hampton Court, Richmond or Windsor in Group 1.

All passes should be purchased thru travel agents or British Rail offices abroad.

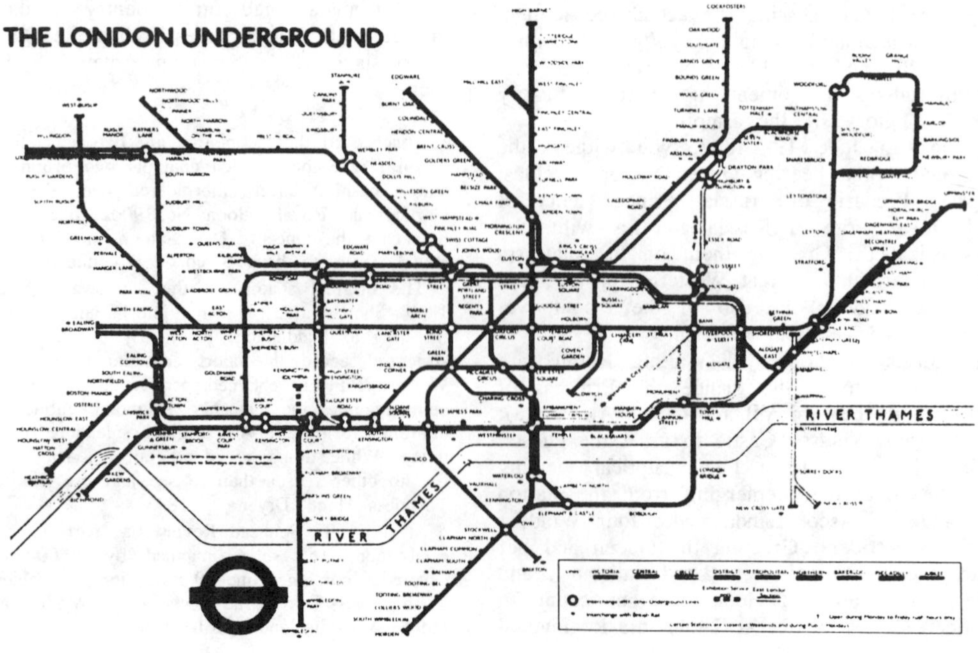

# NORTH EASTERN RAILWAY

18  75

# PENALTIES

*for Breaking*

# RULES & REGULATIONS

OF

## COMPANY'S WORKSHOPS

YORK

| | *Amount of FINE* |
|---|---|
| • *Putting on Coat or making any other preparation to leave Work before Whistle sounds or Bell is rung* ... ... ... | 1 Shilling |
| • *Loitering in the Works or absent without good reason* ... | 6 pence |
| • *Washing Hands in Oil or wasting CANDLES* ... ... ... | 3 pence |
| • *Any Workman creating TUMULT or NOISE* ... ... ... | 1 Shilling |
| • *Removing BURNER from GAS LIGHT* ... ... ... ... ... | 6 pence |
| • *Any Workman SMOKING in the Workshops* ... ... ... | 6 pence |
| • *Defacing the Time Board* ... ... ... ... ... ... ... ... | 1 Shilling |
| • *Using any Stores such as WOOD, IRON, STEEL, OIL, PAINT, TALLOW, etc. Wastefully* .. ... ... ... ... | 2 Shillings |
| • *Any Workman taking STRANGERS into the Works WITHOUT PERMISSION* .. ... ... ... ... ... | 6 pence |
| • *Any Foreman or Hammer-Driver absent without due reason* ... ... ... ... ... ... ... ... ... ... ... ... | 5 Shillings |
| • *Breaking open the Lock or Removing Tools from another Workman's Box* ... ... ... ... ... ... ... ... ... | 2 Shillings |
| • *Any Workman leaving his CANDLE BURNING or neglecting to SHUT his GAS-COCK after work has ceased* ... ... ... ... ... ... ... ... ... ... ... | 1 Shilling |

***Any Man found in a DRUNKEN STATE, or bringing into the Workshops BEER or SPIRITS will be DISMISSED IMMEDIATELY.***

# FRANCE

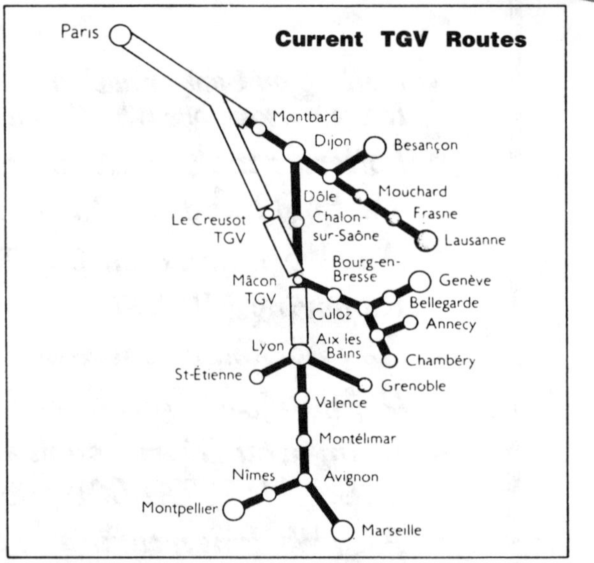


**TGV — *Train A Grande Vitesse***

Currently the world's most advanced coach-type train (no sleepers), TGV is, indeed, *the* Great Train Trip from the standpoint of technology; aerodynamically contoured for minimum wind resistance, it speeds effortlessly (with some sway) and almost noiselessly (thanks to continuous-weld tracks[1]) at speeds up to 168 mph. Glamorous looking in their bright orange outer trim and pleasing, understated interior decor, glamorous sounding as the fastest things on wheels, these electrified TGVs are, in the final analysis, plastic equivalents of planes, a means of fast, comfortable, impersonal and inexpensive transportation — on short runs cheaper and, considering distance of airports from city centers, faster than planes. Certainly if going south of Paris or to Geneva or Lausanne, you shouldn't miss the experience.

Cars are nicely airconditioned, softly lighted and, as mentioned, have attractive beige/gold-trimmed seats and curtains. There are plane-type reading lamps, adjustable window blinds, luggage racks and space between cars for large pieces of luggage. There are automatic doors; articulation rings replace traditional "bellows" between coaches cuts down on noise and draughts; also, bogies are situated between the coaches so that nobody sits over the wheels.

Each TGV train is made up of eight coaches: three first class (111 seats) and five second class (275 seats), each with toilets (spotlessly clean). In first class, comfortable airplane-type seats are 18″ wide (as is the aisle) plus a 3¾″ arm rest and (in rows of two) a 7″ center rest. Rows are 18″ apart, have

[1] Prevalent thru most of western Europe.

Because of the success of this Southeast Route, which cost about $1 billion, French Railroads is developing another TGV line, the 190-mile Atlantique from Paris Montparnasse. One leg will bring TGV trains to Nantes and Brittany by 1989, the other south to Tours and Poitiers, slicing an hour off the Paris-Bordeaux run by 1990. The new trains will be similar to existing TGVs only somewhat faster (188 mph) due to more sophisticated power units and because the route is less hilly.

**TGV Distances/Running Times from PARIS To**

Avignon — 658 km (3:51 one-stop)
Aix-les-Bains — 507 km (3:03)
Chambery — 521 km (3:13)
Dijon* — 284 km (1:38); Lyon* — 417 km (2:02)
Geneva — 551 km (3:32)
Lausanne — 477 km (3:36)
Marseille — 779 km (4:51);
Montpelier — 757 km (4:41)

TGV first class coaches are soothingly decorated, extremely comfortable and almost noiseless.

additional leg room beneath the row ahead. There's a hot meal facility at each seat. A daily average of 900 lunches and dinners are served on TGV runs. These four course, table d'hote meals (with wine) cost about $15. Meals must be ordered when reserving seats.[2]

There are smoking and non-smoking cars for both classes (advance reservations required). Snacks and drinks are served by cart vendors or in the second class stand-up bar.

To/from Paris, the trains traverse some pleasant, undulating rural country, though the scenery between Lausanne and Paris or Paris to Avignon (the two TGV trains we rode) can't compare in dramatic impact with that of the Alpine regions.[3]

### OTHER FRENCH TRAINS

Both domestically and on international express routes, SNCF provides a wide variety of modern equipment: types MU, P and T2 sleeping cars; airconditioned couchette coaches with 36 couchettes in first class, 60 in second. Then there are *CoRail* coaches (first, second class; open or compartment seating) used as a counterpart to TGV on other road beds — along with first and second class lounge-bar cars and deluxe *Grand Confort* coaches and restaurant cars (both first class). And not to forget the previously mentioned Disco Car.

### Customized (Charter) Travel

The foregoing as well as other types of cars listed below are available for group tours, business meetings, conventions and incentive travel. They cannot, however, be used on TGV trains since they are not of similar streamlined design.

Here are some other options:

. . . First class, 54-seat Prestige Coach (similar to TGV).
. . . 32-seat Conference Coach (complete facilities).
. . . Cinema Coach with seating capacity up to 60.
. . . "Club 34" Coach for variable uses: meeting room, cocktails, cinema; all purpose equipment.

Anything from a single car to a made-to-measure train can be obtained for a day, a week or more. Cars can be attached to any scheduled train. Contact French National Railroads offices for further information, costs.

### More About Trains & Stations In France

*Most Important:* As you leave the waiting room, be sure to insert your ticket into one of the one-legged red boxes, *composteurs,* in order to date stamp (and take a small, semi-circular "bite" out of one end). This validation is what the train conductor looks for and woe to you if you've bypassed the *composteur;* dire things are said to ensue.

To facilitate boarding and disembarking of the disabled, vertical transfer devices are used in a number of stations

[2] Hot means an hors d'oeuvre, main course of veal or pork, vegetables, cheese and pastry. There's also a cold lunch with such as a crayfish salad, vegetables, foie gras, cold meats (with, perhaps, an artichoke heart), cheese and pastry. Wines served from a cart. No linens, no crystal glasses yet in good taste.

[3] Actually, the technology is, possibly, as interesting as the ride. Speed and comfort have been combined in smooth-riding cars; noise levels and pollution have been reduced, and environmental factors were considered: the line, as an example, avoids famed Chablis vineyards; livestock and wildlife move *under* the roadbeds thru special passages; hydro-geological studies determined that underground water systems would remain unharmed.

(including Paris, Lyon and Marseille) to raise persons in wheelchairs from platform to car entrance levels in 20 seconds.

Small wheelchairs designed for train aisles and dining cars are now available on several trains. And 57 daily trains have special first and second class accommodations for the handicapped. In first class, an area is reserved for wheelchairs that can be used by those with second class tickets.

New electronic lockers being installed in stations require no keys. Once the correct amount is deposited in any of three locker sizes, lock is activated and a ticket delivered that lists locker row and number plus a confidential 5-digit code which must be keyed in to open the locker. A remote monitoring scanner system controls the lockers, is able to identify any attempted theft or power failures.

Skis can be checked in 10 SNCF stations for 24 hours by placing them in a rack, upper part of which secures them with a locked flap that works like the door of a conventional locker. We saw a similar system at Swiss ski resort stations.

In addition to providing disco cars on some night trains, SNCF has babysitting, too. Summer daytime trains from Paris to a number of destinations have one compartment with changing tables and bottle heaters and a car with a carpeted play area, color TV sets, funhouse type mirrors.

Children under four travel free (but without a reserved seat); by paying one-fourth the adult fare, the child gets a reserved seat or bunk in a couchette compartment on a family train. For a small additional fare, a family of four with at least one paying child under 12 can occupy an entire compartment.

To assist English-speaking travelers, information about fares, schedules et al can be obtained by phone. In Paris, dial 380-5050 and get all the answers — in English; outside Paris, dial 16-1-380-5050.

You can purchase tickets with major credit cards at all SNCF stations or thru travel agencies.

### *France Vacances* (Rail Passes)

Provide unlimited travel for 7 and 15 days or one month in first or second class on all French National Railroads (SNCF) trains, including TGVs. They also entitle you to:

Free round trip transfer by rail from Charles de Gaulle or Orly airports to downtown Paris.

Metropass for 2, 4 or 7 days of unlimited travel on Paris bus and Metro systems.

Free admission to Pompidou Museum, Paris' No. 1 tourist attraction.

Free trip on Provence railroad Nice to Digne (or vice-versa).

Discounted car rentals from French rail stations.

10% discount on French National Railroads bus excursions.

Both first and second class passes are restricted to persons living outside France and are available from SNCF (Societe Nationale des Chemins de Fer Francais) offices abroad or thru travel agents, Also can be bought *upon arrival in France* at SNCF counters in Charles de Gaulle Airport (Terminal 1, gate 28; Terminal 2, gate B6) or Orly (gate H), as well as at SNCF stations in Nice, Strasbourg and Paris (St. Lazare.) Too, Air France and UTA offices abroad issue MCO vouchers exchangeable at airports in Paris and other major cities.

Holders of *France Vacances* must pay extra for reservation fees and sleeping accommodations but not surcharges for fast trains.

### Which Station (*Gare*) For Where:

**Austerlitz** — For Orleans, Tours; Lisbon, Madrid.
**de l'Est** — Reims, Strasbourg; Luxembourg, Frankfurt, Munich, Prague; Basel, Innsbruck, Salzburg, Vienna.
**de Lyon** — TGVs; Milan, Florence, Rome.
**Montparnasse** — For Chartres, Versaille.
**du Nord** — Amsterdam, Brussels; Cologne, Hamburg, Copenhagen.
**St. Lazare** — Le Havre, Rouen, Tours.

### Senior Citizen *Carte Vermeil*

Men 62 and over, women 60 or more may purchase this money-saving card that's valid for one year. With it they may purchase individual point to point tickets at a 50% discount — but travel is limited to so-called blue period that excludes weekends and holidays.

*Carte Vermeil* is obtainable at any SNCF station. Its current price, as well as those for *France Vacances,* is listed in the *Travel Supplement.*

### Other French Rail Passes

*Purchaseable only in France* thru travel agents or at any SNCF station.

*Carte Jeune* (Youth Card) allows 50% discount on all rail fares, first and second class, outside the Paris area; also on Sealink ferries between Dieppe and Newhaven. Valid from June 1 to September 30 for travel during *les jours bleus.*[1]

*Carre Jeune,* first offered in 1984, is similar but offers all year travel. Both cost the same (see *Travel Supplement*).

*Carte Inter-Rail* (obtainable only with proof of six months' residence in France) allows second class travel without further cost on trips outside France for one month — if you're less than 26 years old. Also allows a 50% discount on SNCF domestic routes.

*Carte Couple/Famille* is a free card that entitles a couple to one half fare when one full fare is paid during the blue days; three or more can travel at any time. But for foreigners, proving you're a married couple or family is burdensome; an original marriage certificate with authorized translation is required.[2]

Finally, for groups of five or more, there's *Billet Minigroup* — a 25% reduction on first or second class round trips during blue periods providing you buy the tickets at least two days in advance.

[1] Blue days *are approximately 250 during the year: from noon Saturday to 1500 on Sunday and from noon Monday to 1500 on Friday.* Les jours blancs *(white) are all the other days unless they're* les jours rouges *(red, or holidays).*

[2] *There's also a* Carte Familles Nombreuses *for married couples with three or more children that provides discounts of 30% to 75% — if you have legal, translated proof.*

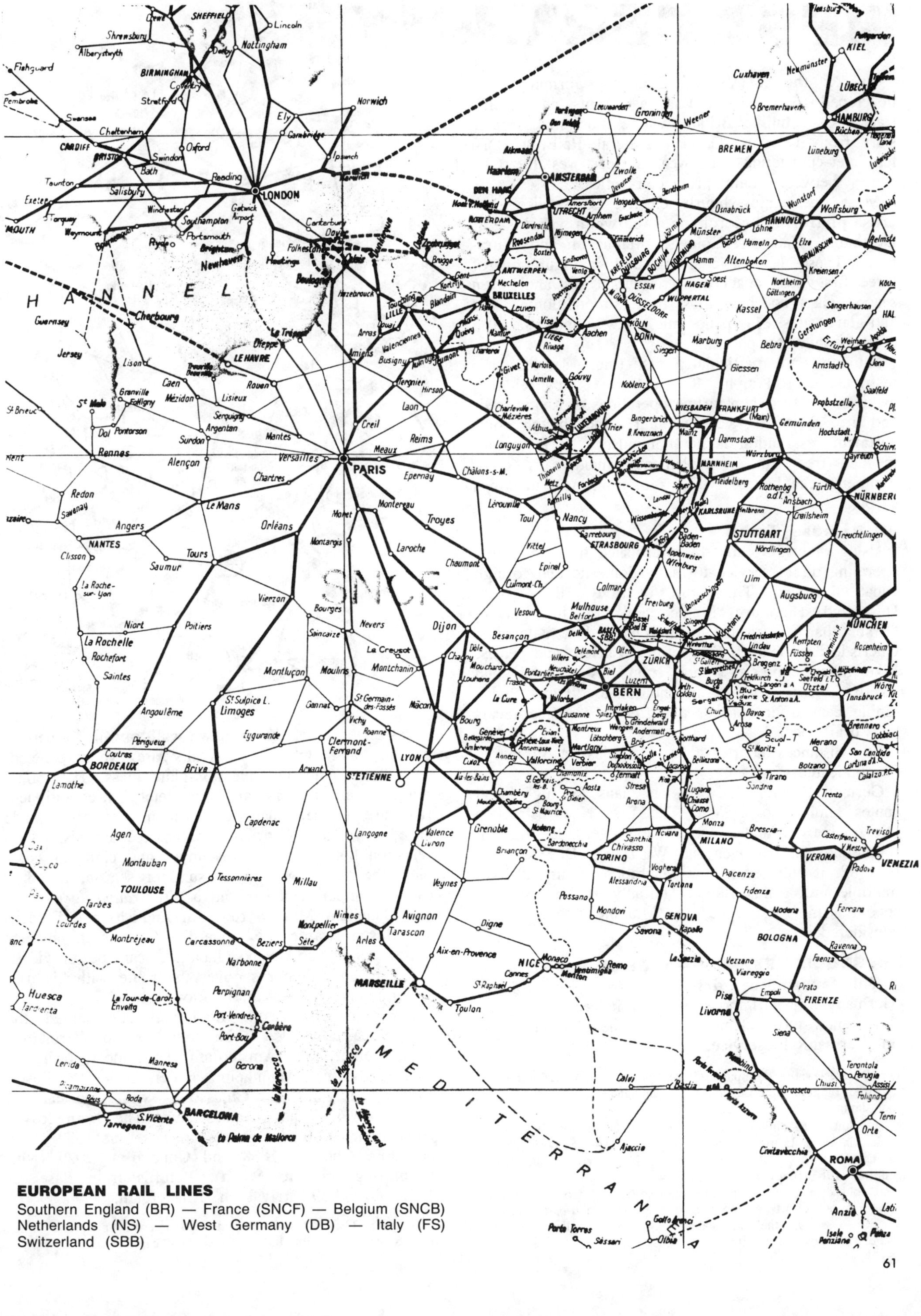


**EUROPEAN RAIL LINES**

Southern England (BR) — France (SNCF) — Belgium (SNCB) Netherlands (NS) — West Germany (DB) — Italy (FS) Switzerland (SBB)

# WEST GERMANY

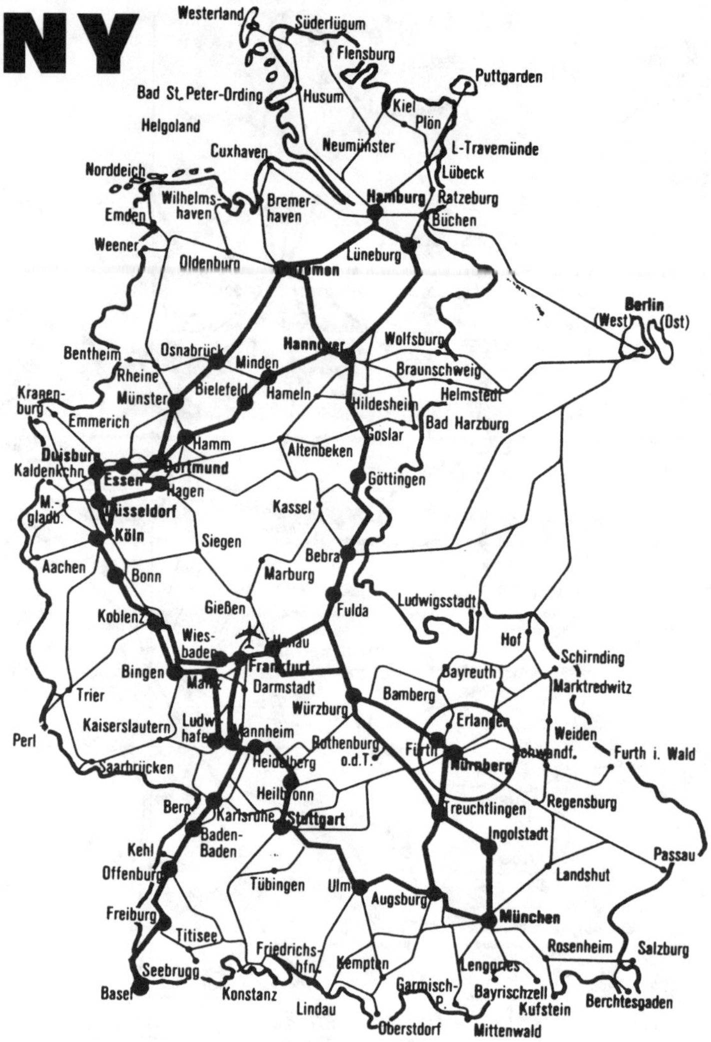


Unlike the TGVs of France, Germany has developed a system of less fast trains on existing track. Also, unlike Britain, where most main routes start from London, German Federal Railway (DB) has inter-connecting north-west and east-west InterCity routes between main provincial cities.

Most lines enjoy hourly electric IC service with cross-platform interchange between routes at Dortmund, Hanover, Cologne, Mannheim and Wurzberg. These ICs have a standard configuration of three first class coaches, a restaurant car and seven second class coaches; most have airconditioning and anti-glare glass in panoramic view windows. And coin-operated telephones.

Although not particularly fast (most services are restricted to 100 mph), IC trains are highly reliable, even in winter (when airline operations are hampered) and are, therefore, very popular. And though compartment reservation is not compulsory, it is recommended (free with IC supplement).[1] Incidentally, compartments can be reserved for mini-business meetings enroute.

### FD Express Trains

Using older IC cars, 18 refurbished trains are now operating direct service to many domestic and foreign vacation areas. They run over IC lines from Dortmund, Hamburg, Munich and Frankfurt but go farther than IC trains: to Berchtesgaden, Konstanz, Obertsdorf, Vienna, Klagenfurt, Zurich and Paris. Like other expresses, each train has a name and its first class cars are airconditioned. "Quick-Pick" dining cars offer snacks, a buffet, one-course meals and draft beer.[2]

For distances shorter than 31 miles, a surcharge is applicable.

German Federal Railways has plans for high-speed routes similar to TGV's. The first Neubaustrecken (New Line) is under construction over the 362 km route between Hanover and Wurzburg. Due to open in 1988, it will see a new generation of aircraft-like, multiple unit trains running initially at 155 mph. A second line, Cologne to Mannheim, is being considered.

### RHEINGOLD EXPRESS—A Great Rail Trip

This revamped, *first class only* version of Germany's most famous train is, indeed, one of the continent's most elegant — and the last TEE now in GermanRail service.[3]

Passenger cars have new wall-to-wall carpeting, curtains and upholstery. Walls are wood paneled, extra-large windows have non-glare glass. The train's nine passenger cars are completely airconditioned: five are conventional compartment cars with side aisles, two are *Grossraumwagen* (center aisle with seats on both sides); a restaurant and club car complete the train. During the summer season, the club car, a compartment car and a *Grossraumwagen* make the Mannheim-Munich run. An English- and French-speaking stewardess is aboard — and with advance notice, one who speaks Japanese can be provided. Multi-lingual brochures cover the route with historic, cultural and scenic information.

For over 50 years, *Rheingold* has served the classic, castle-studded Rhine route, one of Germany's most scenic, from Amsterdam, Dusseldorf, Cologne, Bonn, Koblenz, Mannheim, Baden Baden to Basel, Lucerne, Lugano and Chiasso — with thru cars as far as Brig, Chiasso and Chur. The train leaves Amsterdam at 0750, arrives in Basel at 1532, Brig at 1900, Chur at 1838 and Chiasso at 2029 (with connecting train to Milan). Returns from Basel at 1222 for 1959 arrival in Amsterdam.

[1] DB's reservation computer, linked to corresponding systems in Austria, Belgium and Luxembourg, can handle 21,000 reservations per hour.

[2] In addition to dining cars, an important feature of all European trains is portable food carts — especially so on West German trains where 5.4 million passengers paid the equivalent of $8.2 million (1983 figures) for hot bockwurst and other sausages, hot and cold drinks, chocolate bars et al dispensed from these carts. Now, in an effort to improve service, new mini-bars, weighing 24 lbs. less than the old models, have been installed; they have better thermos units, are easier, faster handling.

[3] Another TEE, *Mediolanum,* runs between Munich and Milan but is operated with Italian first class cars.

*Rheingold's* club car not only provides drinks, live entertainment and multi-lingual travel information but also a kiosk stocked with travel related items. On-board folklore groups present programs relating to the people and regions thru which the train travels.

Besides the "Wunderschoener deutschen Rhein," other scenic routes include Heidelberg-Heilbronn along the Neckar River (known as the Castle Road); Offenburg-Triberg and Freiburg-Konstanz in the Black Forest; Koblenz-Trier along the Moselle and Koblenz-Limburg thru the Westerwald; Lindau-Friedrichshafen-Konstanz along Lake Constance; Freilassing-Berchtesgaden; Munich to Garmisch-Partenkirchen and Mittenwald.

We can highly recommend Garmisch to Innsbruck *as one of Europe's great scenic rail trips.* After taking a bus trip over famed Romantische Strasse (Romantic Road), we continued from Fussen to Garmisch (a terrific drive) which, we observed, is "a bewildering pageant of green slopes and trees intermingled with reds and yellows of falling leaves and o'er topped by white-capped mountains — all blessed by warm, dazzling sparkles of sunshine. In the famous ski resort, we lunched on a restaurant terrace in shirt sleeves against a backdrop of Alpine peaks before taking off for Innsbruck. By train, this is a perfectly stupendous ride, quite beyond adequate description — just one extended panorama of snowy peaks, green valleys, firred forests and sparkling rivers meandering across the valleys, a setting sun to the west, roseate rimmed peaks to the east. Finally Innsbruck, nestled between two Alpine ranges. Nothing can be more thrilling than this two-hour ride."

### GermanRail Tourist Card

Good for nine or 16 days in First Class or Coach, they permit unlimited travel anywhere in Germany — and free motorcoach travel over the Romantic Road (April thru Nov.), on scenic Rhine/Moselle routes (all year). Also reduced fares on many Rhine River steamers (mid-April to mid-Oct.), a substantial reduction on RT rail to Berlin (and free transit visa into East Berlin) and free bicycle rental at rail stations with option to drop them off at another.

*GermanRail* must be used within one year from issuance date, must be validated at a rail station before boarding train for first time. It does not cover reservation fees, sleeping accommodations. Can be purchased from German Rail offices (and travel agents) outside of Germany as well as main rail stations in Germany, including the one at Frankfurt Airport.

There are special weekend RT fares for one or two passengers and for families. Check into these when in Germany.

During Nurnburg's 1985 celebration of 150 years of German railroading, there are not only many special events and exhibits but also rail tours. See *Travel Supplement* for details.

On the FD *Koenigsee Express* between Hamburg and Berchtesgaden, supervised games for kids 4-11, space for them to play and read are available in this Kinderland car. Another FD experiment is a cinema car.

# ITALY

Not only do Italy's trains run fast and on time but also many of them, the Rapidos, are among Europe's most comfortable and luxurious.[1] And so imaginatively named: *Marco Polo . . . Barbarossa . . . Gondoliere . . . Expresso del Levante . . . Genova Sprint.*

On those and other of the Rapidos and Expressos[2] you can see all of the verdant Italian countryside, among the loveliest in Europe, easily and quickly — from the colorful lakes and dazzling Alpine peaks of the north to Taormina overlooking the Ionian Sea in the south. Add Milano, Venezia, Bologna, Firenze and Roma, toss in glorious Amalfi Drive and sparkling Isle of Capri near Naples and you have a superb one-country vacation recipe.

*Rapido* observations cars are distinctively unique, provide wide angle viewing. Note that they are attached to both ends of the train (normally much, much longer than this one).

**More About Italian Railways**

Besides Rapidos and Expresses (*Directissimo*), there are *Directos* (Fast) which, as we've mentioned, are actually the slowest. Rapidos cannot be used by holders of reduced or group fares except by paying full fare plus the Rapido supplement.

Sleeping and restaurant cars are operated by Wagons-Lits.

First class cars do not have luggage storage space except for overhead racks, so large pieces must remain in the aisle or, better yet, checked to your destination.

There are rarely any luggage carts in stations but plenty of porters; usual charge is L1,000 per bag.

In Florence and Venice, tracks are at ground level; in Milan, one level up but there's an escalator in between. Station toilet compartments, with excellent facilities (including a shower if desired) are immaculate. There are first and second class waiting rooms and, of course, bars, restaurants, snack bars,[3] newstands and gift shops.

[1] On a Venice to Milan train, our first class day coach was airconditioned, had a center aisle with two seats to the right, one to the left, each facing another row of three. But the ambience was nil and seat coverings worn though linen headrests were clean — and windows dirty. Not as good as Swiss second class but far better than Italian second. Travel only first class in Italy and be sure to reserve your seats otherwise you'll be crowded out by usurpers.

[2] On the TEE *Vesuvio* (as well as its sisters, *Colosseum* and *Ambrosiano*) from Milan to Naples and on the rapido we took from Florence to Venice, accommodations were exactly the opposite: well-lighted, thick plate glass compartments that were the epitome of first class luxury. The forward observation car with wrap-around front window (above which the engineer and assistant sit in a dome bubble) is unique in our experience. In fact, we were seated in the observation car when our Venice-bound train negotiated the 12-mile Appenine Tunnel, an eerie feeling of wondering when the blackness will end. Four months later, almost to the day, this was the scene of a terrorist bomb carnage.

[3] *Parmalat* picnic meals, put up in bags, are sold by pushcart vendors in large and medium-size stations. Usually include antepasta (appetizers such as salami, olives, etc.), a pasta, meat (like a half chicken), bread, wine, cheese and fruit — for the equivalent of about $3 and as good as dining car food, better than most station dishes (we had the world's worst spaghetti in Venice's station). Pasta and meat course are kept warm on a hot plate (*tavola calda*) inside the pushcart. Plastic utensils and glasses are included.

# SPAIN & PORTUGAL

### *TRANSCANTABRICO*

In this age of the return of romantic train travel, some European countries have brought into service old, narrow gauge railways for short scenic runs of a few hours or a day.

The advantage of such trains lies in their ability to take tight curves and climb steep gradients, thus making them ideal for reaching areas of great beauty inaccessible to conventional trains.

*Transcantabrico* has those characteristics. A tourist train, the only one of its kind in Spain and, indeed, probably all of Europe, it certainly covers the longest distance of any European narrow gauge line — 625 miles. Unique to this type of train, it reminds one of 'ye olden days' when train travel and touring were relaxed pleasures restricted to a privileged few.

To evoke this atmosphere of heady charm and excitement, veteran rolling stock has been resurrected, repaired and fitted with airconditioning, heating, bar, lounge, live music, TV and stereo, piano, showers and restrooms.

The train now comprises six coaches and two vans with maximum capacity of 48 passengers: three sleeping cars and three Pullman lounge cars containing all the entertainment and recreational facilities.

Each sleeping car has eight two-berth compartments (with wash basin, bidet), two showers and four toilets. The vans contain power generators, water tanks, a kitchen for preparing breakfasts and carry the liquor, linens and other supplies.

Breakfast is served on board but lunches and dinners are provided in traditional inns and restaurants along the way. A motor coach with guide and driver that follows the train is used for daily sightseeing. The bar opens for breakfast (to get you merrily on your way), reopens at 1230 each day. After dinner, musicians play until 0100 in the saloon bar; local folk groups also perform on several evenings. The train is halted during the night while passengers sleep.

From May into September, these seven-day trips depart every Saturday afternoon, either from Leon or Ferrol.[1]

The route of *Transcantabrico* is north from Leon to Mar Cantabrico, a portion of the Atlantic Ocean that curves eastward across northern Spain to the

[1] From February to May and October to December, the entire train (or groups of cars) can be chartered for trips of any desired length.

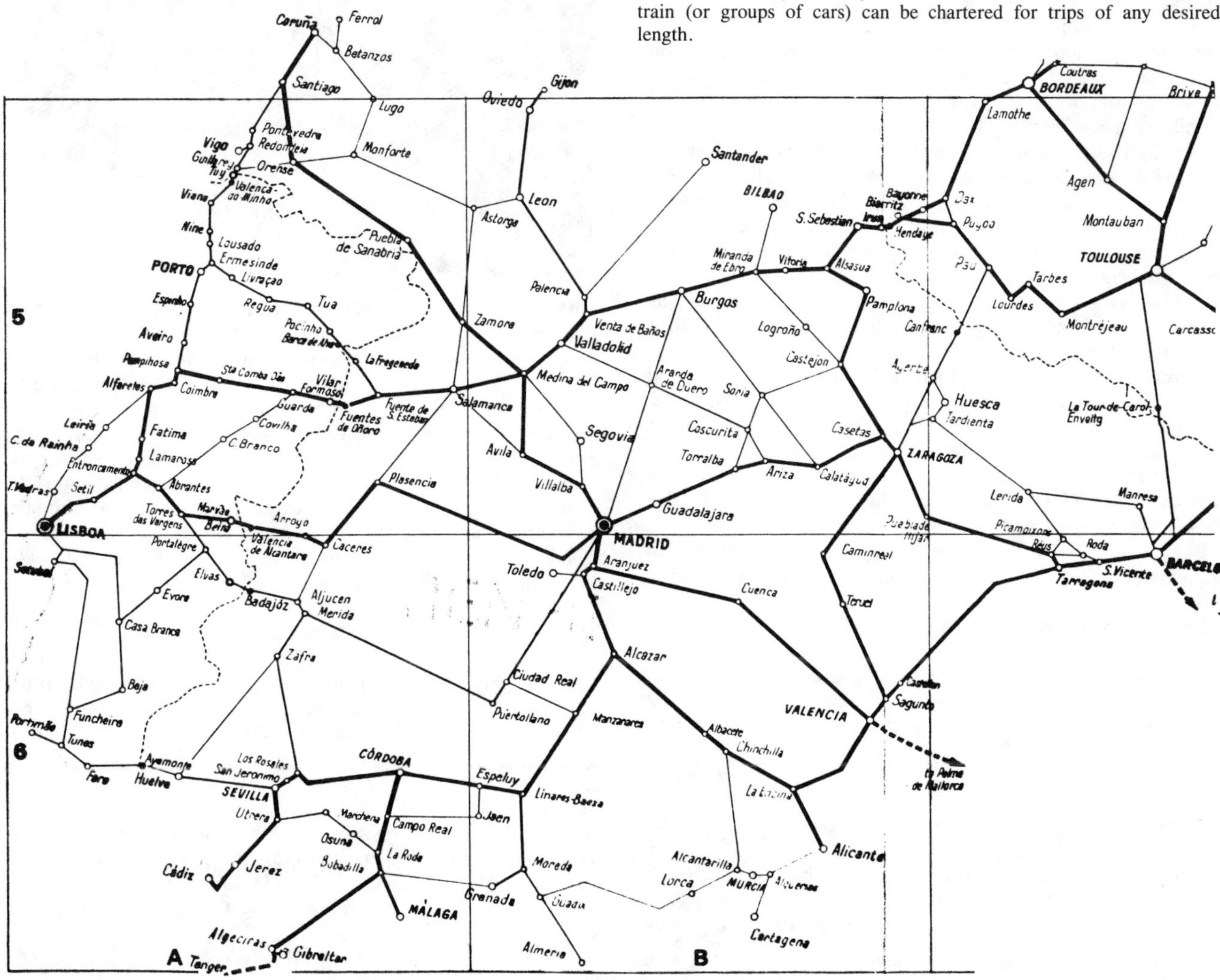

southwestern coast of France. After reaching Bilbao, the train turns westward to Santander then runs along the Cornisa and Costa Verde to Viveiro and finally El Ferrol del Caudillo. In the evening of the same day, the return trip begins.

*This northern region of Spain is an area largely unknown but rich in tradition, natural beauty and fine food. During these seven days, passengers discover at first hand the wealth of enjoyment it offers. We will see caves at Valporquero, the narrow cleft at the Pass of Vegacervera, the ancient coal mines of Leon, fish markets in little Cantabrian ports, the little-known Romanesque in the province of Palencia, and the mysteries of the Pilgrim's Route to Santiago de Compostela. But that's not all. There are the Picos de Europa, the stunning vertiginous views of Fuente De, the Caves Gorge (seventh wonder of Spanish nature), the secrets of Inner Galicia with its* meigas *(witches), old inns from the Middle Ages in the Castile of the Merindades — and more.*

*Passengers will also see traditional folklore in the war dances of the Picayos,* dulzaina *concerts in Leon, the* versolaris *from Cabezon, a Cantabrian game of bowls — plus craftsmanship in wood, ceramics and leather.*[2]

Though we've not taken this trip, we have toured the extreme northwest of Spain from La Coruna to Vigo and spent several hours in Santiago de Compostela. Plan on doing the same to or from El Ferrol, which is about 60 km north by toll road.

This area is ancient Galicia where St. Paul preached to the Galicians and from whence Phoenicians and Romans had, once upon a time, set sail for England. It was here that the Pilgrimage Cathedral of Santiago de Compostela became the last and focal point of a trail of pilgrimage-type Romanesque churches that began in southern France during the 11th century. Masked by imposing 17th and 18th century Flamboyant Gothic, this Cathedral of St. James reveals a severe and little-altered Romanesque interior (other than the main altar and inner tympanum). But the hordes of worshippers, and equal numbers of tourists, are a stirring sight, and surrounding areas of the town are charming. Don't miss it.

Although the *Transcantabrico* trip is not covered by EURAILPASS, it's inexpensive enough to be appealing to anyone who enjoys getting off the beaten track(s). See *Travel Supplement* for current fare.

By planning as follows, this narrow gauge adventure can be extended to a lovely open-jaw rail trip (in either direction):

Madrid to Leon (421 km) is a four hour, 14 min. daytime ride. El Ferrol is but 17 km north of Coruna by rail; change there for Santiago de Compostela (74 km, 1:25). Santiago south to Vigo (105 km) takes 1½ to 2 hours. From there to Porto by another train is a 3-hour run (174 km). Porto, Portugal's second most important city, to Lisbon is a three-hour (339 km) ride on the country's best trains.

If you do come this way, save enough time to take a train from Porto that stops at Coimbra (121 km), then taxi to Bussaco for a memorable stay at the Palacio Hotel. Built in the late 19th century, this was the summer palace of King Carlos until his assassination in 1911, at which

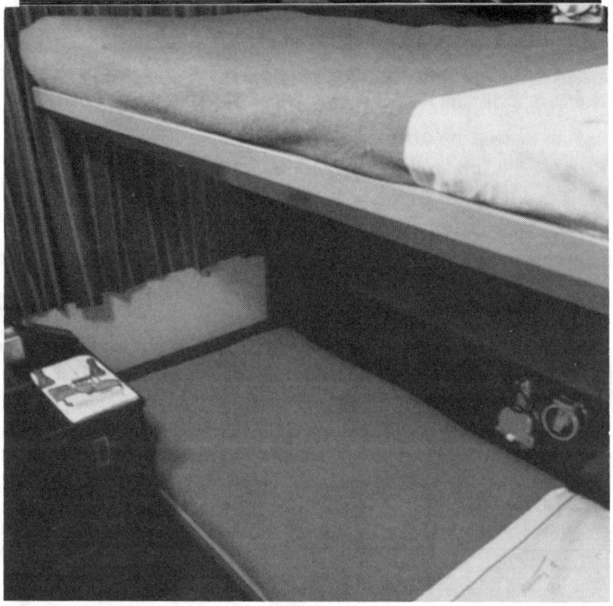

time the Republic of Portugal was inaugurated. Here you live in the early 1900s surrounded by the same inner and outer walls that protected King Carlos; much of the same furniture, antiques, wall hangings, statuary and the magnificent marble staircase remain. The high-ceiling bedrooms are furnished with cut velvet seat chairs, oriental rugs, crystal chandeliers, Victorian furniture — and the bathrooms are HUGE. Dining areas are beamed, ceilings painted, flooring is parquet, walls covered with copies of famous paintings; the tapestry chairs have carved wooden backs. The palace stands in isolated splendor within the surrounding beauty of Bussaco forest.

### More About Spanish Trains

All cities and resorts can be reached by train — very inexpensively, too. Best bets are the airconditioned *Talgo* day trains. From Madrid, they run to Cordoba (5:23) and Malaga (7:41); to Granada in 6:50; to Seville (6¼ hrs.) and Cadiz (8 hrs.); also to Barcelona in 8 hours. There are also night expresses with first class, airconditioned sleepers.

Should you plan traveling only in Spain, where normal fares are extremely inexpensive, there are a number of bargain deals: Chequetren, Blue Days (Dias Azules) travel, Senior and Children's fares. See *Travel Supplement* for details.

Sleepers are operated by the Wagons-Lits Company.

[2] Excerpted from a 4-color *Transcantabrico* brochure (in English).

# AFRICA

## EGYPT . . . First Great Age Of Man

Never has such a high level of civilization been maintained as long as it was in Egypt — from prehistoric times to the beginning of the Christian era — an unbroken chain stretching across 4,000 years. That we, today, may witness phases of this remarkable culture in an equally remarkable state of preservation is a priceless heritage *not to be missed.*

Here, very briefly, are the highlights:[1]

**HOUSES OF ETERNITY . . . THE PYRAMIDS**

Of all man-made structures, the pyramids, particularly the Giza trio of mausoleums — Mycerinus (c 2500 BC), Chefren (2530 BC) and Cheops (2570 BC) — are the most famous. And of the seven wonders of the ancient world, only they have survived destruction by man and nature. Unequalled as engineering projects, they were probably unsurpassed in beauty when, in their prime, the sun's rays danced across the highly polished outer slabs of limestone or granite reflecting the glory, wealth and prestige of pharaohs, the immense capability and dedication of man before his god.

[1] For complete descriptions and background, get our informative booklet, *Destination: Egypt.*

**THAT ENIGMATIC WONDER . . . THE SPHINX**

Perhaps because it has been glorified in the minds of man for so long as the very essence of the greatness of ancient Egypt, The Sphinx (so named by the Greeks) may well be your greatest disappointment. We say this as a precautionary measure, not to take anything away from this architectural wonder. For that it is — 240 feet long, 66 feet high — in the shape of a recumbent lion with a male head, that of Chefren (complete with a curled beard, indicating death), a little more than 13 feet wide. Built contemporaneously with the Chefren Pyramid as a monumental monument for posterity, it was later worshipped as Harmakhis, the Sun God, since it faces east. Over the centuries, sands of the desert seared its face and body, tried to bury it in their drifts. During the Mameluke reign, which ended with subjugation of the country by the Turks in 1517, the face was partially mutilated. Yet it lives, though with a somewhat diminished effect since it now lies, seemingly contentedly, in a sand pit substantially below the current desert level. Shots seen of the mighty head rearing majestically above its surroundings are skillfully angled photography.

**TEMPLES . . . EGYPT'S DEVINE GLORIES**

When viewing their epic proportions and beauty, consider them, as well as the pyramids, as the most significant of man's pioneering achievements.

The temples of Karnak, Luxor, Thebes and Abydos were started and completed between 4,000 and 3,200 years ago.

# THE NILE

## FROM ABYDOS TO KOM OMBO*

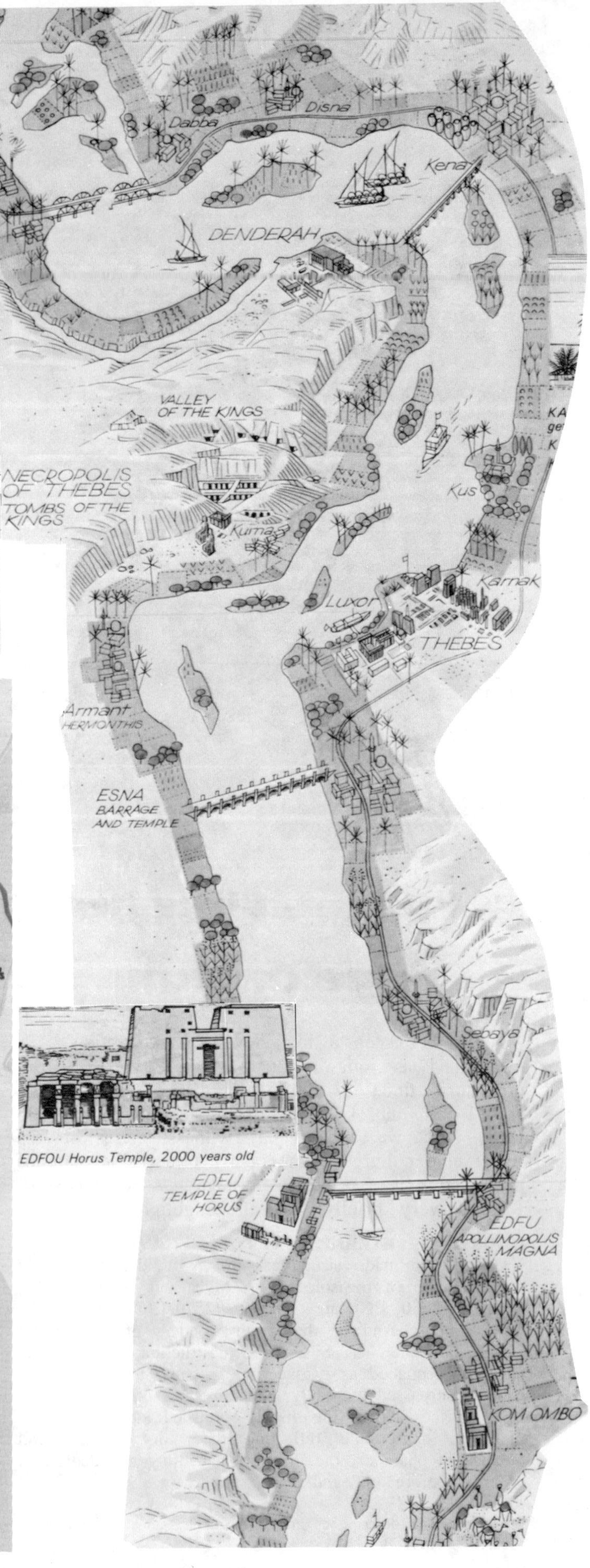

THEBES Mural paintings in the tomb of Nakht, 1400 B.C.

THEBES Temple of Queen Hatshepsut,

LUXOR Amon-Ra Temple, 1350 B.C.

EDFOU Horus Temple, 2000 years old

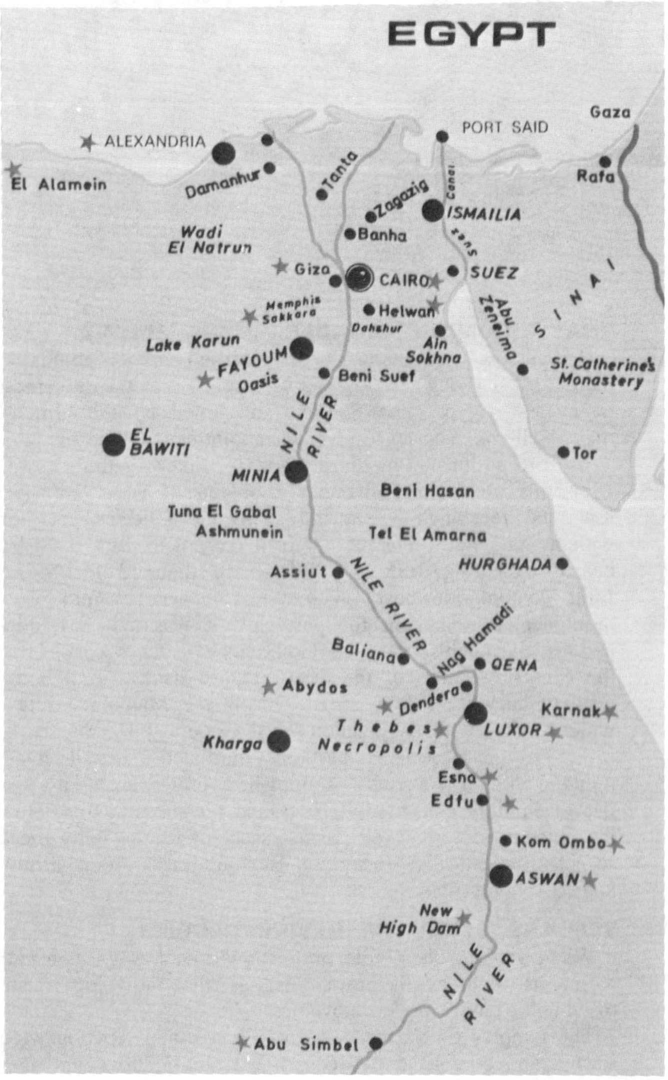

Their architects and builders were unable to computerize their projects to determine what others had done, for there were no others — no Greeks, no Romans, no Christians had yet striven to achieve such grandiose designs. Not only architecturally but, more importantly, conceptually. Here, for the first time, men conceived and then created buildings in which to honor and worship and supplicate their gods in surroundings of grandeur, in a manner commensurate with the divine powers of those gods.

Here, indeed, was something new under, as well as for, the sun. Man's walk on the moon might well be considered less epochal.

### THE MAGNIFICENT TEMPLES OF ABU SIMBEL

For sheer stunning, overpowering effect, we have never seen — experienced is probably a more descriptive verb — anything, anywhere to equal the gargantuan proportions of the Great Temple of Amun and Re-Harakhte. It has been described in many superlative ways — as the most remarkable building in the world, as if Notre Dame Cathedral had been carved out of solid rock. The four colossal figures of Ramses II which form the facade are 67 feet high (larger than the Colossi of Memnon), the temple itself 153 feet wide and 195 feet deep — all carved and hollowed out of an escarpment of solid rock which, originally, stood near the banks of the Nile. Nearby, Queen Nefertari's temple, dedicated to Hathor, seems diminutive in comparison, even though it has a facade 88 feet wide and 39 feet high with six statues 33 feet tall.

"Engineers . . . marvel at the genius of their ancient predecessors who performed this marriage of the colossal with the beautiful, joined science to nature to produce an architectural masterpiece . . . they must have had a profound knowledge of geology, for they knew the rock was of a consistency that could house the interior of the temple and would lend itself to carving of facade and friezes . . . using the more compact strata for ceilings and walls. They must have known about porosity, the solvent powers of the water-table below the escarpment and the possible dissolution of the rock itself . . . about weathering and the durability of stone. Their lives depended on such knowledge, for theirs was the task of building a lasting structure which would embody the immortality of the gods and the Pharoah himself. In doing so, they contrived to fit the designs of the two temples into the landscape, thus creating one of the wonders of the ancient world. They knew enough about astronomy that on two days each year one long beam of the rising sun would penetrate the darkness of the long pillared nave to the innermost sanctuary 200 feet within the mountain and rest upon the silent figure of the sun-god Re-Horakhte."[2]

## CAIRO TO ASWAN BY TRAIN

Majority of group tours fly from Cairo to Luxor, Aswan and Abu Simbel . . . or cruise the Nile from Luxor to Aswan with stops at Esna, Edfu and Kom Ombo. However, there is another option: the daytime or overnight train from Cairo to Luxor and Aswan (but *not* Abu Simbel).

It having been years since we rode the Cairo-Luxor overnight train, we checked with a deluxe tour operator on just how it was today. The reply: "Train itself is very nice — modern, airconditioned sleeping cars with single berth compartments in first class, double berth in second. HOWEVER, the ride is *not good* — very bumpy. Our passengers complain that they are unable to sleep. Food is less than satisfactory (airline type with service to match)."

If you still wish to chance it, here are the schedules:

Train 84 departs Cairo at 1900 for non-stop arrival in Luxor at 0606, Aswan at 1000. Train 86 leaves at 1936 for 0830 arrival in Luxor, 1235 in Aswan. Train 85 leaves Aswan at 1445, Luxor at 1930 for 0640 arrival in Cairo. Train 87 departs at 1745 and 2225 for 0950 Cairo arrival. All trains have a diner. See *Travel Supplement* for approximate fares.

Should you wish a daylight ride, a train (No. 980) with airconditioned first and second class coaches and dining car leaves Cairo at 0730, arrives (after a number of stops) in Luxor at 1830, Aswan at 2320. No. 981 leaves Aswan at 0515, Luxor at 1014 for 2055 arrival in Cairo. Stops are made at Esna, Edfu and Kom Ombo archeological sites north of Luxor.

Cairo to Luxor is 671 km, to Aswan 879.

There's frequent service between Cairo-Alexandria (and vice-versa) with first/second class, airconditioned coaches and diner. This is a 2-hr, 45-min. run.

## ASWAN TO SOUTH AFRICA

It's possible to continue south from Aswan by train for 19 km to El Sadd el Ali and from there to Wadi Halfa by Nile Valley River Transport boat; leaves at 1600 on Saturdays, arrives 0600 on Mondays. On Mondays and Wednesdays, a train (with so-called first class coaches, sleepers and a dining car) leaves Wadi Halfa at 1640, arrives 24 hours later in Khartoum. On Wednesdays/Sundays, it leaves Khartoum northbound at 0645.

Since Khartoum is the end of the line for tourists, they must fly south to Harare (formerly Salisbury) to continue by rail to Johannesburg, a 24-hour journey of 1313 km by the most direct route.

### *Cape to Cairo Express*

This 35-day program by Voyages Jules Verne, offered year 'round (except during summer), is indeed an exciting one — though why it's named Cape to Cairo when it goes in reverse direction we wouldn't know. It includes the night train to Luxor, a three-day Nile boat trip to Aswan, a visit to Abu Simbel and on by air to Khartoum, where the White and Blue Nile meet, Dar Es Salaam, Mount Kilimanjaro, Harare and Victoria Falls. From there it's all the way south by various trains to visit Hwange, Bulawayo, Mafeking, Johannesburg, Kimberley, Cape Town — and back to Johannesburg from Durban by the original Blue Train for the flight back to London. What a way to go!

[2] Bratton's *A History of Egyptian Archeology.*

# SOUTH AFRICA'S
# *Blue Train*

Famed *Blue Train* (actually there are identical twins) is spoken of only in superlatives as the ultimate in luxury equipment. Everything is on a grand scale. Imagine if you can an entire car accommodating only six (or less) passengers — or even cars with the least expensive compartments (Type D) limited to 11 passengers.

The train's 16 dust-free, airconditioned coaches are virtually noiseless and vibration-free thanks to air-sprung bogies — and so arranged as to keep afternoon sun off accommodation areas.[1] And what other train can boast of a suite with tub-shower?

What other train's compartments have five control buttons? No. 1 calls the sleeping car valet-attendant (he serves coffee/tea, shines shoes). No. 2 adjusts the temperature. No. 3 enables venetian blinds on the main window to be raised, lowered and tilted. No. 4 controls musical or radio selection, No. 5 the volume.

The wood-paneled, carpeted and cushioned lounge car has panoramic windows on both sides, a good-looking bar. The attractive dining car, also paneled, seats 46 at each sitting; a head waiter, immaculately dressed in morning coat and striped trousers, visits each passenger to inquire of his preference. There's a choice of international and South African dishes for lunch and dinner, described by one passenger as "undistinguished but copious seven-course meals," though the full, English-type breakfast gets high marks. As does the elegant service.

This is not a high speed train. Rather, it wends its way thru some splendidly scenic areas, particularly in the Hex River Valley (some two hours out of Cape Town), "a small Eden of vineyards and irrigated fruit orchards." Too, there's a dramatic climb thru Hex River Pass when the train loops back on itself 16 times within 15 miles. Beyond that (on the northbound run) is the semi-lunar landscape of the Karoo.

### *Blue Train* Schedule

On the 1,000-mile southbound run, the train leaves Pretoria at 1000, arrives Johannesburg at 1110, departs 20 minutes later. After stopping in Kimberley (at 1831),[2] arrives in Cape Town at 1140 the next day.

Northbound, the train leaves Cape Town at 1030, arrives next day in Johannesburg at 1100, Pretoria at 1230.

From September thru April, there are southbound and northbound departures every other day. From May thru August, the *Blue Train* runs every fourth day of the month, both southbound and northbound.

*Blue Train* reservations can be made up to 11 months in advance — and most advisable to do so as the trains are always heavily booked in advance. For reservations and exact departure dates, contact SAR-travel, 535 Fifth Ave., New York 10017; 800-223-1880.

### Drakensberg Express

With compartments for two passengers and smaller rooms for one, this Johannesburg to Durban train, also with lounge and dining cars, is only somewhat less elegant than the *Blue*. There are toilets and showers at the end of each sleeping car.

Train leaves Johannesburg every Friday at 1745, arrives Durban at 0745 Saturday. Leaves there on Sundays at 1745, arrives in Johannesburg at 0735.

See *Travel Supplement* for train fares.

[1] Corridor windows face the hot afternoon sun side. Too, all window glass, golden in color, was treated with a thin layer of gold to deflect heat and glare.

[2] So as not to disturb sleeping passengers, there are no night stops.

# NORTH AMERICA

"Some of the world's most exciting" is an apt description of Amtrak's long distance trains with Superliner coaches, sleepers, diners and observations-lounge cars. This is the *California Zephyr* near the crest of the California-Nevada High Sierra range of mountains. Other western Amtrak trains with the same equipment link Chicago with Los Angeles, Portland and Seattle, as well as Los Angeles with San Francisco-Seattle and Los Angeles-New Orleans. According to the Jacobs, if you haven't ridden the rails over at least one of those routes, preferably that of the *Zephyr,* you haven't seen the United States at its scenic best.

## UNITED STATES
## CANADA
## ALASKA
## MEXICO

# Amtrak's National Rail Passenger System

## THE AMERICAN TRAIN SCENE

Our fondest boyhood memories include riding the rails all over the continent. And what stands out most vividly are those long-gone dining car breakfasts: immaculate napery, gleaming silver service, cheerful and attentive service by solicitous black waiters, huge strawberries and ice-cold melon, hot and cold cereals smothered in cream, and done-to-perfection eggs, bacon and sausage. Oh, my — we can see and smell them even unto today.

We're speaking of the years between the endings of World Wars I and II. The glory years of all-star trains: *Twentieth Century Limited* (New York Central) and *Broadway Limited* (Pennsylvania RR) between New York and Chicago (20 hours); *Panama Limited* (Illinois Central) from Chicago to New Orleans (16½ hours); Santa Fe's *Chief* and *Super-Chief* [1] and Union Pacific's *City of Los Angeles* from Chicago to Los Angeles (about 37 hours). *California Zephyr* (Bur-

[1] Talk about glamor and celebrities, *Orient Express* had nothing on the *Super-Chief* except age and a few Agatha Christie murders. Hollywood and Broadway stars, captains of industry and world leaders were to be seen (or not seen if anonymity best suited the situation) riding the *Super-Chief.*

## NEW YORK CENTRAL SPECIAL DINNER

SMALL TENDERLOIN OF BEEF SAUTE
FRESH MUSHROOMS AND GRILLED SPANISH ONION
NEW GREEN PEAS WITH MINT — POTATOES FONDANTE

**Choice of**

RICE CUSTARD WITH WHIPPED CREAM — APPLE OR MINCE PIE
STEAMED PLUM PUDDING, HARD SAUCE
IMPORTED CHEDDAR CHEESE WITH TOASTED BISCUITS
BREAD AND BUTTER — TEA, COFFEE, MILK

[$1.35]

## SPECIALS TODAY

| | |
|---|---|
| FRIED FILET OF SOLE, *Tartare Sauce, Julienne Potatoes, Beet and Celery Mayonnaise* | 95 |
| BROILED LAKE SUPERIOR WHITEFISH, *Lemon Butter, Escalloped Tomatoes, Hashed Browned Potatoes* | 95 |
| SADDLE OF LAMB *en Casserole, New Peas, Potatoes, Onions and Carrots* | 95 |
| FRIED MILK CHICKEN, *Salt Pork, Cream Sauce, New Brussels Sprouts, Mashed Potatoes* | 95 |
| BAKED SUGAR CURED HAM *Glace, Bigarade, Creamed New Spinach, Sweet Potato Grille* | 95 |
| SHIRRED EGGS *with Sausage Patties Bordelaise* | 65 |
| FRESH VEGETABLES *with Egg* | 85 |
| ROAST RIBS OF PRIME BEEF *with Potatoes* | 85 |
| ASSORTED COLD MEATS *with Potato Salad* | 85 |
| LETTUCE AND TOMATO SALAD, *Russian Dressing* | 40 |
| CANAPE OF GENUINE RUSSIAN CAVIAR | 65 |
| SMALL CLUB SIRLOIN *Saute, French Fried Potatoes* | 1 25 |
| GRAPE FRUIT, *Iced, Half* | 30 |
| N. Y. C. SPECIAL BAKED APPLE *with Cream* | 30 |

### FROM THE GRILL

Milk Fed Chicken, half, French Fried Potatoes 1 25
Sirloin Steak (for 1), French Fried Potatoes 2 00; (for 2) 4 00
Rack Lamb Chop (1) 40; (2) 75 — Bacon and Fried Eggs 75 — Ham and Fried Eggs 75
Ham 75; Reduced Portion 40 — Bacon 75; Reduced Portion 40 — Country Sausage 60

### FRESH VEGETABLES

| | |
|---|---|
| MASHED HUBBARD SQUASH | 30 |
| BOILED ONIONS *in Cream* | 35 |
| NEW BRUSSELS SPROUTS *in Butter* | 40 |
| WHOLE NEW SPINACH *with Egg* | 45 |
| CELERY HEARTS, *Demi Glaze* | 35 |
| NEW CAULIFLOWER *Au Gratin* | 40 |

Potatoes, Plain Boiled 25 — French Fried 35 — Mashed 25 — Au Gratin 35 — Hashed Browned 35
Stewed Tomatoes 30 — Small Carrots 30
Royal Mushrooms on Toast 50 — Baked Beans, Hot or Cold, with Brown Bread 45

ABOVE PORTIONS PER PERSON ONLY
AN EXTRA CHARGE OF 25 CENTS PER PERSON WILL BE MADE FOR MEALS SERVED OUT OF DINING CAR

In 1931, *Twentieth Century* passengers lived it up at these low depression prices. The $1.35 Special Dinner was actually 15¢ less than it was in 1902. After prohibition repeal, Scotch and soda was served for 60¢. Price of a shave was 25¢, manicure 75¢. Sleeping car porters averaged $5 in tips per run; their average weekly earnings of $38 put them in the upper echelons of Harlem society.

lington, Rio Grande & Western Pacific) from Chicago to Oakland featured (as it still does) the highly scenic 2532 mile run thru the Colorado Rockies and California's Feather River Canyon; in its heyday, six trains of 11 cars maintained a daily run in each direction.

Yes, those were the luxury train days unabashedly appealing to the upper classes. *Twentieth Century,* an extra fare, all-Pullman train that made its first run in 1902 (as did the *Broadway*) the favorite of Chicago's cloak-and-suiters; on Sunday afternoons, the retailers boarded the train (via a red carpet), were greeted by their favorite Pullman porter, served by their favorite waiter, played poker or pinochle thru the night and were ready for a week's buying trip when 7th Avenue showrooms opened on Monday. A Friday afternoon return saw them back in their stores on Saturday morning.

Amenities of crack trains rivaled those of ocean liners, albeit on a reduced scale: barbers, valet and maid service, shower baths, shoeshines, daily papers and, as noted, superb meals (at prices you now weep over). On the *Chief* and *Super-Chief,* dining car stewards solicited your order the night before for Colorado rainbow trout freshly caught the next morning just for you; we can still smell the tantalizing grilled aroma, never quite matched by any in succeeding years. Ah, memories, memories.

In the 50s, trains were constantly being upgraded with vista dome cars, coaches with airplane-type seats, diesel locomotives and such. Yet despite those improvements, despite sold-out train travel during the war years of '42 to '45, the DC-6s and 7s and Constellations that flooded the skies in the years following spelled the doom of boom times for the railroads, just as the coming of jet aircraft sunk trans-Atlantic super-liners. Even the *Twentieth Century* succumbed, grudgingly, in 1967.

The 19th century Age of the Railroad reached its trans-continental zenith in the U.S. during the 1920s. In 1925, there were 65,000 passenger cars in operation, of which 29,000 were coaches, 8,000 sleeping cars, 1,500 dining cars, 1,600 parlor cars, 9,000 combination cars. In 1977, only 5,500 passenger cars remained in service.

Today, Amtrak (National Railroad Passenger Corporation) operates its long and short haul passenger services over almost 24,000 miles of track with a fleet of about 1,500 new or modernized cars: coaches, sleepers (Heritage and Superliner), club, lounges and diners. In the fiscal year ending September 1984, Amtrak carried almost 19½ million passengers, of which well over half traveled the northeast Corridor routes. However, 757,000 took the Great Rail Trip on the *California Zephyr* from Chicago to Oakland/San Francisco. They can count themselves among the most fortunate of rail travelers.

## THE GREAT RAIL TRIP — CROSSING THE U.S. ON AMTRAK

After our summer in Europe, we weren't looking forward to spending three days on two trains versus five hours on a plane. After all, we'd ridden the Orient-Express, TGV, TEE, Glacier Express (not to mention other trains around the world). What, considering all those reports we'd read about Amtrak, did we have to look forward to except boredom? But we had a reportorial job to do. And besides, we had a hunch that maybe, just maybe, Amtrak had been unjustly maligned.

The overnight New York-Chicago ride on the *Lake Shore Limited* did little to recall the glory of the *Twentieth Century* which traversed the same route. It's been described as comfortable, unexciting and, except for those fearful of flying, unneeded. But, after an overnight at that most gracious of hotels, Chicago's Drake,[1] we boarded the *California Zephyr* — and that's where our hunch paid off.

### *California Zephyr* To San Francisco

Let's put it this way: if you haven't traveled this route, you haven't seen the United States at its most glorious scenic best. We had, several times, in bygone years but had simply forgotten, so immersed are we in foreign travel, that here in our own backyard is as magnificent, as enjoyable a Great Rail Trip as anywhere else around the globe.

Matter of fact, you can't *know* the United States without having seen the farms and frame houses and unassuming towns of Illinois and Iowa; here is Middle America, looking strong and substantial and traditional.

You can't realize the scenic grandeur of the Rocky Mountains, the Colorado River, the canyons of Utah, the Sierra Nevadas until they stream past at eye level. From a 747 they're remote, topographical; from the wide windows of a Superliner they are sublime acts of creativity. Here's what we noted along the way:

"Out of Denver, the train climbs and spirals into the mountains along a small but turbulent Colorado River, often almost brushing rock cliffs towering above. If not for our trips thru Switzerland and Norway, this part alone would elicit extravagant exclamations.

"Entire run, Denver to Salt Lake, is the 'Wild West' at its best; many of the towns still look as though the sheriff will come riding up and hitch his horse to the hitching post. True, we saw nary a cowboy or robber, but we did see buffalo and elk — and there are coyotes and varmints and rattlesnakes 'out thar' in abundance. Too, we sightred the LaSalle mountain range in the distance, one of two that run east-west; all other western mountains lie north-south.

[1] A favorite of ours way back when we went there on Friday and Saturday night high school and college dances, it retains an understated charm and elegance that comparatively few hotels in the U.S. can match — and even enhanced by recent renovations by new management, Vista International. The well-furnished rooms and baths are extremely large — hotels can't afford to build 'em that big any more. Our lunch in that Chicago landmark, the Cape Cod Room, was at once elegant, delicious and reasonably priced. Truly, the Drake is one of the world's great traditional hotels in which it's a pleasure to spend one's money.

If this photo, taken thru the window of our Superliner as it rolled along the Colorado River, impresses you with its clarity, imagine how truly impressive are the miles and miles and miles of Ruby Canyon's red sandstone cliffs outlined theatrically by the setting sun.

"Later in the afternoon, shortly before reaching the Colorado-Utah state line, between Grand Junction and Thompson, Utah, Ruby Canyon suddenly surrounded us — miles and miles of red sandstone cliffs and buttes, thru which the Colorado River rushes, paint a stunning, awesome picture similar to Bryce and Zion National Parks but unlike any other rail scenery that, to our knowledge, exists elsewhere in the world. Many of the mounds and ridges have crumbled and eroded over the ages so that huge boulders lie helplessly atop and along their sides — a desolate, moon-surface yet glowing redly in the lowering sun. Except by plane in the Red Centre of Australia, we've never seen anything to match such stark, red beauty.

"Out of Thompson, the ruins of castle-like mountain fortresses run along the train's route as if guarding it — strange, gnarled shapes in a fantasy land punctuated by acres of green ground cover, clumps of yellow black-eyed susans and huge, convoluted rocks, many in the form of elephants' trunks and feet with hide to match.

"In the desert around Grand River, Utah, tremendous sandstone aircraft carriers, battle cruisers and steam engines appeared against the horizon, then a walled city in Tibet, a desert Shangri-La. All in all, a grandiose setting conceived, painted and lighted by a master stage manager, then smashed and battered by some wrathful god only to create yet another masterpiece of tortured rock.

"Morning's dawn brings yet another stage setting: sage-covered desert with barren hills in the distance and, approaching Sparks and Reno, Nevada, a tree-lined Truckee River, backed by tree-clad mountains, rushing beside the roadbed. Then the long climb thru many snowsheds (though, of course, no snow there in September) as the train crests the Sierra Nevada range, looks down on Donner Lake and plunges into the Sacramento delta.

"America the Beautiful . . . from Sea to Shining Sea in three days . . . a glorious experience."

That was the rail trip. But what about the train?

It's comfortable and rides smoothly. Superliner Bi-Level Cars, which Amtrak uses on other medium-distance / long-distance western routes,[2] are aluminum-sheathed double deckers that, aside from TGV cars, are more modern and comfortable than any of Europe's rolling stock.

Coaches have comfortable, well-upholstered, reclining seats with leg and foot rests (two on either side of a central aisle) — the equal of first class slumber seats in a 747. Upper level has 62 seats, lower 14 seats in smoking / non-smoking sections. Five toilets, woman's lounge and limited space for storing luggage are on the lower level. Pillows are provided for overnight travel.

Upper level of sleeping cars has five deluxe bedrooms (A thru E) with toilet and shower; B-C and D-E can be bought as suites. There are 10

[2] Bi-level cars cannot be used on Amtrak's eastern routes — insufficient bridge and overpass clearance. Here conventional cars of the 40s and 50s, refurbished as a series of Heritage cars, are used. Consisting of coaches (with reclining seats), slumbercoaches (very small single or double berth compartments) and sleepers with roomettes (for one) and bedrooms (for two), they are almost as comfortable as bi-level cars, though there's lots of motion at high speeds — but not unpleasantly so. All sleeping accommodations have wash basin and toilet. Our bedroom on *Lake Shore Limited* was about 4 ft. by 6 ft. It was airconditioned (as are all Amtrak cars), had a fan, narrow closet, wash basin, separate toilet space. Lower and upper berths are narrow but comfortable. Specially nice touch: on boarding, conductor and car attendant greeted us by name.

**SUPERLINER ACCOMMODATIONS**

**Economy Bedroom** (right) — 6½′ by 3½′. Does not have toilet. Lower berth is 2⅓′ wide, upper 2′. **Deluxe Bedroom** (left) — 6½′ by 7½′, including closet and toilet and shower. Lower berth is 3′ 2″ wide.

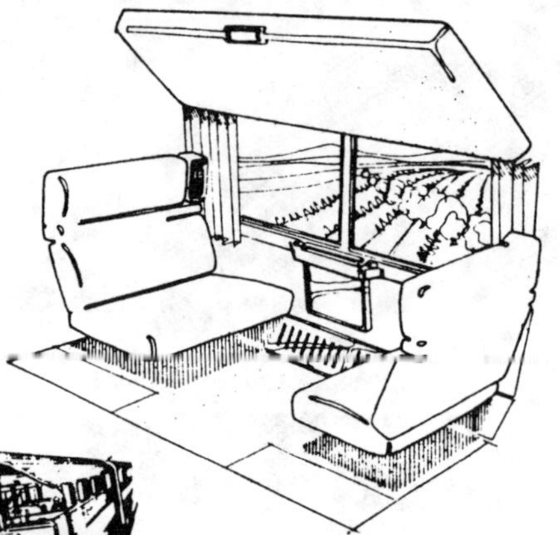

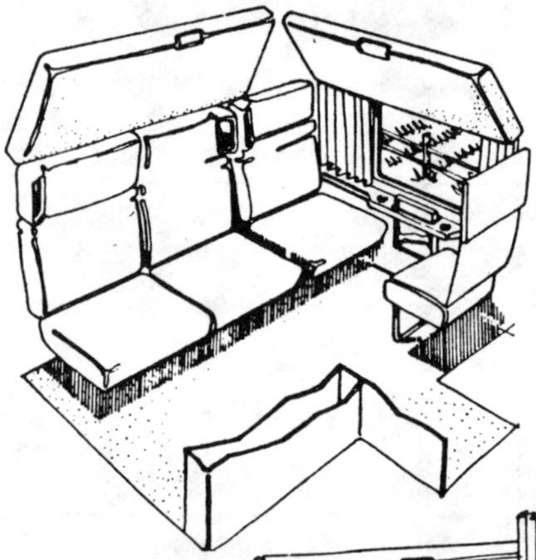

**Diner** — Food prepared in lower level kitchens, moved to dining level by mini-elevator.

**Family Bedroom** (upper left) — Extends width of car, has windows on both sides. No toilet. Two adult berths, two children's berths (4¾′ × 2′).

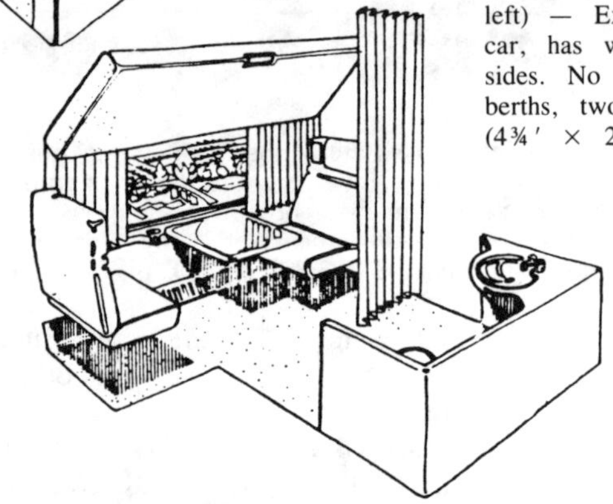

**Coaches** have large windows, roomy reclining seats with leg rests and retractable seatback tray tables, indirect lighting, individual reading lights. Special swivel seat with folding armrests available for handicapped. Rest rooms have built-in infant changing tables; many coaches have women's / men's dressing rooms.
**Special Bedroom** (left) — Lower level room for handicapped and companion. Specially equipped restroom. Car attendants provide meal / beverage service to handicapped passengers.

economy bedrooms on upper level; on lower level, four economy bedrooms, a special bedroom designed for handicapped travelers and a large family bedroom for two adults, two children — plus five public toilets and space for limited luggage storage. Only drawback to an otherwise perfect setup is the narrow, steep staircase between the two levels.

Although the bedrooms for two, on both sides of a center aisle, are small, deluxe bedrooms run the full width of the car (less the two-ft. side aisle), are 7½ feet long. This space encloses a well-lighted, twin-size couch and armchair, drop-down table and wash basin plus a small but adequate toilet / shower room. An upper berth, which is extended at night, is narrow — about two feet wide. Actually, a loving couple can sleep comfortably in the lower.

Service thruout was cheerful and efficient, includes morning coffee / tea and newspaper for bedroom passengers (and cheese / wine basket for those in deluxe bedrooms); if desired, porters deliver a bowl of ice at cocktail times. Overall, the equivalent of first class plane and hotel service.

In all cars — coach, sleeping, lounge and dining — wide view windows, particularly on the upper level, are ideal for sightseeing and photography. We should mention that an interesting commentary over the inter-com system keeps passengers advised of their whereabouts, approaching points of interest and scenic beauty.

The bi-level lounge car, with smoking / non-smoking sections, has an upper level bar, a lower level snack bar serving packaged goodies, excellent microwave oven-cooked hot dogs and hamburgers.

Would we could report that our transcontinental meals equalled those we once enjoyed in bygone years. We can't. First of all, the ambiance of yesteryear is lacking: paper tablecloths and napkins, plastic cups, plates and tableware do not lend themselves to gracious dining.[3] Nor does the food,

[3] Particularly when waiters clear the tables by rolling up the remains in the paper cloth, then throwing the bundle into a plastic garbage bag in full sight of diners.

When this was reported to an Amtrak official, he replied, "You should not have had plastic dinnerware . . . perhaps the dishwasher

*(Footnote[3] continued on next page)*

best described as uninspired mediocrity. Though the menu is well-priced, one wishes that a few well-prepared, higher priced entrees were available.

Attendants solicit lunch and dinner reservations (there are three or four sittings) from each passenger and there are public announcements when each sitting is available. Dining car service is efficient and pleasant, even jovial — but the waiters' short sleeve uniforms could be more attractively designed and colored.

### *California Zephyr* Schedule

A 1440 departure from Chicago on this 2427-mile trip to Oakland, California (or seven miles further by bus to San Francisco) means a 1530 arrival the second day — 45 hours and 50 minutes of leisurely enjoyment. After passing thru Omaha and Lincoln, Nebraska before and shortly after midnight, the train arrives in Denver, Colorado at 0730, Grand Junction at 1545, Thompson at 1705, Provo at 2050 and Salt Lake City at 2225.[4] After Reno, Nevada (at 0823), the train passes thru Sacramento before skirting San Francisco Bay.

### Trip Planning

We'd prefer to take the westbound leg (for that wonderful setting sun lighting from Grand Junction on) since eastbound, under the flat lighting of a noon sun, this dramatic stretch wouldn't be as dramatic.

If time's a factor, start your train ride in Denver. Then, if returning east, take *Coast Starlight* at 0825 from Oakland (it's a night train from Seattle) for the 467-mile ride to Los Angeles. Then board either *The Southwest Chief* to Kansas City and Chicago (old Santa Fe *Super-Chief* route) or *Sunset Limited* thru Arizona and Texas to New Orleans.

A combination of any of the foregoing permits travelers, particularly those from foreign countries, to see a cross-section of western America without which one cannot say, "I've seen some of the most majestic scenery on earth."

### Amtrak Fares

All are based on coach travel — one way, round trip, round trip excursion and others; sleepers use the same base fare plus an extra fare for whatever type of sleeping accommodation is used.

Reservations are required for club / sleeping car accommodations, for coach travel on "All Reserved" trains and are available on other designated trains.

Regular fare coach tickets allow unlimited stopovers; this does not apply to reserved coach, club / sleeping car accommodations,* Metroliners and most excursion tickets (other than Senior Citizens).

Here's a quick look at **Discount Plans,** some of which may have blackout periods:

*Senior Citizens*—25% on round trip travel for those 65 or older. Unlimited stopovers.

*Group* (15 or more)—15% one way, 25% round trip.

*Family Plan*—Husband full fare, spouse and children (12-21), 50%; children 2-11, 25%.

*Children*—Ages 2-11 when accompanied by parent or person 18 years or older, 50%.

*Military* (active duty)—25%.

*Handicapped*—25% on RT travel with guide or hearing aid dog. Special services are available for the handicapped.

Discount plans and excursion fares are not combinable. Only exception is the 50% discount for children 2-11 traveling with an adult.

*This restriction is easily circumvented. For example, if you wish a stopover in Salt Lake City on the Denver-Oakland run, reserve a coach seat Denver-Salt Lake, another (or sleeper accommodation) Salt Lake-Oakland.

All Aboard America Regions from right to left: Eastern, Central, Western

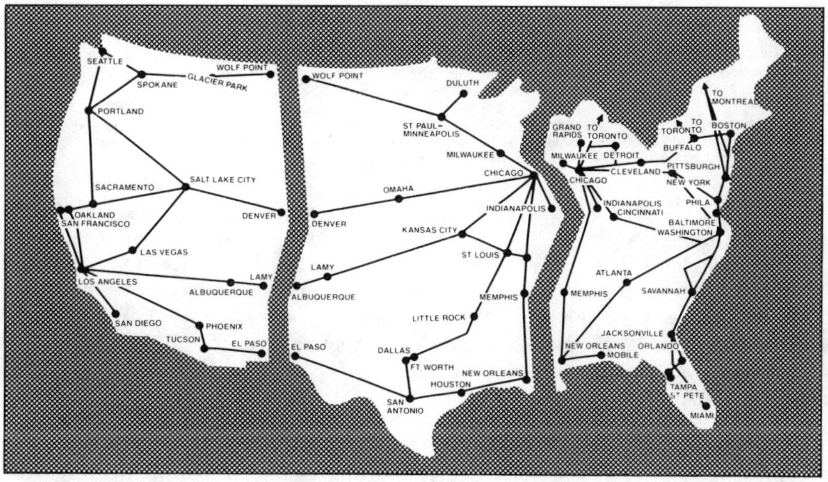


was non-operative that particular day and car."

And to our suggestion of an upgraded dinner service for those desiring same: "We are looking into a first class, one sitting only, higher-cost dinner meal, perhaps at 8 pm each evening, that includes wine, etc. We are also about to launch a more extensive first class amenity service."

[4] Actually, up to this point, the train consists of cars of three trains. *Desert Wind* runs southwest to Los Angeles for a 1405 arrival, *Pioneer* northwest for a 1740 arrival in Portland, Oregon and 2130 at its final destination, Seattle, Washington.

### All Aboard America Fares

Allows unlimited round trip travel for 30 days in one, two or all three regions depending on which fare you purchase (see *Travel Supplement* for exact fares). However, only one stopover is permitted in each direction between departure and turnaround points. Reserved seating is limited; fares are not valid for sleepers from April 5 to 15, December 14 thru January 2. Reservations and tickets must be obtained prior to departure.

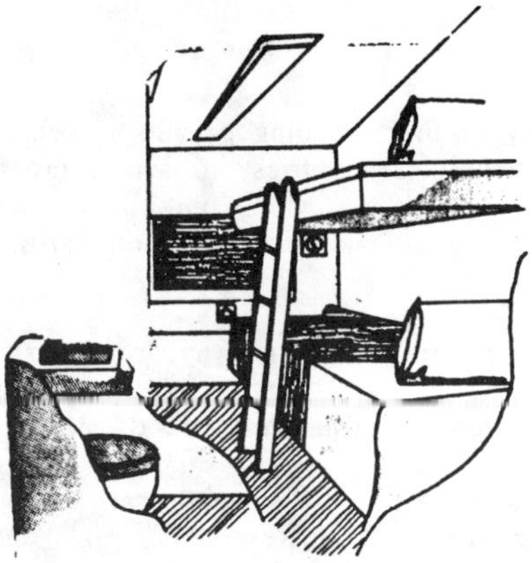

**Bedroom Dimensions**

Room: 7½ x 5'4"

Bed (2): 6' x 35"

Outside aisle: 2'-2'4" wide

**Double Slumbercoach Dimensions**

Room: 6' x 4½'

Bed (2): 6' x 2'

Door: 2' wide

Outside aisle: 2' wide

**Bedroom/night** At night upper and lower berths for two adults unfold. Toilet facilities remain accessible.

**Bedroom suite/night** Two bedrooms adjoined by a sliding partition can be sold as a suite for up to four adults.

**Heritage Fleet** sleeping cars operate on Amtrak overnight trains east of Chicago and New Orleans, plus certain other services. Each sleeper has 10 roomettes and six bedrooms, each with toilet facilities, wash basin, mirror and 110 volt shaver outlet, fresh linens and blankets. Canada's VIA Rail sleeping cars offer similar accommodations. Additionally, Amtrak has Heritage Slumbercoaches consisting of 24 single, eight double compartments with wash basin.

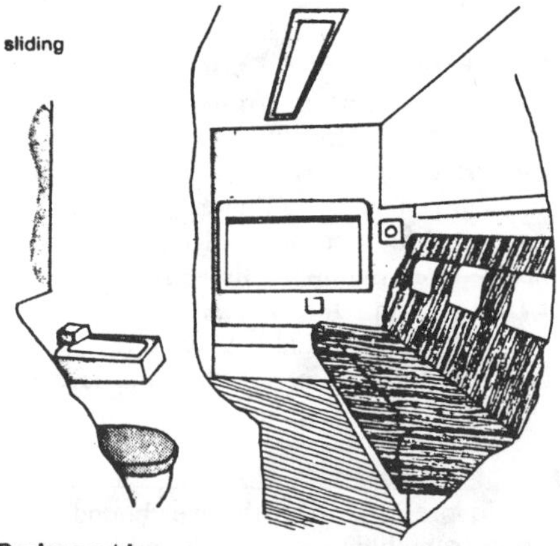

**Bedroom/day** During the day bedrooms provide seating for two occupants in a private room with fully enclosed toilet facilities.

**Roomette/night** At night a full-size single bed lowers. In most roomettes the bed must be raised for night access to toilet facilities. The passenger can raise the bed without a porter's aid if necessary.

**Single slumbercoach/night** (not shown) At night a cot-size berth unfolds. Toilet facilities remain accessible. Double slumbercoach rooms have two berths, with accessible toilet.

**Roomette Dimensions**

Room: 7½' x 3½'

Bed: 6' x 35"

Outside aisle: 2'-2'4" wide

**Single Slumbercoach Dimensions**

Room: 47½"-50½"x43"

Bed: 6'2" x 2'

Door: 19" wide

Outside aisle: 2' wide

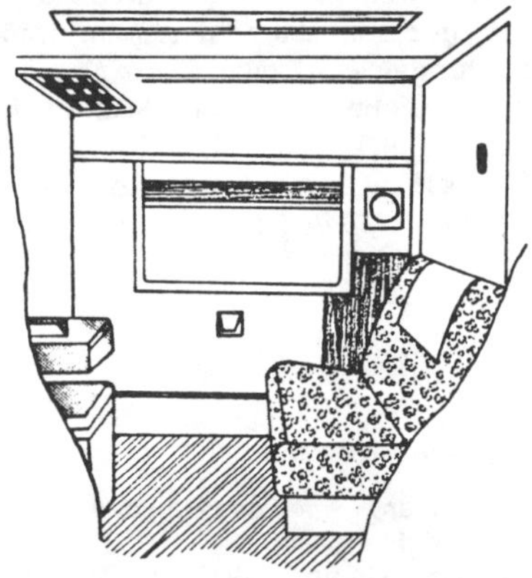

On the U.S. east coast, Amtrak has excellent and frequent services from New York to Washington (2 hours, 49 minutes), including first class club cars; from New York to Boston (4 hrs, 9 min.). There's also Night Owl sleeper service between Boston-New York-Washington, as well as overnight from Washington-New York to Montreal, from where there are frequent connections to other parts of Canada on VIA Rail.

## Washington DC-Florida Auto Train

Take your car along for the overnight ride while you relax, enjoy drinks in the lounge car and dinner in the buffet-style dining car; both dinner (with wine) and continental breakfast are included in the ticket price. After dinner, there's a feature film and complimentary coffee/tea and snacks. Either a reclining coach seat, single roomette or double bedroom are available.

From Boston and New York, there are coach/sleeper trains to Washington, Richmond, North and South Carolina to Florida — Jacksonville, Orlando and Tampa, or Jacksonville to Miami. These are approximately 1½-day trips.

## More About Amtrak Services

**Reservations / Information**—Phone 800-8972-7245 or contact a travel agent, a local Amtrak station. Same applies to VIA (Canada) reservations / information. In Canada, Amtrak is represented by VIA and VIA travel agents. Tickets for both Amtrak and VIA can be purchased U.S. and Canada.

**Credit Cards**—All major ones, including Eurocard, accepted for purchase of tickets and tours at Amtrak ticket offices; also for meals in dining and club cars.

**Personal Checks**—With proper identification, accepted for exact amount of ticket or meal (plus tip).

**Checked Baggage Allowance**—On trains with such service, a passenger may check up to three pieces without charge (not to exceed 75 lbs. per bag or 150 lbs. total). If making stopovers, luggage can be checked to final destination. There are baggage rooms (left luggage) in all Amtrak stations; also self-service lockers for up to 24-hour storage.

**Carry-on Baggage Limitations**—When checked baggage service is available, coach passengers may bring aboard not more than two pieces. Sleeping car passengers may take any pieces that can be stowed safely within their rooms.

**Red Cap Service**—Free baggage assistance is available from porters (with identifying red caps) at most major stations.

Disneyland Railroad, undoubtedly the world's most famous short line, employs four authentic trains of 1890 or earlier vintage to traverse the 1.2 miles of 36″ track to circle Disneyland (Anaheim, Calif.) in 18 minutes. Their locomotives, each named for former Santa Fe RR officials, are authentic reproductions, reassembled with many of the parts of original engines. Main Street Depot (background) is a typical 1900-era brick structure with gabled roof, cupolas and Town Clock.

Elsewhere in California, and in 36 other states and five Canadian provinces, over 100 short line railroads are in operation, most employing steam locomotives, with trips of 15 minutes up to day excursions. These, plus a large number of railroad museums, are fully described in *Steam Passenger Services Directory* ($5 postpaid) published by Empire State Railway Museum, Box 666, Middletown, NY 10940. An invaluable reference.

## PRIVATE RAIL CAR CHARTERS

If you, your company or special interest group would like to travel anywhere in the United States, Canada or Mexico by chartering a car — or even owning one — you should get in touch with David Schumacker, American Association of Private Railroad Car Owners, 3751 E. Dartmouth Ave., Denver 80210.

There are about 300 active and associate members of the Association, approximately 500 privately owned railcars in the U.S., most of which are stationary (converted to restaurants or second homes); possibly 50 are available for charter, meet Amtrak standards for use on its tracks. Most of these are sumptuously restored antiques — real gems. Leasing one of these, fully staffed and equipped, costs up to $3000 per day.

Should you want to own one, the *initial* purchase price ranges from $5000 (at an Amtrak auction) to $100,000; renovated cars may sell for as much as $400,000. One owner, we're told, spends $200,000 a year to maintain and operate his car. Needless to say, most of these lavish cars are owned by businesses for promotional purposes. Incidentally, many individual owners accompany their charters — that's part of their fun.

### Private Car Group Tours

Besides owners who charter their cars, there are a few firms that specialize in booking individuals for rail trips in privately owned cars. Finley Fun-Time Tours[1] have outstanding tours of Mexico, from Los Angeles to the Yucatan and back in their own private (and modern) cars. They also conduct tours of the U.S. and Canada on Amtrak and VIA trains.

Continental Rail[2] has 9-day summer trips from New York to the West Coast in individually-owned cars. This outfit also runs shorter jaunts, as do a few other concerns.[3]

Of those, *American Zephyr,* out of Washington, DC, offers weekend packages to New York or Williamsburg, Va. Two former Amtrak cars, newly refurbished in stunning art deco style, are attached to regularly scheduled trains. Both cars, a 48-seat diner and 50-seat, tavern-style, observation lounge car, gleam with polished wood paneling, etched glass, brass and chrome. For further information, phone 202-223-6026.

[1] 11306 Burbank Blvd, North Hollywood, Ca. 91601. 800-227-1301; 800-831-9668 Calif.

[2] P.O. Box 4225, Grand Central Station, New York 10163.

[3] For listings of others, write David Schumacher at 3751 E. Dartmouth Ave, Denver 80210. Too, the Association is publishing a Charter Referral Guide.

## VIA RAIL ROUTES

## CANADA'S GREAT RAIL TRIP

*Passenger trains touch deep emotions.*

*Few (older) people cannot recall a childhood journey by train: the smells of oiled steel and leather, the feel of the berth that jiggled and sang us to sleep, and the amazing unfolding of a vast country.*

*Today, neither we nor the railroad are the same.*

*We notice that the smell in the washrooms is not at all romantic, and that as the hours pass it seeps into the corridors. Deteriorating roadbeds and worn suspensions transform the jiggling into nasty jerks. The panorama takes too damned long to pass by.*

*Even more painfully, passenger rail service has become an enormous cash drain, absorbing close to $500 million a year in operating losses and $200 million more in capital spending.*

*Via Rail, the government corporation that operates the service, has made some important moves to stem the hemorrhage and capital investments that allow some to ride in the comfort that travellers now demand. To make the service fully modern, Via proposes to crank up those investments to $5 billion over the next 10 years, a prospect that makes the federal government blanche.*

*Even supporters admit that the rail service is not likely, even then, to turn a profit. So why continue to run it when usually profitable airlines and bus companies could provide most of the same services?*

*One reason is our love affair with trains. Via surveys show that 80% of people in all regions of Canada like the trains and favor pouring more money into improving the service. (Perhaps significantly, the survey showed that half the people who say they ride the train are dreaming — they don't according to actual ridership figures.)*[1]

Fortunately, those who wish to see the broad expanses of Canada on a transcontinental rail journey from Montreal to Vancouver (and vice-versa) can do so "in the comfort that travellers now demand" (and without washroom smells) on VIA Rail's crack train, *Canadian* — a four and one half-day (107½ hours) trip that we found both relaxing and interesting. Here are some of our reactions:

"Passing thru the Canadian Rockies, we arrived in Jasper the following afternoon (we left Vancouver at 2200). Disappointed in the scenery which we expected to be spectacular, but at this time of the year (early summer) mountains are almost barren of snow; however, there were some noteworthy vistas as we approached Jasper. We're told that the Lake Louise-Banff area is a considerably more scenic one.[3]

"Meals are adequate, service good. Bedroom berths are comfortable, toilet very small, washbasin small but efficient. Large picture window for easy viewing, railbed quite smooth, the ride fluid.

"On the third day, enroute to Winnepeg, the mile after mile of flatlands are relieved by enchanting vistas of varying shades of greens and field after field of mustard yellow in imposing abstract patterns. In Winnepeg, ate dinner at Hotel Fort Garry near the station.[4] From the little we saw of the city, it has a great deal of gracious stateliness, not at all the Main Street-type we imagined it to be.

"Awakened (fourth day) in a different country, Ontario, to serried ranks of pines and firs, inlets, bays, rivers and ponds — often long stretches of Lake Superior bays. Actually, today's scenery is more pleasing than the Rockies, houses and towns far less stark and austere than those of the Manitoba plains; latter looked like they were inhabited by characters out of Grant Wood paintings.

"Service continues pleasant and efficient. Meals stereotype but nicely edible; breakfast menu reasonable but the same each morning (as on Amtrak)."

### *Canadian* Accommodations, Services & Schedules

There are three types of cars: Day Coaches,[5] Dayniters with roomy stretch-out seating and Sleepers. Latter, usually positioned at rear of train, offer: roomette for one; bedroom for two; drawing room with three beds — all with private toilet, washbasin. Additionally, there are upper/lower berth sections, curtained at night.

In the dining car (called 'meal service car' by VIA), you can choose one of the two full course meals (no a la carte) at breakfast, lunch and dinner — latter two on a reserved seat basis. Train also provides 'bar and take-out snack service cars' as well as 'refreshment lounges' where light meals, continental breakfasts are served.

In Western Canada, there are dome cars to enhance viewing pleasure.

*Canadian* leaves Montreal daily at 1630, arrives Vancouver 0700 on the fifth morning after dozens of stops enroute, a fine way to get closeups of Canadian towns and cities. Leaves Vancouver at 2145, arrives Montreal at 1510 of fifth day (it's three hours ahead of Vancouver time).

An extremely good book, *Scenic Rail Guide To Western Canada,* will add greatly to your enjoyment of this transcontinental journey which, despite the book's title, is thoroughly described and mapped. Also included in the 192 pages, many in full color, is a wealth of interesting rail and road material and maps on other scenic routes in Western Canada, Yukon Territory and Alaska. We consider it invaluable. A companion volume for *Central & Atlantic Canada* is also in print. Each retails for $7.95 (on VIA trains, at VIA stations, in bookstores) in Canada. Cost is $9.95 in U.S. chain bookstores.[6]

[1] Excerpted from an article by Tim Padmore, Business Editor of the *Vancouver Sun.*

[2] From Vancouver, we took Train #4, since discontinued, to Jasper-Edmonton-Regina instead of eastbound *Canadian,* Train #2 (westbound is #1): Vancouver-Banff-Calgary-Regina.

[3] This is one of North America's preeminent resort areas. If you can get hotel reservations (we couldn't), *be sure to stop over for several days.*

[4] Train stops here two hours, 10 minutes. There's time for a British double-decker bus tour if you wish. At Calgary, train stops for 1:10 — time to visit scenic Devonian Gardens, a short walk west of the station, above retail stores and restaurants in Dominion Square.

[5] With smoking/non-smoking sections; also in Dayniters. No smoking in meal service cars except during last sitting.

[6] To reinforce our previous footnote about the beauties of Lake Louise-Banff area, here's what author Bill Coo writes about the train ride from Calgary to beyond Lake Louise:

"This is arguably the most dramatic stretch of track in the world . . . from Banff to Lake Louise the train winds through forests, mountains and valleys . . . terrain changes slightly as you

DAYNITER/SUPERCONFORT

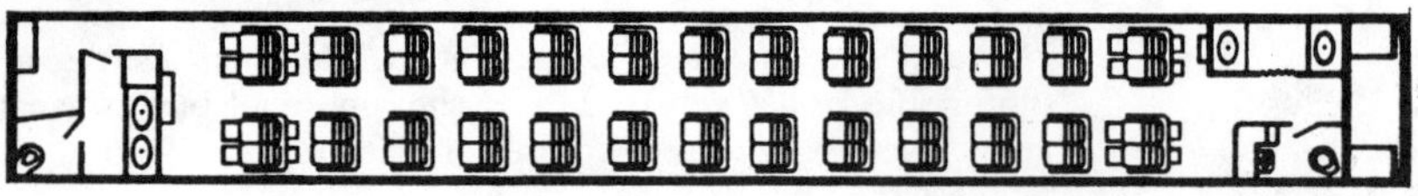

SLEEPER/VOITURE-LITS

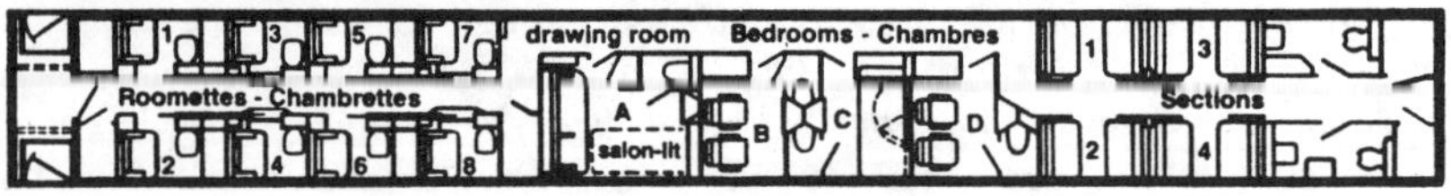


SLEEPER/VOITURE-LITS

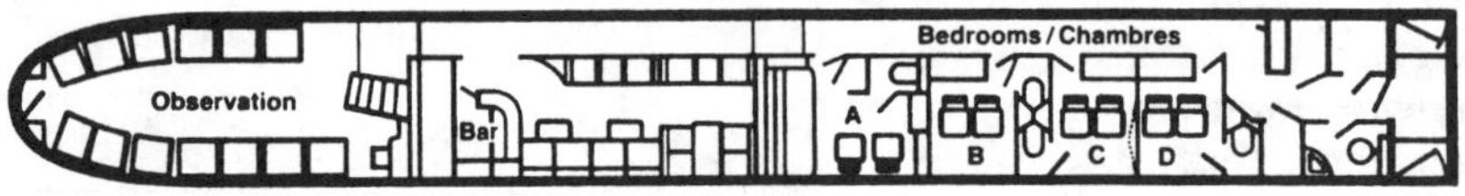


**Other Scenic Routes**

*Cariboo Dayliner* from North Vancouver to Prince George (13 hours) and return over British Columbia Railway tracks that "border water or spectacular canyons and pass through some of the most lonely, breathtaking and varied wilderness to be seen in the Canadian west . . . passengers get a sense of what the west was like early in the century when the first tracks were laid."

*Panorama's* 1750-mile run from Winnipeg and Edmonton to Prince Rupert offers, between Jasper and McBride, "some of the most stunning scenery in the Rockies." Furthermore, it's VIA's newest luxury train (formerly the *Skeena*).

A delightful vacation incorporating the two routes goes like this:

cross the Continental Divide on the stretch between Lake Louise and Field.

"It's wild and rugged country where moose and bear and bighorn sheep roam free. And although other mountains may be higher and individual peaks more beautiful, nowhere in North America, except perhaps Alaska, is there a greater concentration of spectacular mountain scenery then in the Canadian Rockies."

That, we hasten to add, would be especially so during winter and early spring when these mountains are mantled in white.

| | BANFF | CALGARY | CHARLOTTETOWN | CHURCHILL | EDMONTON | FREDERICTON | HALIFAX | KINGSTON | MONCTON | MONTRÉAL | OTTAWA | PRINCE RUPERT | QUÉBEC (STE-FOY) | REGINA | SAINT JOHN, N.B. | ST. JOHN'S, Nfld. | SASKATOON | SUDBURY | SYDNEY | THUNDER BAY | TORONTO | VANCOUVER | VICTORIA | WINDSOR |
|---|---|---|---|---|---|---|---|---|---|---|---|---|---|---|---|---|---|---|---|---|---|---|---|---|
| CALGARY | 130 | | | | | | | | | | | | | | | | | | | | | | | |
| CHARLOTTETOWN | 5293 | 5163 | | | | | | | | | | | | | | | | | | | | | | |
| CHURCHILL | 3167 | 3037 | 5520 | | | | | | | | | | | | | | | | | | | | | |
| EDMONTON | 439 | 309 | 5149 | 3054 | | | | | | | | | | | | | | | | | | | | |
| FREDERICTON | 5293 | 5163 | 467 | 3823 | 5180 | | | | | | | | | | | | | | | | | | | |
| HALIFAX | 6396 | 5220 | 524 | 5577 | 5237 | 555 | | | | | | | | | | | | | | | | | | |
| KINGSTON | 3713 | 3583 | 1549 | 3940 | 3600 | 1580 | 1637 | | | | | | | | | | | | | | | | | |
| MONCTON | 5044 | 4914 | 218 | 5271 | 4931 | 249 | 306 | 1331 | | | | | | | | | | | | | | | | |
| MONTRÉAL | 3998 | 3868 | 1264 | 4225 | 3885 | 1295 | 1352 | 285 | 1046 | | | | | | | | | | | | | | | |
| OTTAWA | 3905 | 3775 | 1451 | 4132 | 3792 | 1482 | 1539 | 190 | 1233 | 187 | | | | | | | | | | | | | | |
| PRINCE RUPERT | 1979 | 1849 | 6689 | 4594 | 1540 | 6720 | 6777 | 5140 | 6471 | 5425 | 5332 | | | | | | | | | | | | | |
| QUÉBEC (STE-FOY) | 4249 | 4119 | 1005 | 4476 | 4136 | 1036 | 1093 | 536 | 787 | 251 | 438 | 5676 | | | | | | | | | | | | |
| REGINA | 895 | 765 | 4366 | 2271 | 783 | 4397 | 4454 | 2817 | 4148 | 3102 | 3009 | 2323 | 3353 | | | | | | | | | | | |
| SAINT JOHN, N.B. | 5187 | 5057 | 361 | 5414 | 5074 | 106 | 449 | 1474 | 143 | 1189 | 1376 | 6614 | 930 | 4291 | | | | | | | | | | |
| ST. JOHN'S, Nfld. | 7773 | 6799 | 2103 | 7156 | 6816 | 2134 | 1579 | 3216 | 1885 | 2931 | 3118 | 8356 | 2672 | 6033 | 2028 | | | | | | | | | |
| SASKATOON | 959 | 829 | 4629 | 2534 | 520 | 4660 | 4717 | 3080 | 4411 | 3365 | 3272 | 2060 | 3616 | 263 | 4554 | 6296 | | | | | | | | |
| SUDBURY | 3033 | 2903 | 2229 | 3260 | 2920 | 2260 | 2317 | 680 | 2011 | 965 | 712 | 4460 | 776 | 2137 | 2154 | 3996 | 2400 | | | | | | | |
| SYDNEY | 5823 | 5693 | 997 | 6050 | 5710 | 1028 | 473 | 2110 | 779 | 1825 | 2012 | 7250 | 1566 | 4927 | 922 | 1106 | 5190 | 2790 | | | | | | |
| THUNDER BAY | 2144 | 2014 | 3118 | 2371 | 2031 | 3149 | 3206 | 1569 | 2900 | 1854 | 1761 | 3578 | 1665 | 1248 | 3043 | 4785 | 1511 | 889 | 3679 | | | | | |
| TORONTO | 3459 | 3329 | 1803 | 3686 | 3346 | 1834 | 1891 | 254 | 1585 | 539 | 446 | 4886 | 790 | 2563 | 1728 | 3470 | 2826 | 426 | 2364 | 1315 | | | | |
| VANCOUVER | 901 | 1031 | 6163 | 4068 | 1340 | 6194 | 6251 | 4616 | 5945 | 4899 | 4806 | 1506 | 5150 | 1797 | 6088 | 7830 | 2054 | 3934 | 6724 | 3045 | 4360 | | | |
| VICTORIA | 1016 | 1146 | 6278 | 4183 | 1455 | 6309 | 6366 | 4731 | 6060 | 5014 | 4921 | 1621 | 5265 | 1912 | 6203 | 7945 | 2169 | 4049 | 6839 | 3160 | 4475 | 115 | | |
| WINDSOR | 3818 | 3688 | 2162 | 4045 | 3705 | 2193 | 2250 | 613 | 1944 | 898 | 805 | 5245 | 1149 | 2922 | 2087 | 3829 | 3185 | 785 | 2723 | 1674 | 359 | 4719 | 4834 | |
| WINNIPEG | 1470 | 1340 | 3823 | 1697 | 1357 | 3823 | 3880 | 2243 | 3574 | 2528 | 2435 | 2897 | 2779 | 574 | 3717 | 5459 | 837 | 1563 | 4353 | 674 | 1989 | 2371 | 2486 | 2348 |

KILOMETRIC CHART Distances calculated using VIA's most convenient routing. Conversion formulas: 1 km = .621 mi 1 mi. = 1.609 km

From U.S., take Amtrak to Seattle, thru Puget Sound to Victoria on *Princess Margaret* (daily; bookable on Amtrak ticket stock); continue by VIA to Courtenay and by bus to Port Hardy. Board a British Columbia ferry for 22 hour cruise up the Inside Passage to Prince Rupert where the *Panorama* takes you into southeast Canada or, at Prince George, *Cariboo* southwest to North Vancouver.

VIA Rail offices can provide information on eastern Canada, particularly the very scenic Atlantic provinces. And on the escorted and un-escorted VIA tours thruout Canada.

**More About VIA Trains**

Most of the cars were inherited from Canadian National and Canadian Pacific roads when VIA was formed in the late 70s to take over their passenger services. However, there have been two newer developments, both popular:

Canadian LRC (Light, Rapid, Comfortable) tilt cars with reclining seats used in densely-traveled corridor inter-city services along with club and club deluxe cars with at-the-seat food service. Between Montreal and Toronto, there's sleeping car service as well.

Double deckers (borrowed from Amtrak) are being tested on Winnipeg-Edmonton run. If demand warrants, such cars will be manufactured in Canada.

A new 160 to 186 mph line is being planned between Toronto and Montreal and possibly another between Calgary-Edmonton where there is now 3¼-hour service with comfortable, reclining seat, self-propelled diesel rail coaches.

Up to 150 lbs. of baggage can be checked to your destination without charge on a full fare ticket, 75 lbs. on half fare.

**VIA Information & Reservations**

In Canada, there are offices in all principal cities — or call 800 Information for proper number from your area. In U.S., call Amtrak.

The elegant *Midnight Sun Express* dome/lounge/diners, attached to daily summer Alaska Railroad trains between Anchorage-Fairbanks, provide expansive viewing of some of the world's most spectacular mountain scenery.

**ALASKA'S GREAT RAIL TRIP**

*''Alaska is a land of contrasts . . . great shafts of light from the aurora borealis frequently tint the sky a beautiful, eerie green. The Alaska Railroad spans the wilderness of this last frontier, rolling through the ever-dramatic and largely unspoiled terrain. The air is so clear, the colors so startling and the space so vast, it's a trip that must be made.''*[1]

And if that isn't enough to whet your travel urges, then take another look at what lies in wait for you:

*''A great mountain-crowned region, presided over by the tallest peak in the northern hemisphere, Denali National Park & Preserve is the magnetic scenic wonder of southcentral Alaska . . . 3,030 square miles of splendor of which the principal awe-inspiring sight is lofty 20,320-ft. Mt. McKinley. Nearby, like sentinels, stand Mt. Foraker (17,000 ft.), Mt. Hunter (14,960 ft.) and Mt. Russell (11,500). These snow-clad peaks form a quartet glorious beyond compare. Throughout the long Alaska summer, the mountains can be seen for many miles, their jeweled, pinkish-tinted heads forming a picture of utter grandeur.''*[2]

That by way of introduction to Alaska Railroad's Mt. McKinley Route served by twin *Aurora* streamliners between Anchorage and Fairbanks, a 9½-hour trip, plus a rail shuttle service (often referred to as the *Glacier Express*) between Anchorage and Whittier, the terminus of the Alaska Marine Highway, State Ferry System — and also port of call for Alaskan cruise liners.

[1] Another quote from Bill Coo's fine book, *Scenic Rail Guide to Western Canada*.

[2] Excerpted from Alaska Railroad information sheets.

From mid-May to mid-September, this 356-mile trip has daily *Aurora* streamliner service in both directions, north and south, between Anchorage and Fairbanks — not at anywhere near TGV speeds but at a nice leisurely, picture-taking pace with frequent stops to pick up passengers along the way. Leaves Anchorage at 0830, Denali Park at 1435;[3] arrives Fairbanks at 1800. The other *Aurora* leaves Fairbanks at 1030, arrives Denali Park at 1355, Anchorage at 2000.

[3] You are well advised to overnight here at Denali National Park Hotel to fully enjoy the scenery and a six-hour wildlife search. Park & Preserve contain 112 species of birds and 335 animal species have been identified there, including Dall Sheep, Toklat Grizzly Bear, Giant Alaska moose and caribou.

Next day, continue your train trip to Fairbanks or return to Anchorage.

On the 141 mile rail shuttle service from Anchorage southeast to Portage and Whittier, a train leaves Anchorage at 1100 (M thru F) or 0400 (Sat, Sun) for Portage from which there are three to six daily round trips to Whittier. However, you can return to Anchorage only at 1950 from Whittier, 2045 from Portage.

Bill Coo thinks that the five miles between Portage and Moraine (enroute to Whittier) "rank as one of the world's most scenic rides. In less than 15 minutes, passengers are treated to the awesome sight of five major glaciers . . . floating icebergs, some weighing millions of tons, are blown about on 600-ft. deep Portage Lake, creating an ever-changing vista of weather-sculptured blue ice . . . then a stunning view of grizzly-filled Bear Valley to the south."

---

"Moose on the right!" yelled the conductor. A huge, shaggy critter with a rack of horns out of a Walt Disney movie went snorting off into the bush as our train sped past. It was our second moose of the day southbound out of Fairbanks aboard Tour Alaska's *Midnight Sun Express* vista dome railcar.

After the excitement of the most recent sighting, we settled back into out deep lounge seats. Some scanned the distant muskeg with onboard binoculars, while others browsed through the library collection. Several groups had started card games. The clickety-clack of wheels on rails was almost totally muffled by thick wool carpeting and suede wall fabrics. Sunlight reflected off brass inlays in the tables, and from the polished flank of a cast brass stag displayed to one side. Just outside, the vast Alaskan Interior flashed by, made all the more wild by the luxurious contrast of our transportation. A Mozart concerto lilted over the railcar's sound system as we spotted two beavers paddling toward their dam.

Stan Freitas, our amiable bartender, had boasted that he made the best Bloody Marys in Alaska. "I've also got the best bar," he added. "The view and scenery are fantastic and on this dome car, it's not just through some window — it's all around you." Stan gestured at the full-length glass domed roof of the railroad car, which curved up from table top level and wrapped overhead. "I can mix drinks, make coffee, and watch bears along the riverbank. Fresh scenery — under glass."

Conductor Steve Hites had been giving a running commentary on the scenic and historic points of interest along the line. Now lunch was being served in the dining room, lower level, and we decided to investigate. As the waiter seated us, we had a sense of deja vue: crisp linens, fresh flowers and sterling bud vases, crystal stemware and bone china decorated in Alaskan blue and gold whispered of other times, other luxury trains. Silverware tinkled against itself as we rounded a curve — just as it must have done when I watched the *Hiawatha* as a boy.* A hot cup of salmon bisque and the tasty Alaskan seafood salad confirmed that the food and service were as special as the nostalgia.

We were nearing Nenana when we re-entered the big dome. Conductor Hites pointed out the location where President Warren G. Harding drove the golden spike completing the railroad July 15, 1923. Then we were on a high single-span steel bridge over the Tanana River. Natives had set out fish wheels to catch salmon below, and we had a bird's eye view of the village of Nenana nestled against the riverbank.

"Just off the bridge you'll get a good view of the train ahead rounding a horseshoe curve" said Hites. "But first, look toward the horizon, on your right. That's Mt. McKinley." Sure enough, like an immense ice cream cone highlighted against the clear blue sky, the "Great One" dominated the scene, forming a backdrop for our train as we made a full 180 degree loop down into Nenana.

An hour later, *Midnight Sun Express* entered Nenana River Canyon, a yawning defile at the edge of Denali National Park. The train wound thru tunnels, over trestles and along a narrow ledge high above the rapids. From time to time we spotted groups of whitewater enthusiasts navigating their rafts thru boulders and whirlpools; they waved as we crawled along, the "Grand Canyon Suite" playing background music for our passage.

"Dahl sheep up on that flat rock." Indeed they were, somehow suspended above us on an opposite cliff high above the river below yet close enough to see their curled horns. Everyone got a prize photo.

At 1355, the train stopped at Denali Park where we would spend the night. Even with a Wildlife Tour up to Mt. McKinley the next day, everyone looked forward to resuming the train ride to Anchorage for it had already meant fine service and grand scenery. A Texan in our group, wearing gold necklace and Rolex watch, summed it up. "I like nice things. This is a nice thing."

* In fact, these superdome cars were originally built in 1952 by Pullman for the Milwaukee Road's *Olympian Hiawatha.* Tour Alaska had three of them rebuilt at a cost of over $1,000,000.

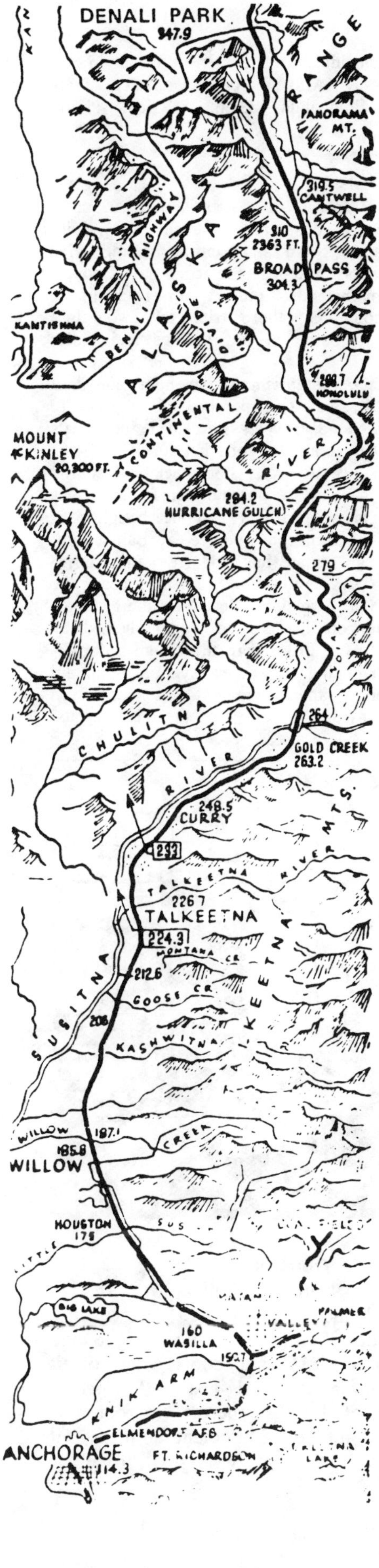


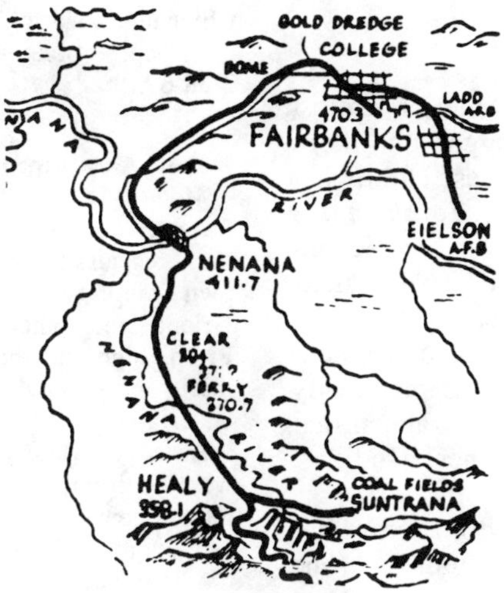


On *Aurora* trains, made up of 10 cars (two of which have small dome sections), all seats are unreserved so during the peak season, there's quite a scramble for choice seats, especially those in the domes. However, as noted on page 84, Tour Alaska[4] has come up with the perfect solution: reserved seats in their privately owned *Midnight Sun Express* 60-passenger bar-salon loungers with comfortable, upholstered seats arranged around coffee tables and contained within a cocoon of vista dome glass. Below, as previously noted, the dining room features gaily striped and upholstered seats and banquettes, table settings in the grand manner and North Country seafood and specialties.[5] These domeliners, the last car or cars of each daily *Aurora* are, without doubt, the most elegant "cabooses" in the history of railroading.

One way adult fare on the *Aurora* (non-reserved seats) between Anchorage and Fairbanks is $74.50 or $51.75 to Denali Park; Fairbanks to Denali Park is $28. Round trip is double OW; children 5-11 half fare. One stopover is allowed per ticket.

*Midnight Sun Express* one way fares (with reserved seating): $125 Anchorage-Fairbanks, $87 Anchorage-Denali Park, $45 Denali Park-Fairbanks. Tickets sold only by Tour Alaska, space available.

[4] Besides running these deluxe cars, Tour Alaska is a prominent Alaskan tour and cruise operator. In fact, *Midnight Sun Express* resulted from a need to care for cruise and tour passengers with something other than long, uncomfortable bus rides. Each cruise/tour package includes the train ride. For further information, reservations: Tour Alaska, 2555 76th Ave. SE, Mercer Island, Wa. 98040 (800-835-8907).

[5] Meals, drinks not included in rail fare.

**ALASKAN RAIL TRIP PLANNING**

It's a long way to go just to take a 356-mile (470 from Whittier) train ride, yet when properly planned it becomes the centerpiece of a complete vacation. Here are the options:

1) By air, stop off in Anchorage enroute to either Europe or Far East.

2) By cruise ship from Seattle or Vancouver and back. As noted, Tour Alaska includes *Midnight Sun Express* in their packages; other cruise packages usually offer the *Aurora* as an optional extra.[6]

3) By world's longest ferry route, Seattle to Skagway (1192 miles) or from Prince Rupert (540 miles) thru the scenic Inside Passage to Skagway (3½ days) via Alaska Marine Highway System's three ships. From Skagway to Fairbanks is a 406-mile bus ride via Whitehorse (change buses). Or cruise to Juneau, fly to Anchorage or Fairbanks.

4) If you're an inveterate rider of the rails, you can reach Fairbanks almost entirely overland except for the Prince Rupert-Skagway ferry segment. VIA's *Panorama* runs from Winnipeg to Prince Rupert (via Edmonton and Prince George) in 44 hours (1477 miles).

British Columbia Railway's *Cariboo Dayliner* takes 13¼ hours along Canada's west coast from North Vancouver to Prince George. There you connect with *Panorama* for Prince Rupert.

After reaching Skagway thru the Inside Passage, take a bus to Whitehorse, an extremely unique 101-mile route that passes thru Alaska (Skagway to White Pass), British Columbia and Yukon Territory. From Whitehorse, you bus to Fairbanks (305 miles).

[6] Two cruise ships, *Cunard Princess* and *Rhapsody* dock at Whittier, enabling passengers to train from there to Anchorage and Fairbanks. Passengers on other cruise ships must fly from Juneau to Anchorage or Fairbanks or travel by bus from Skagway to Fairbanks if they wish to enjoy the train trip.

## MEXICO'S GRAND CANYONS TRIP

Often referred to as one of North America's most spectacular, this rail trip spans the rugged, northern Sierra Madre mountains from east to west, following awesome *Las Grandes Barrancas de la Tarahumara.* These Grand Canyons certainly equal in scenic interest and grandeur those of the Colorado, while their combined length is four times greater!

This Treasure Chest of Mexico (because of tremendous, as yet untapped, natural resources) is practically an unexplored frontier inhabited by aboriginal Tarahumaras or Raramuri (Foot Runner) Indians, most of whom live in caves.

Inaugurated in 1961, the Chihuahua to Pacific RR is an engineering masterpiece of 89 tunnels (one almost a mile long) and 37 bridges (longest about 1/3 mile) between Chihuahua and Los Mochis on the Pacific (408 miles). Crossing the Continental Divide three times, the tracks reach a height of 8,071 ft. and overlook canyons which are over a mile deep. As one travel editor described it:

. . . "we see the wildest sort of country out the window (of the Pullman). Always, across the canyon and above us, is a ledge containing the tracks we have just passed over. We see a long, silvery waterfall; below are curved trestles we next will traverse. Occasional short stops at stations hanging on the edge of cliffs. Highlight of the day is the stop (15 minutes) at Divisadero where we stare awestruck at the walls of Urique Canyon in one grand vista."

However, this trip should be more than a train ride — at least one overnight or longer stop should be made at Creel, Divisadero or Bahuichivo — preferably all three; if only one, then Divisadero for its spectacular panoramic views.

Since the most scenic sections of the rail trip lie between Los Mochis and Creel (about halfway to Chihuahua), people coming from the west could detrain in Creel and return the next day or so.

A Vista-Train leaves Los Mochis 8 am T, F and Sun, arrives Chihuahua 9:50 pm. On M, Th, Sat, Sun. lvs Chihuahua at 8:20 am, ars Los Mochis at 9:51 pm.

Pullman trains, with coach seats, Pullman accommodations and diner, leave Chihuahua at 10:30 pm T and F, ar. Los Mochis 1 pm following day. Return M. Th at 8 am, ar Chihuahua 10:55 pm. There are connecting National Railways trains at Chihuahua from/to Cd. Juarez. At Sufragio, to the west, connections can be made with Pacific RR.

Autovias train (diesel coach) with reserved (reclining) seats departs Chihuahua at 8 am on T and F, ars. Los Mochis at 8:20 pm. Lvs. Los Mochis at 8 am W, Sat. for 8:30 pm arrival. There is separate Autovias service between Chihuahua and Creel, returns same day. Lvs. Chihuahua, M, Th, Sat, Sun. at 8 am; lvs Creel 2:30 pm.

Rail and Pullman rates, regulated by Mexican government, are inexpensive and subject to change, as are rail schedules. Cars can also be transported. Times are Mexican central.

For reservations, schedules or further information on Chihuahua-Pacific Railway: Alfonso Avitia Gonzalez, Traffic Dept, Box 46, Chihuahua, Chih, Mexico. Phone 2-38-67.

### Hotel Accommodations

*Motel Parador de la Montana* at Creel is modern, comfortable and attractive — considered first choice — with bar, restaurant, recreation room and central heating. Has own minibus and station wagons for trips to Copper, Urique and other canyons; also guided horseback tours. From high in the mountains, there trips take you into the tropical lowlands to bathe in hot springs and under waterfalls.

*Hotel Cabanas Divisadero-Barrancas,* an hour and half west by train, is a rustic ranch-type perched cliffside before magnificent panoramas. One traveler described the meals as "exquisite" and raved about the soft, hot tortillas. Here, too, are various excursions afoot, by horseback and station wagon — particularly a visit to Tarahumara Indian caves and dwellings where native artifiсts can be bought.

Another 1½ hours by train and you're at Bahuichivo, 10 miles and a bumpy 45-minute bus ride from the charming, hacienda style (but new) *Hotel Mision* near the 300-year-old Mision San Francisco de Cerocahui. Meals are excellent, hot water on sparse side, rooms heated by quaint, wood-burning stoves. From here there's an unforgettable day trip; a hair-raising 12 miles over a mountain logging road (two hours), then a magnificent view from 7,600 ft. of Urique Canyon. But only for the adventurous.

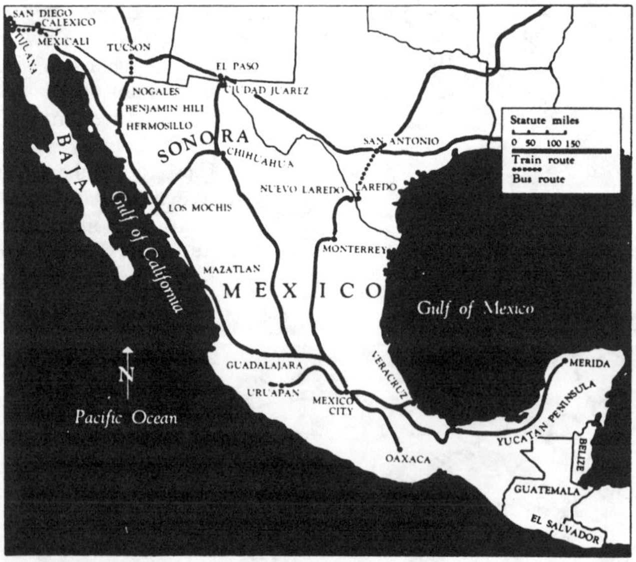


### Other Mexican Rail Routes

On the main routes, National Railways of Mexico (government operated and largest carrier) and Pacific Railroad operate older Pullman, dining and lounge car trains — supposedly AC but don't count on it — for which the fares are still just a few cents per mile (plus cost of Pullman berths or rooms if desired). However, don't for a moment confuse rail travel in Mexico with that of western Europe or Amtrak.

Some 13,000 miles of track connect Mexico City with the U.S. border as well as most major sightseeing attractions — and some offbeat ones, too. One-way fares allow multiple stopovers enroute, *but return fare must be purchased (and Pullman reservations made) at your turnaround point.* Children under five ride free, those from 5 to 12 for half fare. Besides Pullmans, there are unreserved seats, non-AC coaches. Pullman and dining car service is usually good, meals inexpensive but unpredictable — don't depend on getting what's on the menu. Best to bring a supply of water and canned drinks. We've received some reports on deplorable toilet conditions.

Majority of tourists entering Mexico by rail do so independently though there are a number of rail tour operators with some interesting escorted tours (see *Travel Supplement*).

Fares/schedules are subject to constant change, so check same carefully in advance.

Since passengers cannot connect directly with Mexican trains at U.S. border, allow at least two hours to cross into Mexico and check in there.

Principal routes from border stations to Mexico City are:

**Laredo/Nuevo Laredo** — *Aztec Eqgle* takes 23 hours (708 miles). Stops made at Monterrey, Saltillo, San Luis Potosi. There are Pullmans (berths, roomettes, double bedrooms), snack and beverage service, coaches with reserved/unreserved seats.

**El Paso / Cuidad Juarez** — *El Frontizero* stops at Chihuahua, Torreon, Aguascalientes, Leon, Irapuato, Queretaro; takes 36½ hours. Pullmans, coaches, dining car. El Paso is reached by Amtrak's *Sunset Limited* (from Los Angeles or New Orleans).

**Nogales/Mexicali** — From Mexicali (opposite Calexico, Calif.), *El Mexicali* (Train No. 4) takes 18 hours to Mazatlan, 29 to Guadaljara and 40 hours to Mexico City. Stops at Hermosillo, Empalme (for Guaymas), Sufragio (for Los Mochis), Culiacan and Tepic (for Puerto Vallarta). From Nogales, a section of No. 4 connects at Benjamin Hill with Mexicali No. 4. Train No. 2 (all-coach) leaves Nogales in the afternoon while No. 4 departs early morning from both Nogales and Mexicali. Both No. 4s have one thru sleeper to Mexico City plus Pullmans, coaches; dining and club cars for other destinations. Both No. 4 and No. 2 trains are noted for water shortages so bring bottled water.

There's service from Matamoros (opposite Brownsville, Texas) to Monterrey, an overnight train from there to Mexico City (15 hours).

### Rail Routes From Mexico City To

**Lands of the Mayas** — The interesting states of Veracruz, Tabasco, Campeche and Yucatan, along with some amazing rain forests, can be seen and enjoyed via daily Pullman trains *w/o a diner.* Since stops are made at Palenque and Campeche (to mention only the most interesting), stopover sightseeing excursions can be planned. Takes 37 hours to Merida, end of the line and gateway to the Mayan ruins of Chichen Itza and Uxmal.[1]

Return reservations, tickets must be obtained from the Traffic Dept., Ferrocariles Unidos del Sureste, Calles 48 and 55, Merida.

**Veracruz** — One route is via Fortin (270 miles), the other via Jalapa (295 miles). Latter is preferred because you leave Mexico at 7:34 am to enjoy a beautiful 12-hour daylight trip. However, these are antiquated, non-AC coaches.

Adventurous and hardy souls can train from Veracruz to Tapachula (24 hours) on non-AC, non-reserved seat coaches — and no diner. From Tapachula, a one hour plus train ride takes you to Ciudad Hidalgo opposite Cuidad Tecun Uman in Guatemala; from there, if you're brave enough, International Railways takes you to Guatemala City.

**Mexico City to Oaxaca** — This overnight train (14½ hours) is one that gets poor reports (mainly sanitary conditions). Best to fly to this intensely interesting, colorful destination.

### More About Mexican Trains

There are no special or family plan fares, and no commissions granted travel agents. Groups may charter rail cars at predetermined rates. Children under five years ride free, between five and 12 half fare. Two adults may share a lower or upper berth (if able), plus an under-5 child (what fun). Bedrooms require a minimum of two tickets whether single or double occupancy. Roomettes and bedrooms have washing facilities, no toilets; former has one lower, bedroom both upper and lower.

Passengers must provide their own transborder transportation. Car parking facilities are available at or near the stations.

Stopovers can be made at any scheduled point, but sleeping car reservations from each cannot be made in advance but must be applied for at each stopover.

Baggage (110-lb. allowance) can be checked.

Porter service available at major terminals.

Dogs and other small pets can be transported in baggage cars (extra charge), providing you have proper veterinarian's certificate attesting to anti-rabies vaccination.

### Reservations Procedures[2]

For trips originating at border cities, mail space requirements *well in advance* (two to three months); specify type of accommodation required for how many persons — if there are children, give ages. Once reservations have been confirmed, send payment by *cashier's or certified check only* payable in pesos to the railroad. No credit cards, personal or business checks accepted. All necessary tickets are then held for your arrival at the Railway Ticket Office in city of departure.

Return tickets and reservations from Mexico City must be applied for and paid in a like manner. Northbound tickets will be held at First Class Ticket Window No. 2, Buenavista Grand Central Station; open 1:45 to 6:45 pm M thru Sat, 4:45 to 9:30 pm Sundays/Holidays. Cancellation of space must be made at least 24 hours before departure.

All fares, schedules and procedures are subject to change. Always check them in advance.

[1] **Mexico Travel Digest** tells everything you need to know about Lands of the Mayas sightseeing and trip planning.

[2] See *Travel Supplement* for reservation offices.

# SOUTH AMERICA

Picturesque Cuzco is a delight, afoot or from afar. That's Plaza de Armas (left foreground) with La Merced Church at the far end and the Cathedral (left) facing it.

We are often asked, "What is your favorite trip?" Or, "If you had one place to go, where *would* you go?"

Having ranged much of the world, it is impossible for us to pinpoint one place or trip above all others. But this much we can say without equivocation:

"Of all the world's areas, none surpass South America in beauty, few equal it in variety, interest and color."

Our discovery, in the early 1960s, was a revelation. Here was a totally unfamiliar world with eye-popping, mind-boggling impact. And despite many subsequent trips, despite a decided advancement into the late 20th century, particularly in major cities, South America remains one of our prime favorites. We heartily recommend it to you.

There are a number of valid reasons for spending money to discover the southern hemisphere — one of which is that discovery is fairly reasonable. Another is the awesome mountain and rural beauty one encounters. And the totally different life styles, including Indian cultures much as they were lived centuries ago — except for transistor radios. Then there's the colonial charm of old cities, all of whom march gracefully to an ancient Latin beat. Thruout the continent there's a melange of offbeat color and sound that only the Far and Middle East matches in unfamiliar intensity.

But above all, South America offers an almost unmatched series of varied sites and sights, a number of trips that have enriched our lives immeasurably, are indelibly printed in our memories.

Were it not for the colossal Andean mountains raising so many unsurmountable barriers, South America could provide a bonanza of rail trips. As it is, we rank three of them as the most memorable in our experience: two in Peru, the other in Ecuador.

# PERU

## Land Of The Incas

In its glory, it spread from Colombia to Chile, from Peru and Bolivia to Argentina. For the Inca Empire comprised "the four quarters of the world" and four great roads, radiating from Cuzco, navel of the world, led to them — so well constructed that they were "among the most useful and stupendous works ever executed by man."

Between Lima, Peru and Lake Titicaca lies an area of mountainous beauty that absolutely defies description, so huge and panoramic no camera can capture it, so filled with colorful picturesqueness as to be almost unbelievable . . . an astounding blend of the pagan, colonial and modern worlds.

Surprisingly and fortunately, the highlights of this area — Cuzco, oldest inhabited city in the western hemisphere and first capital of Spanish Peru; Machu Picchu, Lost City of the Incas; Pisac, colorful Indian market town; Lake Titicaca, sacred birthplace of the Incas and world's highest navigable lake (12,500 ft.) — are quickly and easily reached out of Lima.

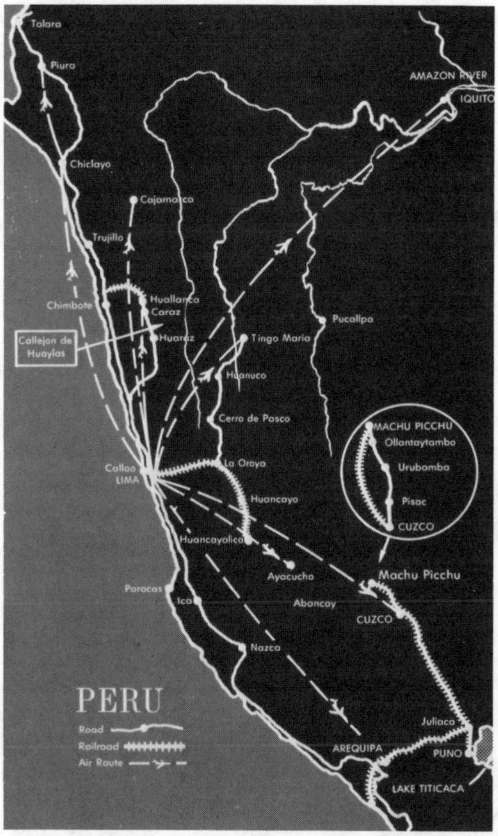


*When Francisco Pizarro and his small band of steel-clad* conquistadores *entered the capital of the Inca Empire on November 15, 1533, the central area of Cuzco, which had a population between 100,000 and 200,000, contained elaborate palaces and temples, beautifully situated around wide plazas, reserved for the emperor (Inca) and his hierarchy.*

*"The capital of the Incas . . . astonished the Spaniards by the beauty of its edifices, the length and regularity of its streets and the good order and appearance of comfort, even luxury, visible in its numerous population. It surpassed all they had yet seen in the New World.*[1]

*". . . the pride of the capital, and wonder of the empire . . . was the temple,* Curiancha, *or Place of Gold. It consisted of a principal building and several chapels and smaller edifices, covering a large extent of ground in the heart of the city, and completely encompassed by a wall which, with the edifices, was all constructed of stone . . . so finely executed that a Spaniard who saw it in its glory assures us he could call to mind only two edifices in Spain which, for their workmanship, were at all to be compared with it.*

*"The interior . . . was literally a mine of gold. On the western wall was emblazoned a representation of the diety consisting of a human countenance looking forth from amidst innumrable rays of light, which emanated from it in every direction in the same manner as the Sun is often personified with us. The figure was engraved on a massive plate of gold of enormous dimensions,*[2] *thickly powdered with emeralds and precious stones. It was so situated in front of the great eastern portal that the rays of the morning sun fell directly upon it at rising, lighting up the whole apartment with an effulgence that seemed more than natural, and which was reflected back from the golden ornaments with which the walls and ceiling were everywhere encrusted. Gold . . . was 'the tears wept by the Sun' and every part of the interior of the temple glowed with burnished plates and studs of the precious metal.*[3] *The cornices which surrounded the walls of the sanctuary were of the same costly material; and a broad belt or frieze of gold, let into the stonework, encompassed the whole exterior . . ."*

*An adjoining chapel of the Moon, mother of the Incas, had a similar plate of silver. Three other chapels, dedicated to the Stars, Thunder and Lightning, and the Rainbow, as well as numerous minor buildings, were likewise richly adorned with gold and silver plate. In fact, pipes that carried water, urns and pools which received it, decorative vases and animals — all were fashioned from these precious metals.*

## CUZCO TO MACHU PICCHU RAIL TRIP

It actually starts from Lima with a spectacular sightseeing flight of 357 miles, first over rural valleys and then, nearing Cuzco, snowy Andean peaks and small lakes before descending into the 11,000-ft. high Cuzco valley slashed by red canyons, accented by tiled roof farmhouses.

Drive from a modern airport into another world — part Indian part Spanish, part yesterday, part today. Where apple-cheeked kids eagerly sell attractive,

[1] These and quotations (in italics) are from William H. Prescott's "Conquest of Peru," a fascinating historical work which should be read by everyone making this trip. Mentor has a fine pocket-size edition.

[2] This was given to a cavalryman, Leguizana, as his share of the booty and was promptly lost in a single night of gambling, giving rise to the Spanish proverb, *"Juega el Sol lantes que amanezoa"* (He plays away the Sun before sunrise.).

[3] It was estimated that about 700 plates, ten to twelve inches wide, were torn from the temple as part of the ransom of Inca Atahuallpa.

handmade bags, llama slippers, alpaca rugs, funny face ski masks. Where new cars honk their way along ancient streets, barefooted Indian women in ankle-length skirts mingle with jean-clad teenagers while buses and trucks burrow under Incan stone arches.

No other city in South America is quite like Cuzco. Still provincial and colonial despite its growth (200,000), it offers miles of panoramic mountain vistas, good shopping, intensely interesting sightseeing: Spanish plazas, palaces and churches, Incan fortresses and ritual baths, fascinating museums. Not to mention its art. Here the unsurpassed Cuzco School of painting and sculpture flourished from the 16th to 18th centuries; many fine examples remain.

Best advice we can offer: *don't treat Cuzco solely as a way to get to Machu Picchu.* It has too much to offer. The usual 3- to 4-hr. City Tour, interesting

Majestic Machu Picchu (foreground), Huayna Picchu (right).

as it is, is insufficient time to see and appreciate this precious relic of the past. *Allow at least two days for Cuzco alone.*

We've been here three times, found it as fascinating in 1980 as we first did in 1964. A German couple said, "We're spending five days here. We didn't come all this way to rush thru one of the world's most unusual cities." Good advice.

Take the Machu Picchu rail trip on the second or third day — you need the intervening time to become acclimated to Cuzco's altitude. It should be noted, however, that you actually *descend* some 3,000 or more feet to reach the rail station below the ruins.

Lest there be any misunderstanding, let's make this clear: though this is a Great Rail Trip, it is *not* by any stretch of imagination a great train trip. In horrible contrast to the sublimity of Machu Picchu is the uncomfortable ride from/to Cuzco. No longer are nice diesel cars in service (except for charter tours); instead, the cars in use are old, dilapidated, crowded and dirty — there's rarely time to clean them. A shame because the scenery is superb. The *ferrocarril* climbs, by a series of switchbacks, above Cuzco for a marvelous view of this red-roofed city (try to reserve seats on the left hand side); it then descends thru lush green forests ablaze with vari-colored tropical plants and orchids and soon races along the tumultuous Rio Urubamba that rushes thru a jagged mountain gorge before reaching the station at the foot of this fantastic mountain hideaway, last refuge of the Incas where only the remains of women and children were found.

Machu Picchu was never discovered by the Spaniards — nor anyone else until 1911 when Hiram Bingham, later a U.S. senator, stumbled upon the 8,875-ft.-high ruins between Machu Picchu (Old Peak) and Huayna (New) Picchu which slopes in terraced grandeur to the Urubamba River below.

Here the Incas succeeded in combining the wonders of nature with those of man. Well-defined traces of the planned city are still evident: House of the Sun, the mile-long aqueduct that brought water from mountain springs, the watch tower, temples, houses and baths, over 100 stairways different from those in other areas, 200 white granite buildings. This fantastic feat of engineering, covering 5 sq. kilometers, was accomplished solely by stone hammer construction — probably over many generations.

But it is the sheer beauty of what we consider the most dramatic place in the world that overwhelms you, keeps you shooting roll after roll of film. Your camera needs a 360° lens to capture it all — and still the magic, the rapture would be missing.

Wear sturdy walking shoes as there's a lot of climbing to reach various sections of the ruins.

*Special Note:* A $10 head tax is assessed every tourist entering the Cuzco area. Funds are destined to finance tourist infrastructure (we hope new rail cars are first priority), restore churches and archeological sites.

Because of worldwide publicity, Machu Picchu during the high season (July-August, October thru March) is overrun with tourists and trekkers; September is a good alternative. Make reservations well in advance thru a Lima tour operator.[4] Usual day package includes train fare, reserved seat, transfers to/from the ruins and your Cuzco hotel and either a table d'hote lunch at the Machu Picchu Hotel or a box lunch; latter preferable during the high season due to the number of people dining on the hotel terrace. English-speaking guides are furnished, admission to the site included. Train leaves Cuzco at 0700, arrives back around 2000.

## CUZCO TO LAKE TITICACA RAIL TRIP

Anyone coming to Cuzco should schedule sufficient time to continue on to the strange world of the *altiplano* surrounding mountain-fringed Lake Titicaca. An 11-hr. train ride to Puno, Peru, plus a day of travel to La Paz, Bolivia, can be combined for another far-out experience.

Here, again, the train has seen far better days — third class in comparison to Amtrak. Buffet cars (22 or 34 seats) are the best of a poor lot; so-called first class cars hold 68, second class (God forbid) 88. In buffet car, lunch, sandwiches, beer, soft and hot drinks are available — or hop out at various stops to patronize food vendors, truly great fun.

But the scenery is magnificent — everything from narrow, tree-studded canyons thru which rivers rage to stunning hill country with grazing cattle, cultivated terraces marching into the sky, jagged glacial peaks; finally onto the prosperous-looking *altiplano* (as high as 14,000 ft.) where Indian women and children herd flocks of llamas, alpacas, vicunas, goats and sheep. Station stops (35 to 37 of them) are kaleidoscopic whirls of action, color; at the longer stops, it's fun to shop for souvenirs, pottery, alpaca hats and rugs, ponchos, shoes and dolls sold by the distinctively clothed Indian vendors. At Juliaca the women wear brown derbies, elsewhere white panamas. Nearing Puno (12,512 ft.), the train skirts Lake Titicaca affording glimpses of reed boats and llamas loaded with reeds.

Train leaves daily (except Sun.) from Cuzco at 0800, arrives Juliaca at 1830 (30-min. layover), Puno at 2000. A private car transfer at Juliaca gets you to Puno in 30 minutes (27 miles over a paved road).

After coming this far, it would be almost criminal not to take the thrilling hydrofoil ride across beautiful Lake Titicaca and on to La Paz, Bolivia. **South America Travel Digest** has complete trip planning information.

[4] North American tour operators invariably include this trip in their South American group tour programs.

# ECUADOR

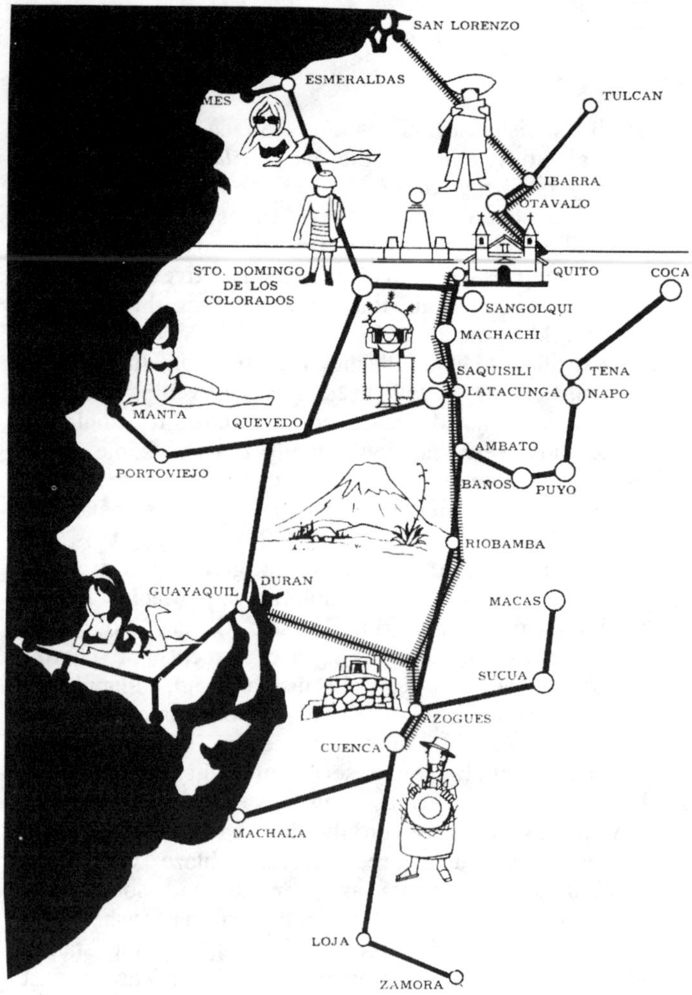


Quito, capital of Ecuador and a living treasure house of the best in Spanish Colonial architecture, art and churches, is a joy to behold, a pleasure to walk around — and one of our most favorite cities.

In 1487, the kingdom of Quito was invaded and conquered by the Incas, who established Quito as the second capital of the Inca Empire and constructed an amazing road system linking it and Cuzco, over which hundreds of *Chasquis* (runners) operated the first walkie-talkie. In 1534, San Francisco de Quito was founded by Sebastian de Benelcazar. It grew up in the image of Spain: narrow, twisting, cobblestoned streets overhung with balconies and grille work, adobe houses built around patios and fountains. And churches! There are over a hundred churches and chapels, monasteries and convents — many with priceless interiors and Spanish Colonial works of art. For the various orders of the Church seemingly concentrated their resources, artistry and techniques in a superb effort to make Quito the Florence of South America, as indeed it is.

Today in the old southern sectors, with steep streets lined with white and yellow houses roofed with red tile, where women crowd the banks of the Machangara River washing clothes with *penco* (cactus) just as their ancestors did for centuries, Quito retains most of its Colonial charm. The air is like wine, the old world atmosphere heady. Those who like to poke around and discover things, or just amble along enjoying and photographing the street scenes, are in heaven here.

You'll be enthralled from the very first. Seen from the air, the Central Valley appears like a giant, irregular checkerboard of muted greens and tans stretching to the sky and touching the clouds . . . surrounded by mountains and volcanoes with snowy domes . . . a majestic setting of simplicity into which Quito, gleaming whitely in the sun, is plumped like a finely cut, sparkling diamond.

One of the great glories of Ecuador, the Avenue of Volcanos, occurs through the narrowing of the central and eastern ranges of the Andes within 25-40 miles of each other to form the Central Valley, the Ecuadorian Highlands and the Shangri-La of South America, down which the Pan American Highway twists — a ride, by car or rail, more grandly beautiful than imagination can conceive. Between Latacunga-Quito-Otavalo, about 125 miles, you see no less than eight majestic, snow-capped volcanos and mountains, including Mt. Illiniza (17,447 ft.), Cayambe (19,161 ft.), and famed Cotopaxi (19,613), world's highest active volcano with a classic cone. On a clear day, a number of these can be seen from Quito which, at 9,000 ft., itself lies in the shadow of 15,706 ft. Pichincha. South of Latacunga are many more, particularly Mt. Chimborazo (at 20,576 ft. one of the continent's tallest) and Sangay, one of the few snow-capped volcanos still in an active state.

Here, then, is the heart of Ecuador, a few miles south of the Equator where, because of it's 0° latitude, you can put one foot in the northern hemisphere, one in the southern . . . where the sun rises at 6 and plunges beyond the horizon at 6 that evening . . . where nearby white capped, terraced mountain slopes and rolling fields dotted with neat, straw-thatched huts and houses and haystacks (with crosses atop), are cultivated as they were in Incan times. We have never visited an area where so much scenic beauty and such a variety of Indian life can be seen so easily, quickly and comfortably.

Otavalo Market basket weavers.

**The Quito-Guayaquil Rail Trip**

Many years ago, we rode a jolting *autoferro* from Quito to Guayaquil, from sunrise to sunset over such an amazingly scenic route that it remains as vividly memorable as if it was yesterday.

Unfortunately, and hopefully temporarily, the trip cannot be duplicated in its entirety during 1985 due to the ravages of *El Nino* several years ago when the storm washed out bridges and track west of Riobamba, including a series of switch-backs around Nariz del Diablo (Devil's Nose) which the train formerly climbed in spectacular fashion until, plunging out of the mountains, it rushed past a desert and down into a tropics of bananas, sugarcane, tobacco and fruit trees.

However, just to ride from Quito along the magnificent Avenue of Volcanos, groan thru a gorge of the Chanchan River and climb to 11,814 feet near Riobamba, at the foot of majestic Chimborazo, is more than sufficient to satisfy the most exacting thrill seeker.

A newer *autoferro* — actually a bus fitted with rail wheels — leaves Quito daily at 0600, covers the 135 miles to Riobamba in about five hours, returns the same afternoon. Those wishing to continue to Guayaquil can do so by public bus or car; incidentally, you'll sight the Devil's Nose enroute. And the cost of this 277-mile trip, Quito to Duran (where you ferry across the Rio Guaya to Guayaquil) is still ridiculously inexpensive; several years ago, the rail trip cost about $4 to $5.

A more comfortable, though less adventurous, way to go over the same route is by *Expresso Metropolitan,* an old car refitted with pullman seats, wide view windows, ceiling fans, rear view observation platform, toilets, and bar — and provisions for a meal and snacks enroute.

Leaving Quito on Tuesdays and Saturdays, *Expresso* parallels the Pan American Highway which, centuries ago, was the Royal Road of the Incas. After skirting the foothills of snow-capped mountains and running thru flower-filled valleys, a stop is made at Latacunga, one of Ecuador's most colorful market towns. Lunch aboard precedes arrival in Riobamba for an overnight hotel stay. Next day's return to Quito by road includes lunch at a hacienda and visits to Indian villages. Or leave Riobamba by road for Guayaquil. Either way, the two-day package, conducted by Metropolitan Touring (old and trusted friends of ours), includes transportation, meals and hotel room — at a very reasonable price. For further information, reservations: Adventure Associates, 5925 Maple, Dallas, Tx 75235; 800-527-2500 or 214-357-6187 in Texas.

## OTHER MOUNTAIN RAIL TRIPS

Two trips which we have not taken, but with which we are very familiar thru first-hand reports:

### Lima To Huancayo, Peru

Spectacular 290-mile, nine-hour trip (leaves Lima at 0740) on world's highest standard gauge line almost *three miles* up in the Andes. Oxygen is carried — and frequently needed. This *Tren De Sierra* is less than a no-frills train and definitely only for the hardy. Try to arrive in Huancayo Friday afternoon in order to attend Saturday morning's market at Chapuca, eight miles away. Or a Saturday arrival in Huancayo allows you to attend its Sunday Indian Market when Calle Real (Main St.) and the central plazas are filled with large-skirted, gaily clad women, men in bright ponchos, all bartering with hardly a sound. Inside the church, a uniformed band plays in front of the altar. In the afternoon, visit the village of Hualhuas, its homes and workshops, where Indians are expert silver engravers.

German-managed Hotel Huaychulo, 12 km from Huancayo, is said to serve good food.

*Tren De Sierra* returns from Huancayo at 0700. Or you can try a *colectivo* (jitney taxi) that run more or less on daily schedules.

### La Paz, Bolivia to Arica, Chile

Years ago, this was known as the smugglers' route and tourists were advised against it. We don't know what it's like today but it's bound to be both scenic and adventurous.

The diesel cars were, supposedly, made in Germany, probably in the late 50s. However, whether or not they are used over the entire 283-mile route we don't know; there's a layover at the Bolivian border town of Charana, presumably to change to the Chilean train from Arica.

There's twice weekly service that leaves La Paz on Tuesdays at noon, Fridays at 0900 with arrival in Arica at 0805 the following day. However, be sure to check current schedule with Instituto Boliviano de Turismo, Casilla 1868, La Paz, Bolivia.

Possibly the most unusual aspect of this rail trip is that it provides access (by bus) from Arica, a seaport at the northern tip of Chile, to Chile's incredible Atacama desert.

Only a comparative handful of foreign visitors have seen this high desert: 600 miles of stark lava fields, soaring volcanos, rolling and trackless dunes, "a vast unadorned waste of grays and beiges, cinders and dust (and nitrates)" called Valley of the Moon and said to be the driest place on the globe as it's never known rain. Except for occasional oases, herds of domestic llama, goats and sheep, nothing lives there, not even insects. The sky is an intense blue, the sun a flame. Winter and spring (June thru October) is tourist season since the weather is cool to cold; in summer it's excessively hot.

Those who've visited this moon-like land come away entranced. "It makes California's Mojave desert look like a garden."

Although the usual trip is packaged out of Santiago, you can arrange with a Santiago tour operator to be met in Arica or Calama, an oasis town of 90,000 and gateway to the Valley of the Moon and San Pedro de Atacama, once the center of a paleolithic civilization that built rock fortresses on steep mountains that nearly encircled the green valley below. Now, within a vast Indian archeological zone, it looks like something out of a Bogart movie. An octagonal-shaped museum houses thousands of dried corpses (many with hair intact), skulls, stone age tools, ancient textiles, ceramics, jewelry, weapons and woodcarvings.

From Calama, it's a 2½-hour flight to Santiago, 1½-hour from Antofagasta, the point from which the usual tour returns. Arica also has flights to Santiago so that it's easy to continue a La Paz-Arica rail trip with or without the desert bypass.

### The Patagonian Express

This is the only South American group tour that covers much of the west coast, from Bogota to Punta Arenas, by rail: Quito to Guayaquil, Lima to Huancayo, Cuzco to Machu Picchu, Cuzco to Puno, La Paz to Arica and Santiago to Puerto Montt.

This 32-day program, conducted by Voyages Jules Verne, is most comprehensive, but, we feel, too physically exhausting — there simply are not enough days of rest following an extremely arduous itinerary at high altitudes. Heart, lungs and stamina must be in good working order before anyone should contemplate this trip, but if they are, you'll see all the best of west coast South America, including the Galapagos Islands.

Although *The Patagonian Express* is solely a west coast program, for the guidance of those who'd like to cross over to the east coast, here's the way to do it:

Return from Punta Arenas by air to Puerto Montt, then take the perfectly gorgeous Chilean-Argentine Lake trip (by boat) to San Carlos de Bariloche. For complete details, see **South America Travel Digest.**

From Bariloche, an airconditioned, first class sleeper train, *Lagos Del Sur,* with dining car service leaves two or three times weekly for Buenos Aires (about 33 hours).

One can also go by bus from Santiago to Mendoza, Argentina; from there by sleeper train to Buenos Aires takes about 14 hours (744 miles). By the way, the drive from Santiago over the Andes and past Christ the Redeemer statue is considered one of the world's most spectacular.

From Buenos Aires north into Brazil is solely by bus or plane. There is train service from Sao Paulo to Rio de Janeiro, from Campinas (near Sao Paulo) to Brasilia via a train with first class sleeping car and dining car — an 820-mile trip in about 20½ hours.

# SOUTH PACIFIC

Ayers Rock now has a resort hotel at Yulara from which guests have a great view of The Rock (partially seen here in the background).

## AUSTRALIA

As with Europe, Canada and the United States, practically all of Australia's tourist attractions can be seen easily by rail — if you have the time and a carefully planned trip. Because there's so much of this continent:

22,874 miles of coastline encircle just about everything the rest of the world has to offer — plus a lot that simply doesn't exist elsewhere. Animals and plants that elsewhere disappeared continued to evolve, others survived in isolation as relics unknown to Europeans in the late 17th century when Australia was discovered. Pouch-bearing marsupials were supposed to be extinct for 25 million years, yet here were 120 species. The platypus[1] was considered a hoax until proved an evolutionary link between reptile and mammal and, they thought, the oldest form of living creatures. Only to discover the lungfish,[2] a cousin to the first fishes to colonize dry land which, apparently, returned to a few rivers in northeast Australia 350 million years ago.

It's a thousand divergent places and things which, like a puzzle, when fitted together add up to one country, one continent (size of the U.S.), one people (just 13,425,000 of them) and one especially fine achievement — more Kentucky Fried Chicken outlets per capita than the U.S.

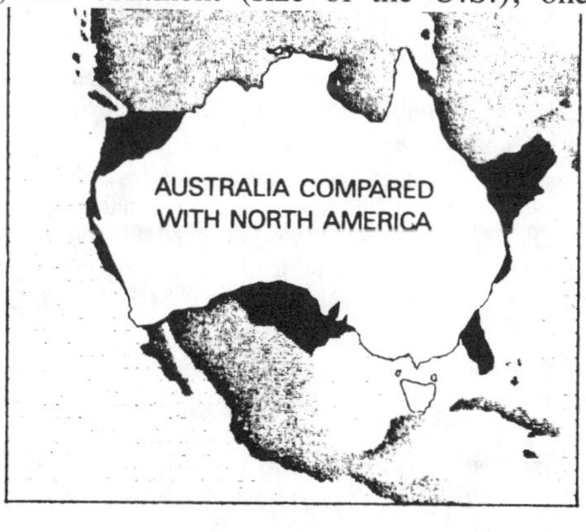


Like the Great Barrier Reef, 1,260 miles of interlaced coral reefs, one of the world's superb natural wonders, the greatest concentration of marine fauna, the most incredible variety of coral configurations to be seen anywhere. "Nobody can adequately describe the reef, and nobody can picture it who has not visited it. You must see it, stand some brilliant blue-and-white day on a gleaming strip of sand, walk carefully among its wonders and explore for yourself the unbelievable richness and strangeness of its teeming life." Only then will you know why your trip of thousands of miles is a glowing success.

Like The Red Centre and other parts of the fabled Outback, a vast area of aborigines and bushmen, boomerangs and kangaroos, searing heat and swirling sand, a ground painted red, eroded mountains etched in crimson purples, solitary ghost gums . . . thousands of miles scarcely touched by man, the heart of a continent almost as it was created — lonely, brooding, stark at one moment, overpoweringly sublime the next. Here the MacDonnell, Musgrave and Krichauf Ranges have been exposed to the elements three times longer than the world has had vegetation. Here the landforms take on grotesque, often majestic shapes: turtle-like domes, endless rows of upended discs, solitary monoliths, miles of evenly spaced waves or gothic castles, piles of stacked cubes.[3]

[1] Has a beaver's fur and tail, a duck's bill and webbed feet, burrows like a rabbit, swims like a fish, hibernates like a bear, lays round eggs like a lizard and suckles its young like a mammal.

[2] Breathes thru gills when underwater, thru a single lung when wriggling on land.

[3] For full descriptions of these and many other attractive destinations, read **South Pacific Travel Digest.**

## AUSTRALIA'S GREAT RAIL TRIPS

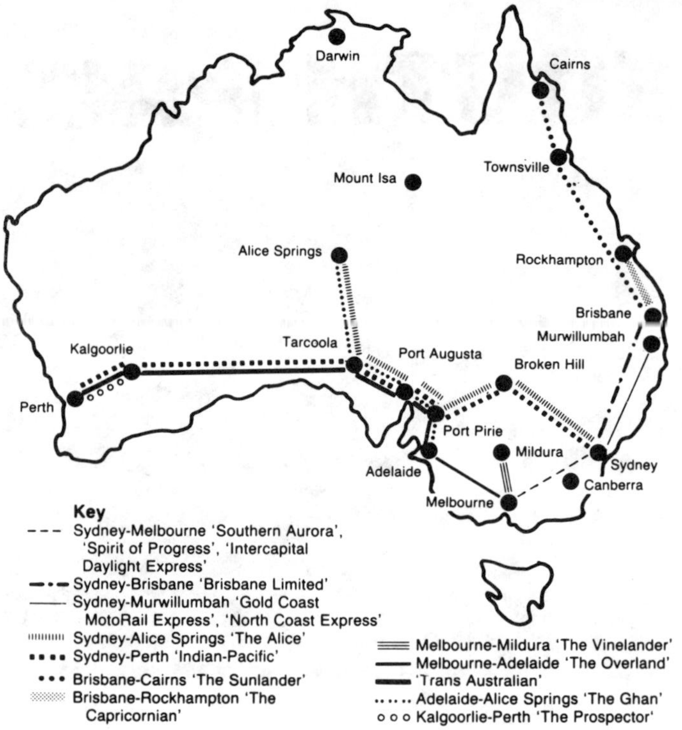


### No. 1 — *The Alice* To Wonderland

No doubt this contrarian choice will surprise those who consider the *Indian-Pacific* one of the world's great trains — which it definitely is. But since *The Alice* is equally as great (equipment is the same on both trains), we rate it No. 1 solely for its destination: The Red Centre, part of a vast desert empire known as Northern Territory.

So, if you have time for just one long train ride in Australia, *The Alice* is it.

We've never seen anything quite like The Red Centre. Not the California desert, the Arizona canyons, New Mexican mesas. Nor the national parks of Utah. Not even all of them put together. Which is not to imply that The Centre is a composite. Its fascination is different, indescribable. Perhaps it lies in the weird shapes of eroded mountains, the simple grace of twin ghost gums, the gasping beauty of sun-drenched rock — or simply the utter vastness surrounding these things and man's courage in coming to grips with it. Whatever, if you dig such scenes, come; despite the flies it'll be an exalting experience.

Center of the Centre, the town you arrive at and from which all tours emanate, is Alice Springs, affectionately called The Alice. She's quite a gal. We certainly enjoyed making her acquaintance.

And then there's the Ayers Rock experience. This immense, sandstone monolith rises 1,143 ft. from the desert plateau like a majestic, red super-whale. There it reposes, all 1,200 acres of it (1½ miles from E to W, ⅝ mile wide, 5½ around), all by itself — absolutely nothing else more than a few feet high for 20 miles around except this convoluted mass of rock. Small wonder it was one of the Aborigines' most sacred places. Not long ago, anyone visiting here was regarded with awe accorded a pilgrim to Mecca. Today, the awesome Rock remains a very unique pilgrimage. Simply nothing else like it.

The 210-mile flight from Alice Springs over the Waterhouse, James and Gill mountain ranges is a succession of weird and wondrous formations: giant roller coasters, battlements, gorges and Great Walls marching off into the eroded distances. To the left, Mt. Connor rears a crew cut head. Then, ahead, the Rock and Mt. Olga — actually a group of 30 or so dome-shaped, reddish brown monoliths to the west — come into view 65 miles away, grow larger, more impressive as your excitement mounts. Finally you're over and looking down on that red, corrugated Rock, swooping left and around the eastern flank of this encroaching monster until you're down on the ground and out — dwarfed by its immensity.[4]

And now for *The Alice.*

As the map illustrates, it starts from (and returns to) Sydney — along the same tracks that carries the *Indian Pacific* as far as Tarcoola, at which point *The Alice* swings north on new standard gauge track[5] to complete its 47-hour (two nights, three days), 1,774-mile trip. There's a sightseeing tour of the mining town of Broken Hill, and the train slows to a crawl for photo-taking purposes at several photogenic spots. In fact, it's a photo-sightseeing trip the entire way as the train climbs into the Blue Mountains,[6] passes settled farm areas, vaster grazing lands and wheatfields, inland gulf waters, migrating birds, enormous lakes and then salt bush desert plains with never-ending horizons.

Operated jointly by Australian National Railways and State Rail Authority of New South Wales, *The Alice* leaves Sydney only on Mondays (at 1340), arrives Alice Springs Wednesday at 1225; departs at 1700 for a 1550 Friday arrival in Sydney.

Australia's newest "hotel on wheels," inaugurated in November of 1983, is the first long distance luxury train since the *Indian Pacific* way back in 1970. Its eight first class, airconditioned sleepers have roomettes (for one passenger) and twinettes — 142 berths in all. Compartments have double-glazed windows, wardrobe, reading lamps, vanity mirror, shaver outlet, chilled water, basin, toilet (plus shower in twinette).[7] There are also some deluxe, more spacious compartments with three-quarter bed and upper berth.[8] A limited number of twinette family units have connecting, lockable doors.

[4] If flying isn't your thing, you can go by car or bus.

[5] Formerly, Alice Springs was served only by *The Ghan* (from Adelaide), a narrow gauge train; it, too, has been converted to standard track. Incidentally, its name derives from Afghanistan camel drivers imported to run the first "train" to The Alice.

[6] For 25 years or more after Sydney was established in 1788 as a penal colony, these massive, tortuous sandstone mountains (blue only because of a bluish haze produced by a dense eucalypt forest) turned back every attempt to penetrate eastward. Even today, just 50 miles from a metropolis, much of the area remains impenetrable.

[7] Twinettes and roomettes are in separate cars; facilities are similar except showers in roomette cars are situated at the end of each car.

[8] Deluxe compartments available only on *The Alice, Indian-Pacific* and *Southern Aurora.*

Lounge and club cars, which we've inspected (also the sleepers) are extremely attractive, comfortable and, above all, companionable — Australians generally are great fun (and great drinkers). Lounge features are a well-tuned piano or organ (for hours of sing-alongs), radio and video-taped TV.

Huge breakfasts and four-course lunches/dinners include freshly prepared specialties, soups, fish, roasts and desserts (the apple pie is delicious) — all included in the fare (but not wine and booze, both reasonably priced).

[9] Should you arrive in Australia at Perth, then *Indian-Pacific* to Tarcoola.

**Planning *The Alice* Experience**

Most people come to Alice Springs to see Ayers Rock. Here today, over the Rock tomorrow, gone the next. Sad, they didn't know how many wonderful sights there are out here, how many unusual experiences await them had they planned the time to enjoy them, to know "this wide, rugged, open-hearted Australia with its nights of brilliant stars and days of beautiful sun."

Plan at least four days here — longer for artist and photographer, those who love to explore the desert. Assuming you board the train in Sydney,[9] there are these departure options: 1) Fly to Cairns, take *Sunlander Express* south to Brisbane with a stop enroute to visit one of the Great Barrier Reef islands (preferably Heron). 2) Take the bus north to Darwin, fly from there to Singapore. 3) Board *The Ghan* for the run south to Adelaide.

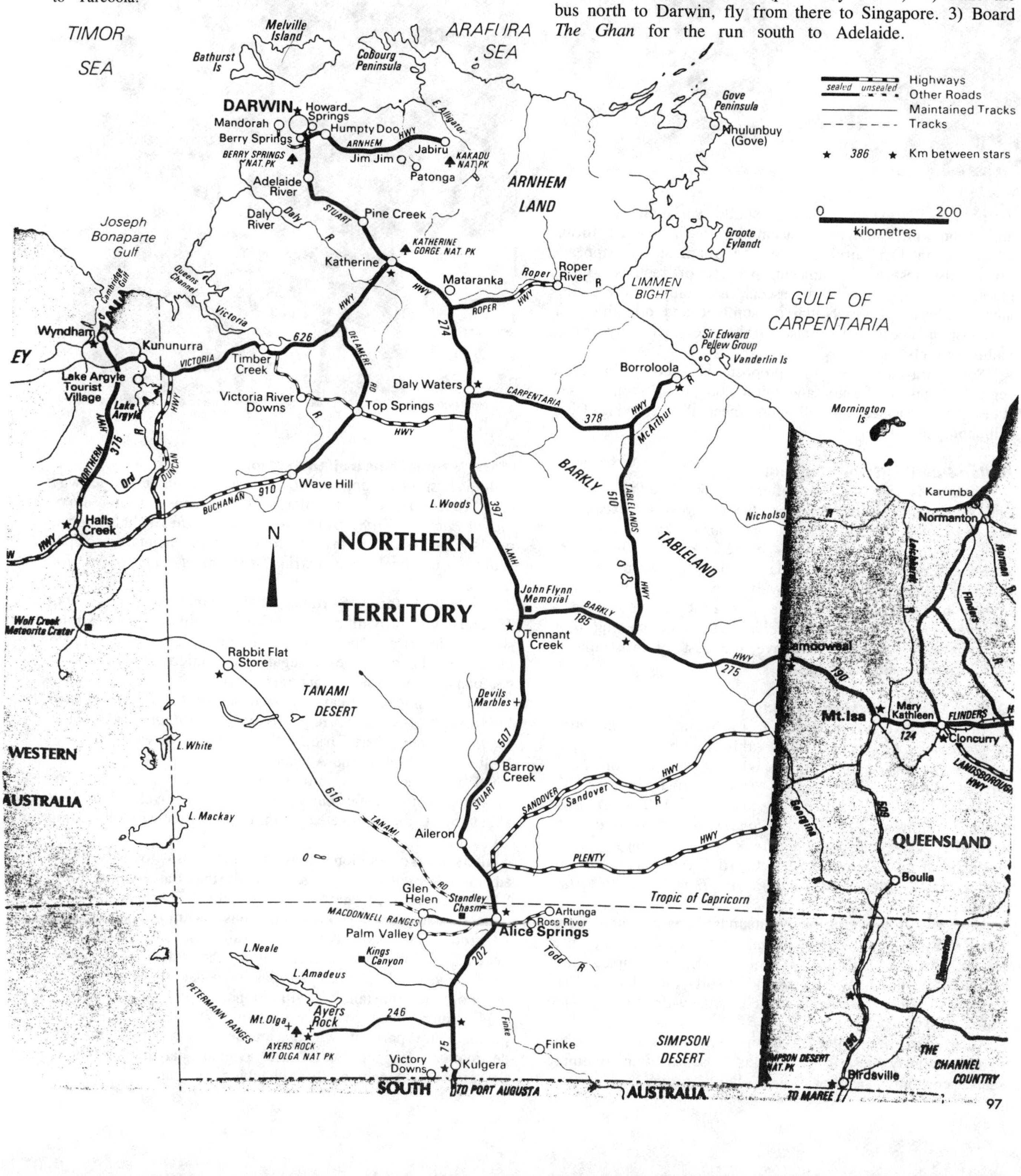

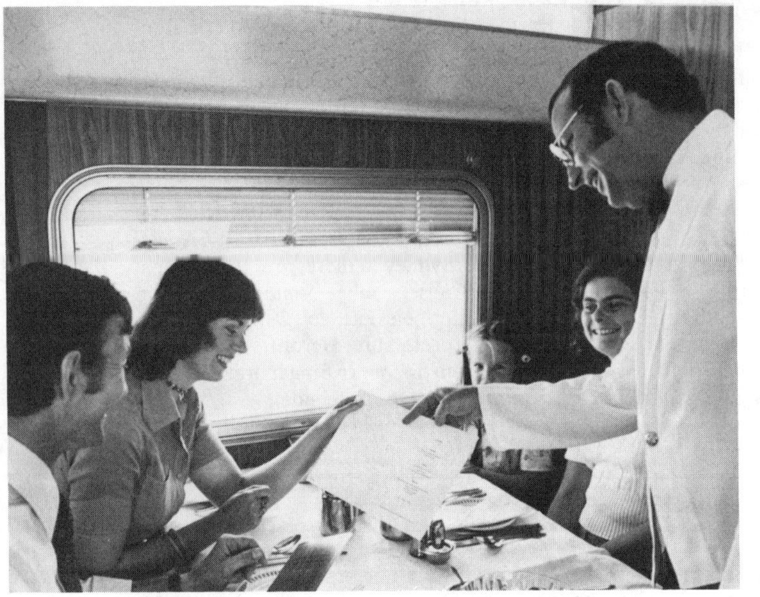

To others it reveals infinitely subtle variations of form and color which hint at the teeming, specialized life forms which do in fact survive in an environment that appears implacably hostile. An amazing variety of reptiles, birds, marsupials, amphibia and insects not only survive the annual inferno of the Nullarbor summer and droughts that can last a decade, but also proliferate incredibly when nature relents.

"Some travelers see the preposterous red plain as a region of austere beauty and miraculous life — others see it as the dessicated gut of a continent slowly dying from millennia of thirst."

### *Indian-Pacific* Trip Planning

Problem is: what to do after reaching Perth? It's the end of the line. You can't go farther west — except by air to South Africa. You can go north, by air or bus, to Darwin — or by air to Singapore. Or return east/southeast to Sydney, Adelaide and Melbourne. But the point is, Perth, though a lovely city, is simply a way station to nowhere except the Far East. If you have a real yen to ride the *Indian-Pacific,* we advise coming *from* the Far East so that you have the rest of Australia to look forward to.

### Other Top Australian Trains

An alternative to departing from Sydney on *The Alice* or *Indian-Pacific* is to follow this routing:

*Southern Aurora* (first class sleeper service) or *Inter-capital Daylight Express* from Sydney to Melbourne. Or *XPT to Canberra* (Australia's fastest at 160 kph) from Sydney followed by *The Vinelander* to Melbourne.

A first class sleeper on *The Overland* brings you to Adelaide from where you can board *Trans Australian* for Perth (1597 miles, 38 hours), or *The Ghan* to Alice Springs.

Way to get to beautiful Whitsunday Passage and Great Barrier Reef is via *The Sunlander* from Brisbane; goes as far north as Cairns (37 hours) with, of course, stops enroute for the many Queensland resorts and Barrier Reef islands. There's overnight service Sydney-Brisbane on the crack *Brisbane Limited.*

All trains are similar in equipment and service to the two previously described — plus coaches with reclining seats, economy sleepers with 3-berth cabins.

Amenities aboard *Indian-Pacific* and *The Alice* rate high among world class trains.

### More About Australian Trains

Both first class and economy fares are quoted one way only; round trip fares are double OW. Fares for *The Alice, Indian-Pacific, Trans Australian* and *Ghan* include berth, meals. On other trains, there's a supplementary sleeper charge and meals are extra. See *Travel Supplement* for fare costs.

Children 4 thru 15 travel at half fare as do students 16 and over providing they have a Railways of Australia student ID card. There are also concessions to organized groups of 12 or more, delegates to conferences, theatrical companies and special interest groups.

You can ship your car via Motorail on the *Ghan* between Port Augusta-Alice Springs, *Trans Australian* and *Indian-Pacific* between Port Pirie-Perth and trains between Sydney-Melbourne, Melbourne-Adelaide.

On mainline routes, stopovers are okay if advance arrangements for same have been made. Travel on a OW ticket must be completed within two months, RT within six months.

Interstate reservations may be made up to a year in advance — particularly essential during Easter, mid-May, September-October and December thru February.

Each state (except Tasmania) has its rail system, each integrated into Railways of Australia. Several states offer tickets for unlimited travel within the state for 14 days to one year. Each has special seasonal tours of a day or more to outstanding attractions.

Maximum baggage allowance is 176 lbs. (80 kg) per person, any part of which can be checked thru to your destination. Baggage carts are available at most stations. So are cloak rooms (for checking baggage).

**Great Rail Trip No. 2 — *Indian Pacific***

*It was fascinating, terrifying and, well, sort of hypnotic.*

*Hell, man, why don't they show movies in the club car?*

*I thought I saw a kangaroo — or d'ya think it was a mirage?*

*By God, sport, they're right. This IS a BIG country.*

Those are typical comments about this 2461-mile, 65-hour crossing of a continent. It's certainly not for everyone and it may or may not be for you, but one thing is certain: this Big Sky Express, as it's often called, is, like *The Alice,* an exceptionally fine train.

The gleaming 12-car steel train (aka Silver Snake) pulls out of Sydney's Central Station every Monday and Thursday at 1515, arrives in Perth's handsome marble terminal at 0700 the third day — one of the world's longest unbroken rail journeys.

Australians view the train as they do a top resort hotel: a delightful opportunity to gorge themselves three times daily (plus tea).

Breakfast: juices, cold cereals and muesli (a notorious porridge); bacon/sausage and eggs with mashed potatoes and onion gravy; sirloin steak and tomatoes (with or without eggs); toast, marmalade (jam), tea, coffee and milk.

Lunch: First soup, then a main course followed by dessert, tea or coffee.

Dinner: Soup, entree and main course (like Weiner Schnitzel, steak,[10] pork chops, roast chicken/chicken cacciatore), then a "sweet."

This is good basic dining served with a little extra flourish by a staff of four waiters and three drink stewards; there are six men in the galley. Forty-eight passengers are served at a sitting. Everything, it's claimed, is prepared aboard.

***Indian-Pacific* — An Unusual Adventure**

Beyond the Blue Mountains for the entirety of the ride, "the countryside streams past like a gargantuan conveyor belt carrying debris of sun-flattened, wind-twisted acacia shrubs, spiky grass thickets and clumps of grey-green saltbush. Who could believe that sheepmen have made great fortunes in this desolation, from gossamer-fine wool grown on pastures so arid that 15 to 20 acres barely suffice to feed one beast?"[11]

In early morning of the second day, the train enters Big Sky country, "the Nullarbor (meaning no tree) Plain . . . so completely flat and featureless that when surveyors determined the route of a transcontinental railroad in 1908, they had only to rule a straight line on the map to delineate 300 miles of track between two camps, called Ooldea and Muringa by nomad tribesmen. The longest railroad 'straight' in the world was built — mainly with pick and shovel — in 1915-16 and the construction gangs toiled in heat so extreme that old-timers on the line used to win bets from newcomers by frying eggs on enameled plates set in the sun.

"No one can ever describe the crossing of the Nullarbor satisfactorily. No two people ever experience entirely similar reactions. To some it is mainly a breath-taking, featureless monotony revealing only vistas of red sand pimpled with parched and dying saltbush blurred by mirage.

[10] 500-steaks are aboard for each run — an average of over three per passenger — not to mention 700 cans of beer.

[11] Osmar White, noted Australian author/journalist.

**Karunda Rail Trip From Cairns**

This is one of the most delightful, enjoyable short rail trips we've ever taken — and next to the Quito-Guayaquil one, the cheapest (about A$6 round trip).

The diesel train climbs thru Barron Gorge, surrounded by tropical rain forests, to a crest from which there's a spectacular view of Cairns, the Barrier Reef and Coral Sea beyond. After 21 miles and one and a half hours of pleasurable excitement, the train glides to a stop at Kuranda's beautifully landscaped station whose gardens of exotic plants, flowers and ferns have won many awards.

There are daily trains (except Sundays, holidays) from Cairns at 0900, 0930 (May-Sept.) and 1540; returns at 1200 and 1912 (May-Sept.).

On the May-September schedule, you can ride the rails all the way to Mareeba, Atherton and Ravenshoe, which is 82 miles beyond Kuranda; arrival is at 1500, return trip starts at 1530.

***Great Indian Pacific Railroad***

Not to be confused with just-described *Indian-Pacific* train, this is another of those comprehensive Voyages Jules Verne group rail tours that combines a circumnavigation of Australia with a jaunt thru the North and South Islands of New Zealand — plus an overnight ride from Mandalay to Rangoon in Burma and the Bangkok to Singapore rail trip described on page 108. For those who don't care to do all that on their own, this 36-day land program covers the essentials thoroughly — though, it should be mentioned, in a go-go-go fashion. Small wonder — it covers a lot of ground (and air).

Landing first in Burma, the tour takes in Pagan, Mandalay, Rangoon before flying to Bangkok and continuing on the overnight *International Express* to Penang. A day train to Kuala Lumpur is followed by an overnight express to Singapore. There's a day of sightseeing at all stops.

After flying from Singapore to Perth, the *Indian-Pacific* takes the group to Sydney. That's followed by a two stage train ride to Cairns: an overnight express to Brisbane and two-day *Sunlander* to Cairns. Here the Kuranda rail trip is enjoyed before flying to Alice Springs-Ayers Rock and then boarding *The Ghan* for Adelaide. A flight to Auckland is followed by a drive to Rotorua, overnight *Northerner* to Wellington, then by ferry and train to Christchurch.

A grand adventure — one that individual explorers might well copy.

# NEW ZEALAND

When people ask for a list of our favorite countries, we unhesitatingly name New Zealand as one of the most beautiful and, for its size, the most varied.

Take California (7,000 miles away to the northeast) for size, flavor with English and Scottish ancestry, add Swiss Alps and Arctic glaciers, English and Irish countryside, Norwegian fjords and Italian lakes, a dozen Yellowstones, a 66½-mile Daytona Beach, a nearby Puget Sound and — well, that's a quick approximation of what awaits you in New Zealand. Plus an uncontaminated environment.

No country offers so much sightseeing variety within such a compact, easily reached area. There are 3,100,000 people and 60,000,000 sheep, 103,000 square miles of mountains and rolling pastureland — much of it spectacular to the extreme — and countless miles of lovely coastline and waterways stretching from the subtropical north to the subtemperate south.

New Zealand comprises two major islands, North (44,281 square miles) and South (58,093), plus a minor one, Stewart (670). North Island is beautiful in a soft, rolling way and the site of an utterly fascinating, unsurpassed thermal area. South Island is so spectacular and massive it boggles the senses. Thus, differences between the two so neatly complement each other *that it's essential to include both in your trip planning.*

For the rail fan, there's an extra bonus: travel by train from Auckland in the north to Dunedin in the south — including one outstanding trip on the *Silver Fern.*

All in all, New Zealand is a prize package that, for unadulterated beauty, interest and unpretentious enjoyment, simply can't be beat. Everyone who visits here loves it, most want to return for another round. Small wonder.

*Silver Fern* negotiating a segment of Raurimu Spiral.

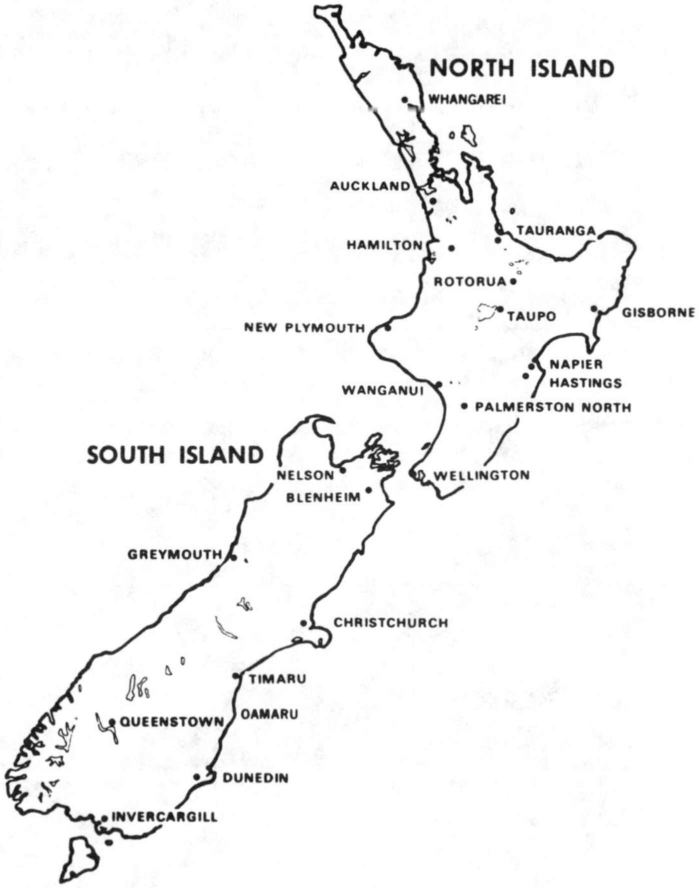


**NEW ZEALAND'S *Silver Fern***

This 422-mile trip thru the North Island's most beautiful scenery is one of the best day trips we've ever taken — a highly recommended way to travel between Wellington and Auckland (or vice-versa).

Both train and scenery are superb. A particular highlight is the famous Raurimu Spiral which was engineered to overcome a sharp rise of 21 meters in six kilometers by traveling a 11½-km loop-the-loop route so that you see the train coming and going at the same time, an absorbing experience.

Diesel-powered cars have large picture windows, comfortable reclining seats. Rows 1 thru 9 (each with seats A, B, C, D) are in the smoking car; next car, rows 10-24, is non-smoking. Seats A & B (on right side of center aisle) have best viewing northbound; C & D southbound. Specify your preference when reserving seats.

Commentaries by well-versed, charming hostesses and guards (conductors) are brief and excellent. Great service — all you have to do is ask just once.

Morning/afternoon snacks are included in the fare. No dining car but you can buy sandwiches or a table d'hote lunch at Taihape (30-minute stop); guard will order the lunch for you in advance. He'll also reserve a taxi in Auckland (or Wellington), make hotel reservations if desired.

*Silver Fern* leaves Wellington at 0820, arrives Auckland at 1930; lvs. Auckland at 0800, ars. Wellington 1902.

**Other New Zealand Rail Services**

The best trains (modern and good) connect Auckland-Wellington and Christchurch-Invercargill. Latter is a 350-mile run by the deluxe *Southerner;* lvs. Christchurch Monday thru Saturday at 0840, ar Invercargill at 1845. You can overnight there, then rent a car and drive to Te Anau-Milford Sound-Queenstown-Mt. Cook and over to Christchurch — a great way to see the best of South Island.

*Northerner* runs nightly between Auckland-Wellington (and vice-versa); has sleeping cars, coaches, dining car and full refreshment services. Lvs. Auckland at 1930, ars. at 0830.

One can ride the rails for almost the entire length of New Zealand's east coast: from Auckland to Wellington in the North Island, from Christchurch to Dunedin in South Island. The gap from Wellington to Christchurch is bridged by the Wellington-Picton ferry followed by a daily six-hour train ride, said to be extremely scenic, from Picton to Christchurch.

New Zealand Railways *Travelpass* is available for eight, 15 and 22 days of unlimited travel on its trains, buses and Cook Strait ferries. See *Travel Supplement* for details, prices.

# FAR EAST

### JAPAN'S BULLET TRAINS

Though even the Green cars, the best, are not deluxe, it's the speed (up to 130 mph) and precision (electronically controlled, trains always stop precisely as marked on the platform) that impresses. And woe to the tardy — trains are programmed to stop for only a minute or two and away they go, with or without you. Yet serious accidents are unheard of.

Most interesting part of riding the rails is the opportunity to observe fellow passengers at leisure, as well as the houses (neo-shrine architecture) and apartments in which they live. Noticeable is the lack of color in the latter — drab monotones of brown and grey — except for colored tile roofs (mostly blue). No squalor nor slums, just depressing mediocrity. Meals are served in dining-buffet cars, but watching people buying ice cream, soft drinks, beer, candy, sandwiches and box lunches from vendors as they wheel their carts up and down the aisles is the most fun.

There are two types of super-express service on the original Shinkansen (New Trunk Line) between Tokyo and Hakata (Fukuoka City): *Hikari,* which makes the 730-mile run in six hours, 56 minutes with only seven stops (Nagoya, Kyoto, Osaka,

On a clear day in Japan, you get a grand view of famed Fuji from the Bullet Train. Enroute to Kyoto, try for a grandstand seat on the right hand side.

Economy Class car on the Bullet Train.

Okayama, Hiroshima, Kokua and Hakata). *Kodama,* which covers various segments of the run, stops at all stations, takes three hours, 56 min. for the 319-mile run from Tokyo to Kyoto.

On the Hikari Super Express, cars 1 thru 5 have non-reserved seats, cars 6 and 7, 10 thru 16 reserved seats. One of those cars are for non-smokers (76% Japanese men smoke, only 15% of the women). Green Cars (with four-leaf clover emblem) are 11 and 12. 8 and 9 are the dining and buffet cars.

Another bullet train, Tohuku Shinkansen, links Omiya, a suburb of Tokyo, with Morioka, 290 miles NE, making the trip in about four hours. Special relay trains carry passengers from/to Tokyo. In August, many festivals are held in this northern area where hot springs spas are located; in winter, Tohuku's ski resorts are an attraction.

Another new bullet train line is Joetsu Shinkansen with two-hour service from Tokyo to Niigata, bordering the Sea of Japan. Cars on both Tohoku and Joetsu lines are ivory color with light green stripes.

Work is nearing completion on an extension beyond Morioka thru the new 54 km underwater tunnel to Sapporo, Japan's winter sports center.

Because of engineering improvements over the years, trains on the two newest routes can run at speeds up to 162½ mph — about 30 mph faster than the Shinkansen bullets.

All cars are numbered as are station platforms (to show where you enter each car).

Cars on long distance trains have toilets (Japanese style at one end, western at other) and public phones.

You're allowed to board with two large pieces of luggage; additional bags can be checked thru to your destination (preferably a day in advance) and, for an extra fee, delivered to your hotel.

*Don't throw away your tickets after boarding* as they must be surrendered to platform gateman at final destination.

*Strict rule:* no tipping on trains. Station porters charge Y250 per bag; worth it to see them carry bags fore and aft by head straps.

If you have difficulty climbing stairs (or aren't supposed to), don't travel by train. Usually you'll have to walk up and down stairs to reach the platforms. Porters normally available to carry luggage — but we suggest a tour operator transfer service at each destination.

For night travel, there are A class sleepers with roomettes, lower and upper berths and B sleepers w/3-bunk berths.

Seats can be reserved in advance thru travel agency offices in Japan or, in the U.S. and Canada thru Japan Air Lines (if flying JAL). Japan Travel Bureau, in New York, Los Angeles and San Francisco (800-223-0266 exc. NY), is another reliable source, as is Nippon Travel Pacific.

Japanese National Railways' Super-Expresses depart from Tokyo Central Station (Nihonobashi), northern trains from Ueno Station. In addition to JNR, there are private railways operating deluxe limited-express trains to Hakone, Nikko and Nara — with English-speaking female guides. Japan National Tourist Organization's *Train Guide* lists all JNR stations from which trains depart.

For extensive train travel, you'll want a Japan Railpass. See *Rail Pass Supplement* for details.

Japanese section of **Far East Travel Digest** tells you what to see and how to plan your trip.

# *People's Republic of* CHINA

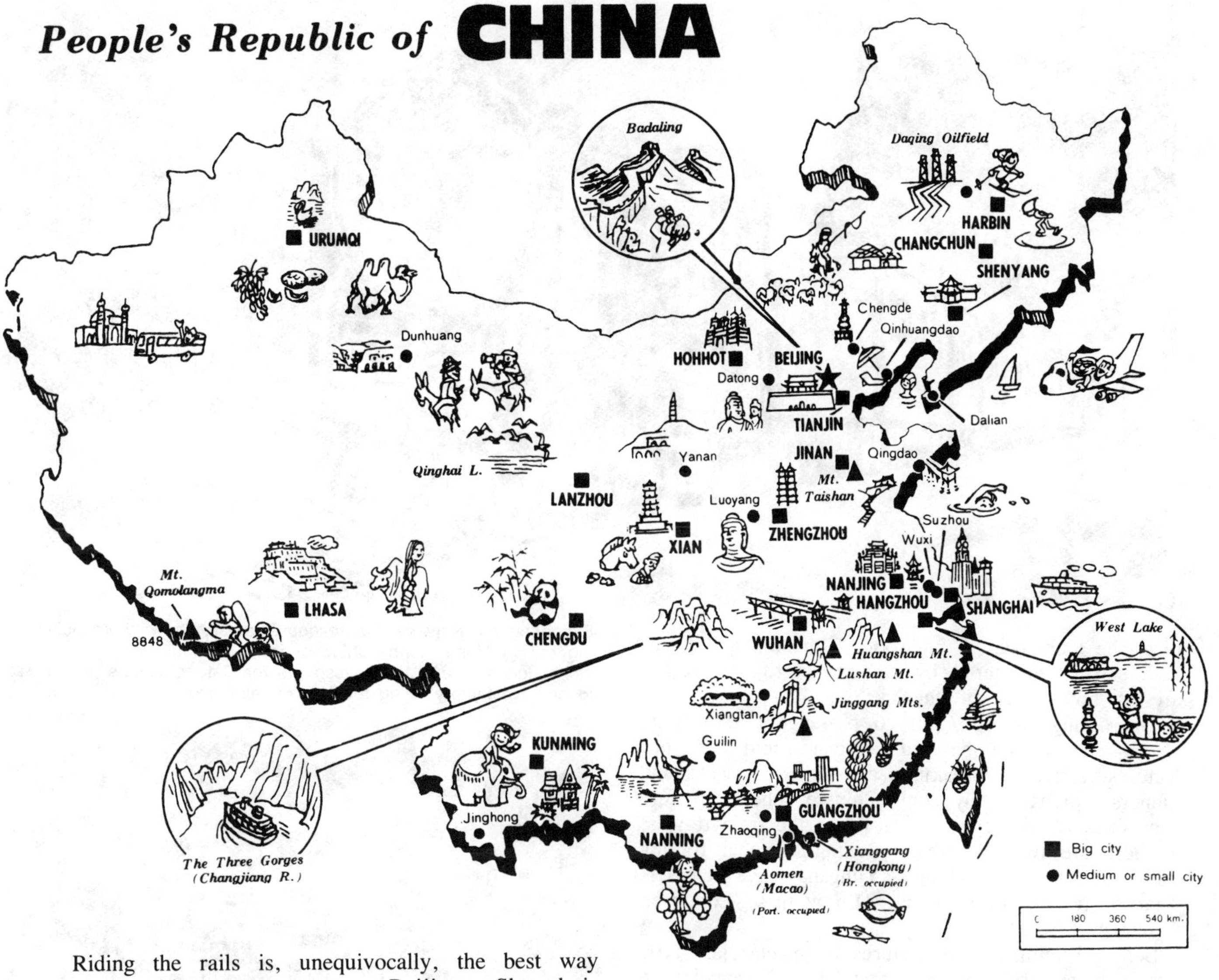


Riding the rails is, unequivocally, the best way to see this vast country. Beijing, Shanghai, Guangzhou and other large cities are, of course, important pieces of the Chinese puzzle . . . but to complete the picture satisfactorily, you must see the rural countryside, villages and people.

But that's not the only reason. Chinese trains are a pleasure: comfortable, well maintained and generally on time; the same cannot be claimed for domestic planes. Day coaches have wide picture windows, swivel chairs (not reclining), the inevitable lace doilies and tea mugs. Soft class sleeping car compartments for four, two lowers and two uppers, have bright comforters, clean sheets and comfortable pillows, vase of flowers, big thermos of hot water, tea mugs and tea bags. With a congenial couple, you'll have a ball. Meals could be better. Johns are okay (one at each end of the car) as long as you don't patronize the Chinese-style one; some even had an adjoining washroom.

Because Chinese Railways connect many of the most interesting and scenic tourist destinations, there are scores and scores of group tours booking two, three or more day or overnight trains between stops; a few operators tour the country solely by rail. And if you're the more adventurous type, arrangements can be made for individuals to tour China on your own.[1] However, since the majority of visitors prefer a group tour, here's a rundown on the best ones conducted entirely by rail:[2]

### *Imperial Peking Express*

Society Expeditions' 16-day program is the epitome of luxury train travel in China. Just 26 passengers can be accommodated in the two VIP sleeping cars (normally used for transporting dignitaries) and private dining car which are attached to scheduled trains.

Each sleeping car has eight double compartments (unusually elegant for China) with upper and lower berths; during the day, compartments, become a sitting room with couch, easy chair and writing table. Dark walnut paneling and polished brass fittings com-

[1] Make arrangements months in advance thru a wholesale tour operator specializing in China. Particularly well qualified is Lindblad Travel, 8 Wright St., Westport, Conn. 06880 (800-243-5657)

[2] See Trans-Mongolian Railway to Beijing for additional tours.

plete the ambience. A bathroom with sink and hand-held shower is shared by two compartments; toilets are at both ends of the car.

The dining car seats all 26 passengers at a time, also serves as lounge and seminar room for staff lectures. American breakfasts are served; lunches and dinners, prepared by top Chinese chefs, feature specialties of the regions thru which the train travels.

There are two itineraries. Beijing-Shanghai routing includes visits to Datong's Yungang cave temples, Xian's terra cotta army, Luoyang's Longmen Grottoes.

Beijing-Kunming line features a spectacular 1100 km segment thru mountains that has 427 tunnels and 653 bridges; includes stops at Luoyang, Xian and the great Buddha at Leshan.

*Imperial Peking Express* can be teamed with previously mentioned Society Expeditions' Trans-Mongolian *Paris to Peking Express* in August and September.

Also refer to the Trans-Mongolian Railway section for details concerning Globetrotters Tours' and Voyages Jules Verne's programs which includes extensive train travel within China. Another program by Globetrotter, a 32-day *China-USSR Explorer* from Hong Kong to London, has a very comprehensive China segment: Guangzhou, Guilin, Shanghai, Suzhou, Grand Canal Cruise, Wuxi, Nanjing, Xian and Beijing before going to Ulan Bator, Irkutsk et al.

Smithsonian Institution had an excellent *China by Train* tour (26 days) in April of 1984; check whether it's being repeated. Also check Finlay Fun-Time's 25-day China Rail Tour.[3]

A two-week *China-Japan Rail Trek,* designed to accommodate a small group of 12 steam railroad buffs and escorted by train buff Dave Checkley, is an October offering by Kim's Travel.[4]

Excepting the *Kowloon-Guangzhou Express,* shown here pulling out of Hong Kong, Chinese trains are still powered by steam locomotives. Which accounts for Datong's huge steam locomotive factory being the last remaining one in the world.

[3] Smithsonian National Associate Program, A & I 1270B, Smithsonian Institution, Washington 20560. Finlay Fun-Time Tours, 11306 Burbank Blvd., No. Hollywood, Ca. 91601.

[4] 603 Stewart St., #619, Seattle 98101.

### *Kowloon-Guangzhou* (Canton) *Express*

Next to Japan's Bullets, this is the most famous train in the Far East. With diesel engines and airconditioned day coaches, it speeds three times daily between Hong Kong and Guangzhou (182 km) in two hours, 40 minutes.[5]

Pre-1949, this Kowloon-Canton Railway, a Hong Kong entity, lived up to its name. After the communists came to power, passengers had to change at the border, walking between LoWu and Shenzhen to board the Kowloon train's Red counterpart — which we did in 1979 — notable for its loudspeakers blaring *The East Is Red* and attendants sloshing hot water into passengers' teacups.

What a difference today. Loud speakers have been replaced by Japanese color TV sets mounted on the walls and hooked to a central videotape system showing traditional Chinese opera. Trains no longer stop at the border; *Express* passengers go thru customs and immigration in the Kowloon and Guangzhou stations. And snacks and drinks are sold aboard.

But *the* highlight, the reason for many to take the train, is duty free shopping: French perfumes, Martel Napoleon brandy (about $11 US), US cigarettes (about $6 US per carton), scotch and other liquors. All, by the way, sold only for Hong Kong dollars.

Trains from Guangzhou sell popular Chinese products such as thousand year old eggs (pickled for two months) and dried fruit; latter is especially attractive to Hong Kong residents. "Hong dou, you peng, you leng" the vendors cry in Cantonese. "Dried dates, they're cheap, they're pretty." And so they are — about 50¢ for a pound bag.

For all those reasons, this link between the two Chinas is being used more and more frequently by tour operators to move groups from or into Hong Kong. We commend it to you — it's a slice of color you'll long remember.

**ELAPSED TIMES (Hours) & DISTANCES (Kilometers)**

**Beijing To:**

| | |
|---|---|
| Chongqing—43 (2552) | Nanning—37 (2565) |
| Datong—5:30 (382) | Qingdao—17:30 (887) |
| Guangzhou—34 (2313) | Shanghai—19 (1462) |
| Guilin—32:40 (2134) | Suzhou—18:40 (1376) |
| Harbin—18 (1388) | Tianjin—1:51 (137) |
| Jinan—6:45 (494) | Wuhan—16 (120) |
| Lanzhou—33 (1811) | Wuxi—18 (1334) |
| Nanjing—16 (1157) | Xian—17:40 (1206) |

**Shanghai To:**

| | |
|---|---|
| Guangzhou—33 (1811) | Suzhou—1:15 (86) |
| Nanjing—5 (305) | Wuxi—2 (128) |

## HOW TO PRONOUNCE CHINESE NAMES

In 1978, the State Council decreed that all Chinese proper and place names were to be romanized thru a system called *Pinyin* (literally *spelling*), replacing traditional names given by a British linguist, Wade, over a hundred years ago.

For easy recognition of places you'll visit and read about, we've included a list of cities and provinces with Pinyin and Wade systems of phonetic spelling, designed to approximate Chinese pronunciations.

### Traditional City Names (with Pinyin equivalents)

Canton—Guangzhou
Chenchiang—Zhenjaing
Chengchou—Zhengzhou *(chung-joe)*
Chengteh—Chengde
Chengtu—Chengdu
Chinhuangtao—Qinghuandao
Chunking—Chongquing
Foochow—Fuzhou
Hangchow—Hangzhou *(hong-joe)*
Hotei—Hefei
Hong Kong—Xianggang
Huhehot—Hohhot
Kirin—Jirin
Kweilin—Guilin
Lanchow—Lanzhou
Liuchou—Liuzhou
Loyang—Luoyang
Macau—Aomen
Nanking—Nanjing
Peking—Beijing
Shaosing—Shaoxing
Sian—Xi'an
Soochow—Suzhou *(Soo-joe)*
Talien—Dalian
Tatung—Datong
Tientsin—Tianjin
Tsinan—Jinan
Tsingtao—Qingdao
Urumchi—Urumqi
Wuhsi—Wuxi
Yangchou—Yangzhou
Yenan—Yan'an
Yentai—Yanti

[5] This Chinese operated train has 10 AC coaches (total of 640 passengers), first class only. Leaves Guangzhou at 0845, 1030 and 1839 daily; departs Kowloon at 0825, 1305 and 1435 daily. In Hong Kong, reservations made thru China Travel Service in Kowloon or Central District. Round trip fare is about $36 US.

## HOW DOES ONE GET TO CHINA?

Best way, by far, is with a tour offered by North American tour operators and/or airlines who have an official quota of group visas issued by China International Travel Service. As previously noted, individuals can tour China on their own by making arrangements with tour operators authorized to do so by CITS.

When booking a tour, you receive a visa application form which you fill out and return to the tour operator (together with passport) who then obtains a group visa listing each tour member by name. On entry into China and subsequent travel therein, always as a group, you retain your passport, but the tour leader takes care of all formalities; individual registration at hotels is rarely required.

For groups with specialized interests (teachers, doctors, lawyers, etc.), there are two ways to go: have an airline or tour operator assign one of their tour dates to the group, or apply to China International Travel Service, Hsitan Building, East Chang An St., Beijing, for a special tour. In latter case, state purpose of the proposed visit, for how long, what the group wishes to study and, if known, what cities are preferred. Group cultural exchange programs can also be initiated thru various official Chinese agencies. Should a favorable reply be received, application for visas must be made to the Embassy of the People's Republic of China, 2300 Connecticut Ave. NW, Washington 20008, or, for Canadians, at 100 Bronson St., Ottawa. When forms are received and filled out, return with required passport photos and individual passports. There's a fee for each entry, exit and transit visa. An exit visa, obtainable thru CITS, must be obtained before leaving China, the rules thereon strictly followed.

With the granting of visas, CITS will then proceed with final tour schedules, hotel accommodations (assigned, not chosen), sightseeing tours, transportation and transfers, guides, etc. — all paid for *in advance* thru a tour operator or travel agent, preferably one with prior China tour experience. Obviously, the foregoing requires months of advance negotiating and planning.

Chinese embassies in Washington and Ottawa have a quota of visas for overseas Chinese, both individual and group types; these can be issued within two weeks if quotas are not used up. Travel is then arranged by CITS if English speaking or Chinese Travel Service (same address) which furnishes Chinese-speaking guides only. Overseas Chinese usually stay in less expensive hotels, travel in smaller groups and are able to visit relatives in areas that might otherwise not be open to foreigners.

Chinese People's Institute of Foreign Affairs, Ministry of Foreign Affairs, Beijing is the agency normally responsible for inviting VIPs, governmental, business and public figures as well as journalists. Individual visas are then issued by the People's Republic of China Embassy.

## BANGKOK TO KUALA LUMPUR & SINGAPORE

This romantic-sounding rail trip is certainly one of the most way out and a great way to see lushly tropical landscapes and seldom-visited places — but here's what our Bangkok correspondent has to say:

"From the standpoint of luxury, *International Express* is definitely not one of the greatest experiences. Facilities are quite basic. There are two types of sleepers: those with airconditioning (1st class) are simple but modern and mostly too cold since there are no individually controlled thermostats. Non-airconditioned sleepers (2nd class), made of wood, are older but nicer. Restaurant cars, and their food, are elemental; nonchalant waiters dispose of leftovers by tossing them out the window.

"Since the train runs on a narrow gauge track, speed does not exceed 60 kilometers (about 37 mph) and poor suspension systems provide a far from smooth run."

*International Express* leaves Bangkok at 1610 on M, W and Sat, arrives Butterworth, Malaysia (station for the resort island of Penang) next day at 1845. If not stopping over, take the *North Star* departing at 2200, arriving Kuala Lumpur at 0700, Singapore at 1325. From Butterworth, there's also the *Rakyat Express* departing at 0815 that gets into KL at 1435, Singapore at 2135. Between KL and SIN, there are six daily trains in both directions.[1]

*International Express* leaves Butterworth M, W, F at 0755, arrives Bangkok 0645 next morning.

In either direction, we recommend breaking the rail journey in Kuala Lumpur and Penang.

Since the State Railway of Thailand requires full prepayment of rail and sleeper fares at time of making reservation, best to use the services of a Bangkok travel agency when southbound.[2]

An alternative to the Bangkok to Singapore train trip is Diethelm Travel's 8-day *Overland Discovery Tour* that leaves on the *International Express* then continues the next morning by air conditioned bus with overnight stops in southern Thailand resorts, flies to Penang then overland by bus to Cameron Highlands, Kuala Lumpur (sightseeing tour) and Singapore. Good hotels, all meals and transportation included at about $100 per day. If you wish to see little visited southern Thailand as well as the west coast of Malaysia, this is an excellent way to go.

Next to Bangkok, Chiang Mai to the north is Thailand's most interesting destination. There's a night train (with 1st, 2nd class sleepers) departing Bangkok at 1800, arriving Chiang Mai at 0750. The same express returns at 1650 for 0630 arrival in the capital.

Suggested reading to learn all about this area: *Far East Travel Digest.*

[1] Rail buff Ed Benson and wife Sheila report that the 488 km, 9-hour ride on the *Kuala Lumpur-Singapore Express* is excellent: good roadbed, new Japanese cars with reclining seats, piped music and video facilities — and fares extremely reasonable.

[2] We recommend Diethelm Travel, 544 Ploenchit Road, Bangkok as a thoroughly reliable source for all travel in Thailand.

---

## BRIDGE ON THE RIVER KWAI (Khwae)

In Kanchanaburi Province, some 80 miles west of Bangkok, a picturesque area of wild jungle and rugged hills, stands this memorable landmark of World War II, immortalized by the award-winning movie (based on a novel by Pierre Boulle) starred William Holden, Alex Guiness and Jack Hawkins.

The Bridge, constructed by Allied POWs to complete the 415-km Thai-Burma Railway for the Japanese Imperial Army, was never actually blown up by British commandos but was partially destroyed by Allied bombers on November 28, 1943 and later reconstructed by the Japanese (in steel instead of the original teak) as part of their war indemnity. Thailand purchased the Bridge for $2 million from the Allies. It now serves the State Railway of Thailand as far as Nam Tok, 210 km from Bangkok but no longer into Burma. Actually, the Japanese amassed a huge army of Allied prisoners and Asian laborers, of whom some 16,000 prisoners and possibly 40,000 laborers died, to build this "Railway of Death" thru the Kwai Valley and, ultimately, to the Rangoon-Maungye Railway in Burma as an assault route on India; without such a land link, Japan's supply line by sea would have been vulnerable to Allied subs.

The Bridge is about 2 kilometers from the town of Kanchanaburi, a cross between old New Orleans (overhanging wooden balconies) and frontier shanty town. Nearby is the Allied Soldiers' Cemetery where some 9,000 prisoners are buried.

A special tourist train leaves Bangkok Station on weekends and holidays in the morning, returns in late afternoon. Thrice daily, a third class train makes the run in 2:34 in both directions. Most tourists, however, take a one-day or longer bus tour to the Bridge and River Kwai Village resort hotel.

# INDIA

Anyone who has visited India will tell you it is one of the world's most colorful countries — if not *the* most — what with its teeming, varied population. But not everyone enjoys the kaleidoscopic melange of poverty and wealth, modernity and backwardness, of religious art and scenery of great beauty contrasted with hordes of physically handicapped and deformed. Whether you wish to view this amalgam — and, we hasten to add, India is a very popular tourist destination — is a matter for you to decide. Our job is to tell you how to see the country by rail.

India Railways is the nation's largest employer — some 1,600,000 persons oversee 38,000 miles of track, 7,072 stations and take care of 10 million passengers and 740,000 tons of freight *per day*. With such traffic (almost four billion passengers a year), you can expect almost anything to happen when traveling by rail — like a two-hour dead stop in the middle of nowhere for no apparent reason; you're never sure if the train will start in two minutes or, possibly, two days.

Most trains are badly in need of upgrading. For that matter, so is much of the country. But you can't beat the local color, particularly in the stations. Calcutta's Howrah is India's largest and a village in itself where, as in most stations, you see people cooking, eating, washing and sleeping, sacred cows foraging for scraps. However, Victoria Terminus in Bombay is imposing, while Hazrat Nizam station in New Delhi is the best organized. Varanasi's station may well be the most interesting. It looks like a Hindu temple and like one it overflows with holy men, pilgrims and sacred cows; in fact, it's home for the latter.

Basically, India's rail network is a British system begun in 1853 to connect Bombay, Calcutta and Madras. By 1869 there were 4,000+ miles of broad gauge track, but to reduce track-laying costs, narrower gauges were introduced, mostly between 1870-1900. In 1956, much of the one meter track was converted to broad gauge so that main lines out of major cities are almost completely wide track. Electrification was begun in 1920; today, all main trunk lines have been or are being converted.

To fully appreciate this vast network, despite its drawbacks, one must realize that construction of a transcontinental rail route across the United States (and Canada) was a pipe compared to the incredible distances and difficulties encountered in India.

### *Palace On Wheels*

The richly decorated steam engine is called *Desert Queen*. Behind it are 14 ivory-colored, luxuriously redecorated sleeping cars, beautifully appointed with crystal chandeliers, embroidered curtains, plush furnishings and wall to wall carpeting. Each of these one-of-a-kind coaches was especially made for its royal head of state. The oldest one, which belonged to the Maharajah of Bikaner, dates back to 1898, but even the newest is of 1935-36 origin. In other words, this was India's 1982 answer to the Oriental Express.

To give you an idea of how sumptuous the cars are, the original coach of Bhavnagar State, built in 1929 for the agent of the Governor General, features solid brass pillars, metallic ceilings and a side verandah. It, like all the others, sports the coat of arms of its former owner.

Despite their uniqueness, the sleeping cars do have similarities. Each has four double compartments and two full bathrooms complete with shower. Each carries two full-time attendants, has a small lounge in which breakfast and afternoon tea are served from a kitchenette and mini-bar. "Good morning, Sir . . . good morning, Madame . . . your breakfast is ready." Ah, but what's a heaven for?

A well-traveled rail buff who's ridden the Nostalgic Orient Express, Trans-Siberian Special and Palace On Wheels confides that the latter is his favorite despite heat, dust and lack of airconditioning. For there's

a crew of 60 (porters, assistant porters, waiters, cooks and chefs) to cater royally to the comfort and convenience of passengers (maximum of 110 but often less).

A travel agent says, "The experience is unforgettable, sightseeing unbelievable and service very good but the accommodations are not up to brochure hyperboles. When these salons were constructed, they were certainly fit for maharajahs, but American tourists expect superior accommodations. Eight persons sharing two bathrooms is not exactly palatial. However, there is no more efficient or convenient way to see this part of India."

A travel writer, on the other hand, was utterly intrigued by the romantic ambiance of it all, said not a word about inadequate accommodations. "Outside (the train at night) the ghostly outlines of bullocks and pipal trees hanging just out of sight; the smell of steam and sandelwood and *kheema muttar* wafting back from the dining saloon. Like a thirsty animal, sometimes the train would glide to a halt to take on water in some tiny settlement. There would be a moment of silence, then voices on the platform would start to murmur. Platforms were never quite still, even in the deepest night. Someone was cooing to a baby, someone was singing softly, someone was splashing his ankles in a fountain."[1]

Many consider this tour of the state of Rajasthan, which borders Pakistan to the northwest, *the* highlight of the entire country as major cities have fantastic palaces, museums and forts. Further, they lie amidst a desert landscape of great beauty. Perhaps to compensate for the starkness, the people are among the most colorfully dressed of all Indians: men might wear flaming rose turbans, women the brightest of saris. Here, too, the use of camels is not uncommon, nor is the sight of peacocks.

The observation/lounge/bar car is Indian art deco at its fascinatingly imaginative best: rose-colored velvet banquettes, inlaid tea tables, 14 revolving ceiling fans (with which sleeping cars are also equipped).

**_Palace On Wheels_ Itinerary**

Day 1 — Dinner at Delhi Cantt Station from 2000 to 2230. Embarkation, departure at 2245.
Day 2 — Jaipur. Lunch at Rambagh Palace Hotel (fabulous dining). Tea, dinner at Man Singh/Nahargarh (originally Royal Fort).
Day 3 — Morning free in Udaipur. Depart at lunch time for Jaisalmer.
Day 4 & Sightseeing, camel ride in Jaisalmer. Dinner at Moomal Tourist Bungalow.
Day 6 — Jodphur. Lunch at Umaid Bhawan Palace Hotel, once the Maharaja of Jodphur's Palace.
Day 7 — Bharatpur & Agra. Breakfast in Bharatpur Bird Sanctuary. By bus to Fatehpur Sikri, a ghost city founded and deserted by Akbar the Great, a Mughal Emperor. Lunch at Clarks Shiraz, Agra followed by sightseeing and dinner at Mughal Sheraton.
Day 8 — Disembarkation in New Delhi after breakfast.
*** Unless otherwise listed, meals are served on board.**

In the two dining cars, Indian chefs prepare regional dishes, Rajasthani and Western specialties, while in the lounge/observation car, passengers watch historic and culturally rich northwest India glide by — at a stately 24 mph; if the engine went faster, vibrations might damage the venerable cars.

As a joint venture of Indian Railways and Rajasthan Tourism Development Corporation, a seven-night tour — from Delhi to Jaipur, Udaipur, Jaiselmer, Jodhpur, Bharatpur, Agra Fort and back to Delhi — is scheduled 23 times between October and March. Departures are on Wednesdays. Included in the fare are all meals on board, sightseeing in best available buses, an elephant ride at Amber in Jaipur, a camel ride in Jaisalmer, boating at Udaipur and Bharatpur, Indian dance and theater entertainment.

**Palace On Wheels Tour Programs**

During the coolest time of the year, January-March, Society Expeditions charters the entire train once each month, and again in November, for a 16-day tour that spends four nights aboard the train, the balance in hotels in Bangkok, Delhi and at several of the train destinations. On the train, only lower berths (a single and double) of each sleeping compartment are used, thus limiting group membership to 88.

There's extensive sightseeing programs in Delhi and all other stops under the guidance of expert American

[1] *Stephanie Brush in Signature,* July 1984.

lecturers. An outstanding day is spent at the exceptional Bharatpur bird sanctuary at the peak of the migratory season, in the ghost city of Fatehpur Sikri and finally viewing the Taj Mahal.

An optional 5-day extension to Kathmandu and Tiger Tops is available.

Hemphill-Harris Travel has eight deluxe 16-day tours, Oct. 27 to March 23, that utilize some of the Palace sleeping cars exclusively for its members. Before the seven-night train trip, three days are spent in Delhi; afterwards there are three nights in Bombay.

A less expensive (and less elegant) 13-day tour, similar to the Society Expeditions program but utilizing the scheduled Palace departures, is conducted by Tours of Distinction.

### *Great Indian Rover*

This modern, first class AC train, consisting of nine sleeping cars plus restaurant and lounge cars, departs each Thursday from Calcutta after a city tour. Five nights are spent aboard; during the day, the route to Gaya, Varanasi and Gorakhpur to the northwest of Calcutta follows in the tracks of Gautama Buddha, visiting such venerated places as Rajgir, Nalanda, Bodhgaya, Lumbini (where Buddha was born) and Kushinagar (where his body was cremated). There's an optional extension, by air and motor coach to Delhi, Agra, Jaipur and back to Delhi.

Each well-appointed sleeping car accommodates 14 people (five lower and upper berth compartments, one four-berth), has a wardrobe, cupboards, dressing table with full-size mirror, dressing table and stool, good-size picture window. Each coach has two toilets with wash basins. Dining car, featuring Chinese, Indian and Western cuisines, can accommodate only 20 at a time, no doubt a problem with a full complement of 126 passengers.

But the lounge car is the *piece de resistance* and quite unique by any standard: one section is the bar and bar lounge, while at the end of the second lounge section is a prayer hall, in the center of which a brass Buddha statue stands on a pedestal under a wooden pagoda.

### Raj Express

Billed as "A passage across the Indian Subcontinent," by its operator, Voyages Jules Verne, it is exactly that — an amazingly complete 40-day, all-rail program (except for London to Rawalpindi and Colombo back to London by air) from Pakistan to Sri Lanka, from one side of India to the other. Just about everything and every place of interest is included, even a narrow gauge, overnight rail trip to Silguri, from there to Darjeeling and then down to New Jalpaiguri on the "toy train." You ride such name trains as the *Khyber Mail, Amritsar Mail, Raidhani Express* to New Delhi, *Taj Express* to Agra, *Gujarat Mail* for Bombay. No question, it's a program that will make any hardy rail enthusiast drool.

### Other Indian Trains

Other than *Palace On Wheels* and *Great Indian Rover,* the Delhi-Varanasi-Calcutta *Howrah-Kalka Mail* is probably the most satisfactory train ride. It has AC chair and sleeping cars plus a pantry car; food is cooked there, waiters carry meals on trays to the passengers. The 263 kilometers is run in about 17½ hours.

There's an *International Express* from Pakistan to Amritsar in India but it's very slow, its coaches battered. *Madras-Janata Express,* from Delhi to Madras, could be the world's slowest; stops at every station along the 1400-mile route, takes several days to make its appointed rounds. *Khyber Mail,* from Pakistan to Lahore, India, in 8¾ hours, has AC compartments.

But according to dedicated Indian rail fans, the country's narrow gauge trains offer the best, most exciting veiws. The so-called "toy train" from New Jalpaiguri to Darjeeling in the hill country is a precious heirloom of the past; its four coaches, pulled by small, blue steam engines, are filled with a cross-section of India that produces colorful scenes matched only by the dramatic views. There's a stop at Ghum, India's highest rail station (7,407 ft.), followed by the famous Batasia Loop descent to Darjeeling during which the train snakes around so that the engine seems about to collide with its caboose. This 54-mile run (in about 7½ hours) is a remarkable feat of engineering. So is the five-hour run from Kalka to the hill station of Simla in a 20-seat rail car. *Howrah-Kalka Mail* leaves Delhi in late evening in time to connect with 0630 departure for Simla.

Food is served aboard. A waiter takes your order; at next major stop, he brings your meal on a tray — usually a vegetable tali as well as rice, salad and unleavened bread (cooked, baked or fried). Unless you can eat as Indians do (with your fingers), bring tableware. Tea and soft drinks available.

#### More About Indian Trains

You can travel anywhere in the country by rail, *but be sure to do so only in first class,* preferably by airconditioned sleeper and/or chair car; both of these can be reserved at nominal charge up to 360 days in advance (without charge if you have an *Indrail Pass*).[2]

For extensive rail travel, from seven to 90 days, *Indrail Pass* is most economical. Can be purchased *only in India* and *only with foreign hard currency* thru recognized travel and railway agencies. India Government Tourist Bureau offices have listing of same.[3] See *Travel Supplement* for costs of *Indrail Pass* and addresses of Tourist Bureau offices.

[2] Be sure to make sleeper/chair car reservations well in advance at time of purchasing *Indrail Pass* or regular tickets. Airconditioned (A) and first class (1) cars are convertible to berths for overnight travel on Mail and Express trains; two or four berths to a compartment in A class; four, five or six in first. Bedding is furnished in A, costs extra in other classes.

[3] Two responsible agents we know about: Indian Air Travels, 101 Hemkunt House, 6 Rajendra Place, New Delhi 110008; SITA World Travel, F-12, Connaught Place, New Delhi 110001. Bookings can also be made thru Central Reservations Offices, Rajasthan Tourism, Chandralok Build 36, Janpath, New Delhi.

## INDIA

### *Indrail Pass* (U.S. Dollars)

*AC First Class w/Sleeper:* $160 (7 days); $200 (15 days); $240 (21 days); $300 (30 days); $450 (60 days); $600 (90 days).

*First Class and/or AC Chair Car:* 50% less than above. Children (5-12) pay half the adult fares.

Indrail Pass holders are *not* subject to normal supplementary or extra fees of any type. Pass can be used within one year of issuance date, at which time the issuing agent should insert validity dates on the Pass and also make seat/berth reservations for your entire itinerary. If no reservations are made, then Pass holder must have train conductor validate the pass *before start of first train trip.*

### *Palace On Wheels* Fares (Indian Rupees)

Lower berths, Luxury Cabins — Rs 2050

Four berth Luxury Cabins — Rs 1400 per lower, 1200 per upper (Rs 5200 total)

Two berth Compartment — Lower Rs 1400, upper 1200.

Single Supplement — Rs 2050.

### INDIA TOURIST OFFICES

New York 10020 — 30 Rockefeller Plaza
Chicago 60601 — 230 N. Michigan Ave.
Los Angeles 90010 — 3550 Wilshire Blvd.
Toronto — 1016 Royal Trust Tower, Dominion Center

### INDIA TRAVEL-FACTS

**Airport Exit Tax**—Rupees (Rs) 100 (about $8).

**Climate & Clothing**—October thru March best months; pleasant days, no rain. April to June is summer — and HOT. End of June to September is monsoon season, wettest and greenest period — but best time to visit Kashmir (no monsoons).

**Currency**—Foreign currency must be declared on arrival; no restrictions on amount. Keep exchange receipts to reconvert rupees on departure.

**Entry & Customs Regulations**—Passport plus tourist visa; latter requires one photo, costs about $1.50, is good for three months, extendable for another three. Collective visas issued for groups.

Cholera, typhoid innoculations not required but are advised for your protection.

On arrival, fill out Tourist Baggage Report Form so you can take out your cameras, radios, binoculars, jewelry, etc. If any are stolen or lost, obtain a police report; without that, you could pay 100% duty on the items. Gold, antiques, animal skins cannot be exported.

**Tipping**—Keep plenty of one and two rupee bills in your pocket (ask for them when changing money or buying things) for tipping whoever is helpful: one or two Rs per bag to porters, bellboys; Rs 5 to 10 maximum to waiters in good hotels, restaurants; Rs 2 to 5 for taxi drivers.

**Transportation**—Driving is to the left. City taxis, scooter rickshaws are metered — but always check first as to approximate fare.

**Water**—Use bottled only — or the purified water in good hotels/restaurants.

# TRAVEL SUPPLEMENT

**PHOTO CREDITS**

We are grateful to the following organizations for their cooperation in furnishing photos and diagrams for the pages listed below:

AMTRAK — 71, 72, 76, 77, 78
Australia Tourist Commission — Inside Front Cover; 95, 98, 99
British Rail — 5, 113
The Budd Company — 8
Thomas Cook — Negatives for 11, 53
Danish Tourist Board — 49
Disneyland — 79
French National Railroads — 58, 59, 60
German Federal Railways — 63
India Air Travels — 109
*International Railway Traveler* Newsletter — 64
Intraflug — 23
Japan National Tourist Organization — 103
New Zealand Gov't Tourist Commission — 101, 102
Norwegian National Tourist Office — 44
Queensland Gov't Tourist Bureau — 100
Society Expeditions & Wolfgang Kaehler — 1, 2, 22, 24, 25, 31, 110
Swiss National Tourist Office — 19, 38
Tourist Organization of Thailand — 108
Venice Simplon Orient-Express — 10, 28, 29
VIA Rail — Inside Back Cover; 80, 82



Another view of British Rail's *Advanced Passenger Train (APT).* Three pre-production prototypes have been built for passenger evaluation on the 400-mile route between London-Glasgow. APT is capable of taking curves 20% to 40% faster than conventional trains by tilting each car's body inward to maintain passenger comfort. It can operate now at speeds above 125 mph on existing tracks and within the capacity of current signalling.

Material on pages 126 & 127 come from *TRAVEL ANSWER BOOK,* a handy 4″ × 5½″ booklet containing 64 pages of vital travel information. Available at $1.50 postpaid from Travel Digests, 30695 Ganado Dr., Rancho Palos Verdes, Ca. 90274.

## RAIL TOUR OPERATORS

### Globetrotter Tours

P.O. Box 6145, Auckland, New Zealand

*Grand Tour of China, Mongolia, Soviet Union*

Hong Kong to London—$4300; to Copenhagen—$4230; to Helsinki—$3950.

*Grand Tour of USSR*

Tokyo to London — $2900.

*The Fast Track*

Hong Kong to London — $3200.

### Hemphill-Harris Travel Corp.

16000 Ventura Blvd., Encino, Ca. 91436
800-421-0454; 800-252-2103

*Palace On Wheels*—$2590 (plus airfare)

*Blue Train*

Eight different African tour programs, ranging from 20 to 44 days ($2990 to $6880 plus air), include the Johannesburg-Cape Town run. Departures from January thru October (not all tours depart every month).

*Indian-Pacific*

South Pacific Adventure tour (33 days) includes the Perth-Adelaide segment. $5060 plus air. Departures in February and October.

### *Highland Belle*

Charterbarge Ltd, Henbant, Crickhowell
Powys, Wales. United Kingdom

One Week Charter (6 passengers) — $14,880. Six nights from 1600 Wednesday to 1245 Tuesday.

Two week charter is $28,868.

**North American Agents:**

Autoventure, 920 Logan Bldg., Seattle 98101
800-426-7502

Frontiers International, Box 161, Wexford, Pa. 15090
800-245-1960

### Intraflug AG

Tagernstrasse 12a, CH-8127 Forch / ZH, Switzerland
01-980-1772

*Nostalgic Orient Express* Charters

Society Expeditions

Excalibur Ltd, Bournemouth, England, has a Paris-Istanbul trip October 2-6, 1985.

Tapis Rouge International, Paris, has a deluxe Paris-Monte Carlo-Paris trip March 7-12, 1985 for Monte Carlo's "Ball de la Rose."

For *Trans-Siberian Special,* Intraflug is skipping 1985 but plans one for September, 1986.

### Maupintour

1515 St. Andrews Drive, Lawrence, Ka. 66044

**Europe** (May-Sept. departures)
Prices do not include airfare.
*Britain by Rail*—17 days. $2128-$2148
*Grand Highlights by Train*—17 days. $2498-$2568
*Art of Paris & Southern France*—18 days; $2798
*Swiss Alpine Resorts*—15 days; $1898-$1978

**Africa** (Departures all year)
*Cape to Cairo*—24 or 29 days; $3458/3958
*Southern Africa*—22 days; $2948

**Canada** (May-Sept. departures)
*Trans-Canada by Train*—16 days; $2058, $1968

### Voyages of Discovery

737 Pearl St., La Jolla, Ca. 92037; 619-459-7250

*Round The World*

San Francisco/Return to L.A. — $2995 (w/o meals).
Short Version (from New York) — $1895 (w/o meals)

### Olson-Travelworld

5855 Green Valley Circle, Culver City, Ca. 90230
800-421-2255; 800-421-5785 Ca. Agents

*Famous Places & Famous Trains* — $2998 (plus air)

*Blue Train* African Tours:

"From The Blue Nile To The Blue Train," a 26-day program (Feb. to Dec.) — $3790.

"African Adventure" — $3690 (24 days), $4690 (31 days). Year 'round (except April, May).

"African Escapade" — $3295 (21 days), $4295 (28 days). Feb.-Dec.

Airfare not included in these prices.

### Osborne Travel

3379 Peachtree Rd. NE, Atlanta 30326

**Great Trains Series** (Land only)

*Eastern Europe* (16 days) — From $2,197 per person.

*Great Trains & Grand Hotels* (18 days) — From $3997.

*Northern Europe* (9 days) — Germany, France, Belgium and Holland; *Nord Express* to Paris, *Brabant* to Brussels. From $1367.

*Romantic Inns & Castles* (16 days) — Germany, Austria, Switzerland and France riding *Donau Kurier, Transalpin* and *Glacier Express* from Chur to Zermatt. From $2597.

### Society Expeditions

723 Broadway East, Seattle, Wa. 98102
800-426-7794; 206-324-9400 (Wa)

**Tour Tariffs***

*Nostalgic Orient Express*
Paris-Istanbul—$4990; Istanbul-Paris—$4490
Paris-Vienna (OW)—$1790; RT—$2390

*Trans-Siberian Special*—$2990

*Imperial Peking Express*—$3990

*India Palace On Wheels*—$3650

*Land arrangements only; airfare extra.

### Venice Simplon Orient-Express

One World Trade Center, Suite 2841, New York 10048.
800-223-1588; 212-661-4540 (NY State).

Sea Containers House, 20 Upper Ground, London SE1.
(01) 928-5837.

**Rates (per person / double occupancy):**

From London to: Venice—$770; Innsbruck—$650; Zurich—$550.

*Supplements:* Single Cabin—$150; Single in Double Cabin—$450. Southbound Stopover—$100.

*Daytime Sector Rates* (in Day Car): London-Paris or Zurich-Venice—$250; Zurich-Innsbruck or Innsbruck-Venice—$200. With cabin accommodation, $100 more.

Children 12 or under, 50% discount. During July & August, free travel for child under 12 in double cabin.

*Day Trip Rates* (in England): Canterbury, Hever Castle—$110 per person; Folkestone, Leeds Castle—$125; Bath / Bristol—$145; Beulieu (group booking only)—$135.

### Voyages Jules Verne

10 Glentworth St., London NW1, England (01-486-8751)

**North American Agents:**

Bayliss Int'l Journeys, 2392 Telegraph Ave., Berkeley, Ca. 94704
415-849-4333

Express International, P.O. Box A, Saltillo, Pa. 17253
800-458-3606

Great Journeys Ltd, 2 W. 45 St., New York 10036
800-223-5336; 212-719-4780 NY

Voyages of Discovery, 737 Pearl St., La Jolla, Ca. 92037
619-459-7250

**Tour Rates:**

*Cape to Cairo Express*—$5390; *Flying Scotsman*—$2500
*Central Kingdom Express*—$4320 ($5670 RTW)
*Indian-Pacific Railroad*—$6800; *Istanbul Train*—$2995
*Night Train From St. Petersburg*—$2450
*Patagonian Express*—$5300; *Raj Express*—$4170
*Red Arrow Express*—$3900 (RTW); *Tian an Men*—$3000
*Victoria Falls to Cape Express*—$3100

## OTHER TOUR OPERATORS WITH RAIL TOURS

Amity Tours, 1 First St., Los Altos, Ca. 94022
800-523-8406; 800-227-6928 Ca; 415-941-9275

Anniversary Tours, 250 W. 57 St., NY 10107
800-223-1336; 212-245-7501

Cartan Tours, One Crossroads of Commerce, Rolling Meadows, Il 60008. 800-323-7888

Challenger Tours, Box 8965, Trenton, NJ 08650
609-586-4664

Citizen Exchange Council, 18 E. 41 St., NY 10017 212-889-7960

Club Universe, 1671 Wilshire, Los Angeles 90017
800-431-0231; 800-252-0682 Ca

Crown Line Tours, 3300 S. Gessmer, Houston, Tx 77063
800-722-6737

Esplanade Tours, 38 Newbury St., Boston 02116
800-343-7184 (except Ma)

Exprinter International, 500 Fifth Ave., NY 10110 800-221-1666

Extra Value Travel — 437 Madison Ave., NY 10022 800-223-1980

General Tours, 711 Third Ave., NY 10017.
800-221-2216; 800-442-4200 NY
2029 Century Park East, Los Angeles 90067.
800-426-7136; 213-553-5222 Ca.

International Cruise Center, 185 Willis, Mineola, NY 11501.
800-221-3254; 516-747-8800

Osborne Travel, 3401 Northside Pkwy NW, Atlanta, Ga 30327.
800-241-2512 (ex Ga)

Rail Study Tours, 1401 Wilson Blvd, Arlington, Va. 22209
703-998-2362

Russian Travel Bureau, 20 E. 46 St., NY 10017.
800-847-1800; 212-986-1500.

Security Travel, 1625 Eye St. NW, Washington 20006.
800-424-8892; 206-324-9400

Smithsonian Associates Travel Program, A & I Smithsonian Institution, Washington 20560. 202-357-2477.

Tour Designs, 713 6th St. SW, Washington 20024
202-554-5820

Travcoa Travel, Box 2630, Newport Beach, Ca 92660.
800-854-7204; 800-432-8873 Ca.

Voyages of Discovery, 737 Pearl St., La Jolla, Ca. 92037
619-459-7250

---

## Eurail Ticket-Issuing Offices*
### U.S. & Canada

**French National Railroads**
New York 10020—610 Fifth Ave. (212-582-2110)
Miami 33134—2121 Ponce de Leon (305-445-8648)
Chicago 60603—11 E. Adams (312-427-8691)
Beverly Hills 90212—9465 Wilshire (213-272-7967)
San Francisco 94108—360 Post (415-982-1993)
Montreal H3A IR3—1500 Stanley (514-288-8255)
Vancouver B6C 1Tw—409 Granville (604-688-6707)

**Germanrail**
New York 10017—747 Third Ave. (212-308-3100)
Boston 02116—625 Statler Office Bldg. (617-542-0577)
Chicago 60603—104 S. Michigan (312-263-4423)
Houston 77002—1121 Walker (713-224-8781)
Santa Monica 90401—520 Broadway (213-394-0293)
Toronto M5R 2C3—1290 Bay (416-968-3272)

**Italian State Railways**
New York 10103—666 Fifth Ave. (212-397-2667)
Bensonville, Il 60106—765 Rt. 83 (312-860-1090)
Encino, Ca. 91436—1760 Ventura (818-783-7245)
Montreal H3A 1V4—2055 Peel (514-845-9101)
Toronto M4Y 1W4—13 Balmuto (416-927-7712)

**Swiss Federal Railways**
New York 10020-608 Fifth Ave. (212-757-5944)
Chicago 60603—104 S. Michigan (312-641-0050)
San Francisco 94108—250 Stockton (415-362-2260)

**Great Britain**
London W1V OBA—179 Picadilly (French Nat'l Railways)

**Individuals can purchase passes, EURAIL or those for individual countries, from local travel agents.*

## EUROPEAN RAIL PASSES & FARES

### *EURAILPASS* (First Class)
$210 (7 days*); $260 (15 days); $330 (21 days); $410 (Month); $560 (2 months); $680 (3 months).
*Sold only in conjunction with a land package.

### *EURAIL YOUTHPASS* (Second Class)
$290 (Month); $370 (2 months).

### *Austrian Network Pass* Fares (in Austrian Schillings)
**First Class**—2,160 (9 days); 2,940 (16 days); 4,560 (month)
**Second Class**—1,440, 1,960 and 3,100 respectively.
***Austria Ticket*** (Youth Pass) costs 950 (9 days), 1,350 (16 days) for second class travel, ages 6 to 26.

### *France Vacances* Fares
**First Class**—$170 (7 days); $220 (15 days); $345 (Month). Children (4 thru 11): $105, $135 and $205 respectively.
**Second Class**—$115 (7 days); $150 (15 days); $230 (Month). Children (4 thru 11): $70, $90, $130 respectively.

### Other French Passes
Sr. Citizen ***Carte Vermeil*** — Francs 61
***Carte Jeune, Carre Jeune*** — F120 each
***Carte Inter-Rail*** — F1250

TGV passengers traveling with either a EURAILPASS or France Vacances pass are eligible for 15% to 30% discounts on room rates in Frantel hotels in Besancon, Dijon, Lyon, Marseille, Montpelier and St. Etienne.

*Rail Your Way Thru France* is a joint program of French National Railroads and France Accueil hotel chain: seven days of unlimited rail travel and accommodations for six nights in family-run, two and three star hotels. Breakfast and dinner are included in these low-priced packages (some average less than $50 a day per person).

SNCF has also adopted the word Accueil, meaning service or welcome. It appears on information centers in stations served by TGV trains, and employees wear orange Accueil buttons.

Nor will you have difficulty finding a TGV station; those letters are prominently displayed on road signs near the stations.

### *GermanRail Tourist Card*
**First Class**—$165 (9 days); $215 (16 days).
**Second Class**—$120 (9 days); $155 (16 days).
Half fare for children 4-11.

A 4-day Card has been added at $100 (first class) and $70 (second class) for unlimited travel without supplements.

With a *GermanRail Tourist Card,* you're eligible for specially priced tour packages at Romantik Hotels (small inns, guest houses) or luxury Steingenberger Hotels.

---

## Other European Railroad Offices
### In U.S. & Canada

**Belgian National Railroads**
New York 10151—745 Fifth Ave. (212-758-8130)

**Brit Rail (Great Britain)**
New York 10017—630 Third Ave. (212-599-5400)
Chicago 60601—333 N. Michigan (312-263-1910)
Los Angeles 90014—510 W. 6th St. (213-626-5104)
Dallas 75258—World Trade Center (214-748-0860)
Toronto M5R 1A3—94 Cumberland (416-929-3332)
Vancouver V6C 1T2—409 Granville (604-683-6896)

**Netherlands Railways**
New York 10036—576 Fifth Ave. (212-223-8141)
San Francisco 94105—605 Market (415-543-6772)
Toronto M5H 2R2—327 Bay St. (416-363-1577)

**Austrian Federal Railways**
No offices in U.S. or Canada. *Network Pass* available in Austria and at Central Rail Stations in Frankfurt, Munich and Zurich. *Youth Pass* available only in Austria.

On December 7, 1935 the first German railway was opened between Nurnberg and the city of Furth six kilometers away, an event that marked a technological breakthrough for Europe.

To commemorate this and subsequent developments, 150 Years of Railways in Germany is being celebrated in Nurnberg from May 15 to August 18, 1985 with a mammoth exhibition in the 30,000 square meter Transport Museum, some weekend Parades of Locomotives. Railway of the Future can also be seen at Nurnberg-Ost station. At nearby Neuenmarkt-Wirsberg is the German Museum for Steam Locomotives.

Seven special day tours thru some of Bavaria's most scenic areas, featuring steam locomotives and vintage cars, are scheduled from mid-May thru September. First class fares range from DM30 to DM94, second class from DM24 to DM74; children ride for half fare and there are Family Fare discounts. Special trains with historical steam, diesel or electric locomotives are also available for groups/conventions.

## GREAT BRITAIN

### *Britrail Pass*

**First Class**—$155 (7 days), $230 (2 weeks), $290 (3 weeks), $335 (month).

**Economy**—$115, $175, $230 and $260 respectively.

**Youth**—$95, $150, $190, $225 respectively.

**Senior Citizen**—Economy fares but permits first class travel.

### *Britrail Sea Pass*

$26 OW, $52 RT to the Continent; $11 extra OW for Jetfoil. $38 OW, $76 RT to Ireland.

### *Triple Ticket*

$50 for an adult, $25 for child (5-15).

### *Scottish Highlands & Island Travelpass*

$68 for five days, $113 for 10. Valid March-October.

To determine if Britrail Pass is a money-saver for your itinerary, compare it to the following examples of Round Trip Rail Fares. To approximate one way fares, divide by two (actually, RTs are slightly less than double OWs).

| Between London And... | First Class | Economy Class |
|---|---|---|
| Bath | $ 50.00 | $ 33.00 |
| Brighton | 25.00 | 16.00 |
| Cambridge | 26.00 | 18.00 |
| Canterbury | 26.00 | 18.00 |
| Chester | 83.00 | 59.00 |
| Edinburgh | 154.00 | 107.00 |
| Glasgow | 145.00 | 99.00 |
| Inverness | 196.00 | 131.00 |
| Penzance | 139.00 | 93.00 |
| Plymouth | 102.00 | 68.00 |
| Stratford-Upon-Avon | 45.00 | 31.00 |
| York | 93.00 | 62.00 |

### Sleeping Car Fares

Britrail Pass holders can book a first class single compartment for as little as L5; second class compartments have been eliminated on night trains.

Without a Pass, sleeper accommodations include rail fare. As an example, a London-Glasgow twin compartment costs L36.50 per berth, or L55 for single berth compartment. During the day, a London-Edinburgh first class, airconditioned coach seat costs L17 one way.

### Holland *Rover Tickets*

Allow unlimited travel, including from/to ports and frontier crossing points. Passport photo or your passport number required. 7-day Rover costs florin (f)158 first class, f107 second.

3-day Rover: f116 and f77.50. Day Rover: f80 and f53.50.

There are, as well, *Teenager Rover* (ages 10 to 19) for unlimited travel in second class for four days (f40) and 4-day *Family Rover* (f200 first class, f140 second), both during the summer.

## ITALY

### *Italian Pass*

**First Class**—$114 (8 days); $139 (15 days); $166 (3 weeks); $202 (month).

**Second Class**—$72, $87, $102, $127 respectively.

Passes must be purchased outside Italy.

### *Biglietto Chilometrico* (Kilometric Ticket)

In US, costs $140 first class, $79 second class. Dur to devaluation of the lira versus the US dollar, best to purchase in Italy; passport needed.

### *Carta d'Argento* (Silver Card)

Sold only in Italy for equivalent of about $5. With it, senior citizens save 30% on regular rail fares.

## SCANDINAVIA

**Scandinavian Railpass** is valid for unlimited travel on the railways of Denmark, Finland, Norway and Sweden for 21 days at an approximate cost of $235 in first class and $155 in second.

Scandinavian Railpass is also valid for passage on certain ferry crossings in Denmark and allows a 50 percent reduction off the price of sailings between Denmark and Sweden, Denmark and Norway and Sweden and Finland.

The pass can be purchased at any railway station in Scandinavia.

**Danish Rail Pass.** Ticket entitles holder to one month's unlimited travel on Danish State Railways and domestic ferries. It is priced $170 for first class travel and $134 in second class. Children under 12 pay half price. Danish Rail Pass can be purchased at any railway station in Denmark.

**Danish Railways Group and Sr. Citizen Reductions.** Danish State Railways discounts fares for groups of three or more people traveling together and offers senior citizens over the age of 65 half-price tickets.

Travel is valid only during off-peak periods. Inquire at any railway station in Denmark.

**Finnrailpass.** Finnrailpasses are good for unlimited travel on all passenger trains in Finland for specified periods.

Eight-day tickets are priced $90 for first class train travel and $60 in second class; 15-day tickets cost $132 in first class and $88 in second class; 22-day tickets cost $177 for first class travel and $118 for second class travel.

Finnrailpass can be purchased at any train station in Finland or through Holiday Tours of America, 40 E. 49th Street, New York, N.Y. 10017.

**Finland Senior Citizen Rail Discounts.** Senior citizens' cards cost about $4, and entitle the holder to 50% off on any trip in Finland that's at least 47 miles one way. The card is not valid during weekends and certain holidays when a surcharge will be added.

**Group Rail Tickets.** Group tickets, available through Finnish State Railways, are valid for three or more people traveling together for a distance of at least 47 miles in Finland.

Tickets are valid for one-month's duration and travel must be on the same train in the same class.

Reductions are 20 percent for three people, 25 percent for 10 people, 30 percent for 25 people. A group of at least 10 students can receive a 30 percent discount.

**Finland Bus Senior Citizen Discounts.** A senior citizen card is available for $1 that entitles holders to a discount of 30% for a ride that must amount to at least 47 miles one way.

**Iceland Omnibus Passport.** Unlimited travel on any and all bus routes.

One-week ticket is priced at about $112, two-week ticket costs about $150, three-week ticket costs about $180 and a four-week ticket is priced at about $208.

Icelandair Offices in North America have additional information about Omnibus Passport.

**Full Circle Passport.** The holder of a Full Circle Passport is entitled to one full trip on the Ring Road completely around Iceland traveling in either direction from Reykjavik. There is no time limit. Tickets are priced at about $112 per person.

**Norwegian Bargain Rail Pass.** Two versions of this rail ticket can be purchased at any train station in Norway.

A one-way ticket valid for seven days and good for travel of up to 470 miles costs about $320. A one-way ticket valid for seven days unlimited travel is priced about $430.

Unlimited stopovers are allowed and the ticket is not valid during some peak travel and holiday periods.

**Norwegian Senior Citizen Rail Discounts.** The Norwegian State Railways allow a 50 percent discount on any train travel in the country for visitors over age 67. Tickets are available at all railway stations in Norway.

**One Way Fares From Oslo* To**

Andalsnes — $68, $45 (1st, 2nd class)
Bergen — $69, $46
Copenhagen — $74, $38; Stockholm — $61, $39

***RT is double OW fare.**

**Swedish Railways Reduced Rate Card.** This discount card entitles the holder to a 40 percent reduction on all rail fares in Sweden for a period of 12 months. It is priced $23 for first class travel, and $14 for second class travel. The card can be purchased at any railway station in Sweden. Prices approximate.

**Swedish Railway Family Reductions.** Three or more family members traveling together by rail receive a 45 percent reduction on fares with this reduced rate card. Chilldren's fares are also offered.

Tickets are available at railway stations in Sweden or from Swedish travel agents.

**Swedish Railways Senior Citizens Reductions.** Senior citizens over age 65 receive a 45 percent reduction on all rail travel in Sweden.

Swedish State Railways (SJ) operates an all first class *City Express* Mondays thru Thursdays between Stockholm and Goeteborg with two daily morning and evening runs in each direction — 300 miles in four hours.

Trains have comfortable, refurbished, 1960s cars with compartments and, in club cars, plush armchairs. For business meetings, half of one coach has a conference room (with audio-visual equipment, tables and chairs) that rents for about $300. For larger meetings, five conference cars are available.

Breakfast and afternoon coffee are included in the round trip fare of about $100 (versus RT air of about $130). There's on board telephone service, attractive hostesses, bar-equipped diner. Dinner costs extra but, it's said, well worth it for gourmet type meals planned by some of Sweden's famous chefs. Credit cards are accepted.

*City Express* proved so successful that it was added to the Stockholm-Karlstadt route.

## PORTUGAL

### Special Fares

*Kilometric Ticket* — Permits Express train travel (3,000 km) for three months. Costs Escudos 12,020 first class and 8,020 second.
*Tourist Ticket* — Unlimited travel in first or second class. Costs E4,585 (written 4.585$00) for 7 days; 7,320 for 14; 10,455 for 21.
*Family Ticket* — Minimum of three persons for trips of 150 km or more. Full fare for one adult, half fare for others; one-fourth fare for children 4-11.
*Group Ticket* — Minimum of 10 persons for trips of 100 km or more. 20% off first or second class fares. One person free for groups of 15 to 50.
*Senior Citizen* — 50% discount on regular fares.

Super-Express trains *Douro, Miragaia* and *Tejo* run one-stop between Lisbon and Oporto in three hours. First class only; El,730 OW; additional E340 for seat in lounge car with bar service.

*Rapido Sotavento* connects Lisbon with the Algarve. Takes 3:55 to Faro; costs E1450.

Electric trains run between Lisbon and Estoril or Sintra, both in 25 minutes.

*Lisbon Express* leaves at 0730, arrives Madrid at 1838. One way first class fare, E2847; second, E2037.

*Lusitania Express,* with first class, airconditioned sleepers, leaves at 2100, arrives Madrid 0900 next morning. First class fare is E2609 plus 1001 per person for double compartment, or 2502 for single.

*Note:* We're told that 1985 fares in both Portugal and Spain may be as much as 30% lower than previously quoted ones.

## SPAIN

### *Transcantabrico* 7-Day Trip

68,900 pesetas (about $400 @ P170 to US $) per person; supplement for one person to a compartment (instead of two), P15,000. Fare is all-inclusive except for two meals, coffee and drinks.

For reservations, additional information: Marsans International, 3325 Wilshire Blvd., Los Angeles 90010 (800-525-5515). Or FEVA, General Rodrigo 6, Madrid 3, Spain.

### Special Fares

***Chequetren*** — By purchasing these discount tickets (which can be used by up to six persons) for 17,000 or 21,250 pesetas, you get a "passbook" worth 20,000 or 25,000 pesetas which can be used to buy first or second class fares, sleeping accommodations, reservation fees, supplements. There are no time or distance limits as long as the book is used in Spain over RENFE (Spanish National Railways) routes.
***Blue Days*** — There are 305 Dias Azules a year on which the following discounts apply: 25% off round trip fares of more than 100 km in each direction; 20-30% discounts for groups of more than 10; family discounts whereby one member pays full fare, rest of family 50% upon presentation of *Tarjeta Familiar* (Family Card) which costs 50 pesetas (with proof that all members live in same residence).

Seniors, 65 and over, get 50% off regular fares on Blue Days upon presentation of Gold Card (obtainable for 25 pesetas at any RENFE office).
***Children's Fares*** — Those under three ride free (but no seat); those from 3 to 7 (4 to 10 with international ticket) half fare with seat; over 7 (12 with international ticket) full fare.

Seat reservations can be made up to 60 days in advance at a charge of 30 pesetas.

## SWITZERLAND

### Swiss Holiday Cards

Good for *unlimited* travel in Switzerland by rail, lake steamer and about 180 postal bus lines. Also entitles you to reductions of up to 50% on private mountain railroads and cable cars. Anyone living outside Switzerland / Liechenstein may purchase Holiday Cards at Swiss Federal Railways offices in foreign countries *or upon arrival at Zurich and Geneva airports.* No passport photo needed. Your passport number and name are entered on the Holiday Card which is validated at a Swiss rail station on your initial day of travel. Here's what it costs:

1st Class: 4-day—$94; 8-day—$109; 15-day—$131; Month—$183.
2nd Class: 4-day—$63; 8-day—$74; 15-day—$90; Month—$124
Children 6-16, half fare; those under six, free.

### Half-Fare Travel Cards

Entitle you to 50% reduction on one way or round trip tickets purchased in Switzerland for railroads, lake steamers and postal buses. Must be purchased *before* your arrival in Switzerlland. Costs $24 for 15 days, $31 for 30 days. 30-day Junior Half-Fare costs $16.

Women 62 and over, men 65 or older may purchase Senior Half Fare Travel Cards, good for one year, for $55. Senior Card also entitles holder to reduced hotel rates at participating hotels.

### Supplemental Travel Cards

Holders of Half Fare and Sr. Half Fare Travel Cards can purchase (in Switzerland) Supplemental Cards entitling them to unlimited travel on days of their choice over much of the rail system.

If you're going to be in one or two of the following regions, it might pay to purchase a *Holiday Season Ticket* good for discounted excursions within the regions. Rates (in Swiss Francs) range from 38 to 106 for each of these regions: Bernese Mittelland, Bernese Oberland, Chablai, Grisons, Lake Lucerne, Locarno/Ascona, Lugano, Montreux/Vevey, Sarganserland/Walensee. Vouchers, exchangeable in Switzerland for these Season Tickets (1st or 2nd Class for varying number of days) can be purchased outside of Switzerland, or the Tickets themselves at any Swiss Railways station.

For those with limited time in Switzerland, there are day excursion fares from major cities/resorts; Zurich, for example, is an excellent base for round trip day excursions to Luzern, Basel, St. Moritz and other Swiss highlights.

#### *Glacier Express* One Way Fares

St. Moritz-Zermatt — $61, $39 (1st, 2nd class)
Chur-Brig — $40, $25; Andermatt-Brig — $17, $11
Brig-Zermatt — $21, $13; Brig-St. Moritz — $54, $35
Brig-Basel — $36, $23; Brig-Bern — $26, $17
Brig-Zurich — $39, $25; Zurich-Zermatt — $58, $37

### *Gotthard Pullman Express*

If you're not taking one of the Orient Express Great Rail Trips, here's a chance to sample them on the cheap — by riding one of Intraflug's authentic 1930s Pullman lounge cars. We did from Lugano to Goschenen, enjoyed the luxury of the ride and the bar service of a smartly uniformed attendant.

The Pullman car is attached to the daily train from Basel (at 0700)-Lucerne (0824)-Goschenen-Lugano (1126) to Chiasso (1155) at the Swiss-Italian border. Leaves there at 1459, arrives Basel at 1954. You can, of course, ride one way or round trip, board or disembark at any scheduled stop (including Airolo for our recommended bus ride across St. Gotthard Pass).

First class ticket (or pass) plus supplement of SF20 OW buys this bit of nostalgia at any Swiss Railways station. However, at press time, Intraflug had not finalized 1985 plans — so be sure to check this out.

Ideal for day trips are airconditioned *Panoramawagens* (double decker, vista dome cars) attached to these regularly scheduled trains:

*Gotthard-Panorama* — Lv. Zurich at 0904, ar. Lugano 1210 and Chiasso 1236. Lvs. at 1811 and 1836 for 2150 arrival in Zurich.

*Lotschberg-Panorama* — Lv. Zurich at 0725 for Brig; change there to BVZ narrow gauge for 1245 arrival in Zermatt; lv. latter at 1510, ar. Zurich 2029. For those with little time, a great way to see a segment of Glacier Express route. But if that isn't intriguing, you can continue on the Panorama to Domodossola and Locarno (1348 arrival), lv. at 1831 and be back in Zurich at 2150.

Passengers holding first class tickets (or passes) pay these Panorama surcharges: Bar Section, SF10; Dome Section (no smoking), SF15. Second class ticket holders pay SF15 and 25 respectively.

Make reservations thru Swiss Railways offices or direct to Reiseburo Mittelthergau, CH-8570 Weinfelden, Switzerland (072-22-46-77).

### USSR FARES (In Rbls. per person)

#### Trans-Siberian Train

Moscow-Khabarovsk-Nakhodka—184.50 first class; 139.50 second.
Moscow-Irkutsk-Khabarovsk-Nakhodka—191.40 or 144.80.

Train-plane combinations on this route are 10% to 18% less.

Deluxe A or B cabins on Nakhodka-Yokohama ships 325 and 280 respectively per person; 745 and 560 to Hong Kong.

#### Trans-Siberian *Rossiya* Schedules

**Moscow to Nakhodka** — Leave by Train #2 at 1000 Moscow Time. Arrive Novosibirsk, Day 3, at 1545 (1945 local time). On Day 5, arrive Irkutsk at 0100 (0600 local time). Arrive Khabarovsk at 1740 (0040 of Day 8, local time). Lv. by Train #4 at 1125 (1825 local time) to arrive Nakhodka at 0240 (0940 local time of Day 9).

**Nakhodka to Moscow** — Train #3 lvs. at 1300 (local 2000) to arrive next day in Khabarovsk at 0410 (1110 local). Train #1 lvs. at 0640 (1340) arrives Irkutsk at 0012 (local 0512) on Day 5; Novosibirsk at 0938 (1338) on Day 6; Moscow at 1505 on Day 8.

#### Intourist Offices

New York 10111—630 Fifth Ave. 212-757-3884
Montreal H3A 2A5—2020 University Ave. 514-849-6394

---

### SAMPLE ONE WAY RAIL FARES* (1st/2nd Class)

**Paris to:** Amsterdam—$64/$43; Athens—$238/$154; Basel—$58/$39; Berlin—$128/$86; Brussels—$35/$24; Budapest—$165/$110; Copenhagen—$160/$107; Frankfort—$74/$49; Geneva—$66/$44; Innsbruck—$106/$71; Istanbul—$233/$151; Luzern—$75/$50; Madrid—$134/$93; Lausanne—$60/$40; Munich—$110/$73; Rome (via Milan)—$138/$86; Salzburg (via Switzerland)—$126/$89; Stockholm—$214/$141; Venice (via Germany)—$114/$73; Vienna (via Germany)—$109/$70; Zagreb—$144/$92; Zurich—$73/$49.

**London to:** Amsterdam $67/$50; Dublin (via Liverpool)—$86/$70; Paris—$74/$57, or $65/$54 via Dieppe.

**Rome to:** Amsterdam—$194/$123; Barcelona—$129/$82; Basel—$91/$54; Brussels—$156/$98; Copenhagen—$246/$157; Frankfurt—$136/$83; Geneva—$87/$51; Munich—$77/$46; Venice—$40/$22; Vienna—$89/$53; Zurich—$87/$51.

**Vienna to:** Amsterdam—$159/$108; Athens—$132/$89; Basel—$85/$57; Belgrade—$63/$43; Berlin—$71/$47; Brussels—$134/$90; Bucharest—$82/$55; Budapest—$26/$18; Copenhagen—$179/$120; Frankfurt—$83/$56; Hamburg—$133/$89; Istanbul—$127/$86; Munich—$47/$32; Warsaw—$58/$40; Zurich—$74/$50.

*Note:* On longer trips, such as Paris to Vienna or Rome, sleeper supplements, single or double occupancy, cost about the same as first class hotel accommodations for one or two persons.

Individual seat reservations on certain express trains can be made up to two months in advance for a fee of $2. Supplements for TEE/IC and some other express trains include the fee.

Group reservation fee is $1 per person (adult or child) OW, $2 for RT or circle tour. Full passenger list must be submitted to issuing office not later than four weeks prior to first day of travel.

First class supplements on TEE trains run from $2 to $21 (highest in Italy) with average around $7 or $8 (depending on distance traveled). On IC trains, first class supplements cost $2 to $8, second class $2 to $5.

Sleeping car supplement for a single compartment is the most expensive — about 15% more than the combined supplement for two in a double compartment, while a Special is about 15% less than a double. Second class tourist supplement is about one-third less than first class double. Of course, cost for all of these is dependent on distance traveled. On Spanish trains (RENFE), supplements for airconditioned cars are higher.

On Cross-Channel ferries with cabin accommodations, there are also supplementary fees with night service about twice as much as daytime crossings for same types of cabins.

---

## SOUTH AMERICA

#### PERU Train Packages*

**Cuzco-Machu Picchu** — About $55. Includes round trip train, transfers, admission to ruins and box lunch.
**Cuzco-Puno** — About $19 for coach seat, $27 for buffet car seat.
**Puno-La Paz** — About $133 by hydrofoil; by catamaran, $70.

***Obtainable thru Lima tour operators.**

## NORTH AMERICA

### AMTRAK FARES

#### *All Aboard America*

$150 for one region, $250 for two, $325 for three.

#### *One Way Coach*

Oakland to Chicago — $238
Oakland to New York — $365

Comparing these, it's obvious that *All Aboard America* is the best buy between Oakland-New York (even traveling just one way), whereas the one way fare to Chicago is $12 cheaper (if not doing a round trip).

#### *Sleeping Car Supplements*

Oakland to Chicago — $125 per person for Economy Bedroom; $354 for Deluxe Bedroom (one or two persons).

Chicago to New York — $32.50 for single Slumbercoach, $56 for double. $102 for Roomette and $187 for Bedroom (one or two persons).

#### Amtrak Reservations

400 N. Capitol St. NW, Washington 20001
800-872-7245 Cont'l U.S.; 800-523-5731 Maine
800-263-8130 Ontario, Quebec
800-263-8170 Balance of Canada

### VIA FARES

The basic standard fare permits travel in regular day coaches with supplements payable for all other accommodations. Vancouver to Montreal (and vice-versa): Basic—$123; Bedroom—$217; Roomette (one person)—$99; Section (lower/upper)—$114; Dayniter (per person)—$23. Those are Canadian dollar fares. They are slightly lower between January 4 and May 31 (except over Easter) and between October 1 and December 15.

*CANRAILPASSES* — Unlimited travel within various geographical areas for designated number of days (from 8 to 30). For example, you can travel anywhere in Canada during the high seasons for $435, or $110 from Edmonton-Calgary west for eight days. *Senior Citizen* (60 and over) discount of 33% is available on basic fares (but *not* on supplements).

### Mexican Rail Tour Operators

Following operators offer a number of departures for what we consider to be well-planned tours of varying types to various parts of Mexico. Finlay uses private Pullmans to insure good accommodations and food. Others specialize in rail car transportation of cars and recreational vehicles.

Consisting of everything from weekends to trips of 24 days, they range in price from $15 a day per person on up — even way up. Price depends on distance, number of included meals, extent of inclusive sightseeing trips, types of accommodations. Evaluate carefully and compare before choosing the tour that most appeals to you.

Basic tour is down the west coast of Mexico from Mexicali or Nogales to Mazatlan/Guadalajara/Mexico City and on to the Land of the Mayas. Many include Copper Canyon — or simply Copper Canyon only.

Baja Adventures — 10100 Santa Monica Blvd., Los Angeles 90067 800-421-0454; 800-252-2103 Ca.
Barney Thompson — Box 3422, San Ysidro 92073
Caravanas de Mexico — 3801 N. Piedras, El Paso 79930
Finlay Fun-Tours, 11306 Burbank, No. Hollywood, Ca. 91601
Don Quixote World Travel — 100 N. Stone, Tucson 85701
Simpatico Tours — Box 642, Northridge, Ca 91325
Town & Country Tours, Box 32307, Phoenix 85064 800-528-0421; 800-352-6509 Az (ex Phoenix)

### Where To Make Reservations

Two travel agents handle train reservations for a fee:
Orozco Travel — 202 S. Broadway, Los Angeles 90054 (213-262-2291)
The Travel Co. — 33 N. Stone, Tucson 85704 (602-624-5586)

Reservations by mail should be directed to:

Mexicali — Sr.Jose M. Salgado, Traffic Superintendent, Sonora-Baja California RR, P.O. Box 182, Mexicali, BC., Mexico. Phone 2-6175 or 2-8502 before 3 pm (1:30 pm on Sat.). Also Box 231, Calexico, Ca. In Mexico City, Navarra 210 (phone 530-0936).
Nogales — Sr. Francisco Hernandez, Ticket Agent, Pacific Railroad, Calle Internacional 10, Nogales, Son., Mexico.
Nuevo Laredo — Sra. G.C. de Lopez, Foreign Agent, National Railways of Mexico, Box 595, Laredo, Tx 78040.
Mexico City to U.S. or Other Destinations — Sr. Raul Holguin Lopez, Chief Passenger Traffic Dept., Buenavista Grand Central Station, Mexico 3, D.F.
Ciudad Juarez — Sr. A. Barrazas, Foreign Representative, National Railways of Mexico, Box 2200, El Paso, Tx.

## SOUTH PACIFIC

### AUSTRALIA

#### *Austrailpass* Fares (in Australian $)

14 days—$A320; 21 days—$A400; Month—$A510;
2 months—$A710; 3 months—$A820.

Berths and meals on all trains cost extra. From Sydney to Perth on *Indian-Pacific,* berth costs $A66, meals $A71.50. From Sydney to Alice Springs, meals are $A49.50, berth $A40.

#### *Budget Austrailpass* Fares

14 days—$A230; 21 days—$A290; Month—$A370;
2 months—$A520; 3 months $A600.

Economy berths available on *Indian-Pacific* (once weekly), *Trans-Australia* and *Ghan* at $A18 per night. Meal charges obligatory.

#### One Way Fares From SIDNEY To*

Alice Springs on *The Alice* — $311.50
Perth on *Indian-Pacific* — $451.50 (via Broken Hill)

***In Australian dollars. Include sleeping berths, meals.**

| Major Rail Services | ADULT FC** | ADULT EC | 4 yrs to under 16 yrs FC** | 4 yrs to under 16 yrs EC |
|---|---|---|---|---|
| Sydney-Melbourne | $A 75.00 | $A 53.00 | $A 37.50 | $A 26.50 |
| Sydney-Brisbane | 75.00 | 53.00 | 37.50 | 26.50 |
| Sydney-Murwillumbah (Gold Coast) | *** 50.50 | 36.00 | *** 25.25 | 18.00 |
| Sydney-Adelaide (via Broken Hill) | #0 159.50 | 93.00 | #0 94.00 | 46.50 |
| Sydney-Adelaide (via Melbourne) | 134.00 | 95.00 | 67.00 | 47.50 |
| Sydney-Alice Springs (via Broken Hill) | ## 311.50 | — | ## 200.50 | — |
| Sydney-Perth (via Broken Hill) | ## 451.50 | ## 348.50 | ## 294.50 | ## 237.00 |
| Brisbane-Cairns (1 night berth, a.m. dep.) | + 102.80 | + 68.50 | + 51.40 | + 34.25 |
| Brisbane-Cairns (2 night berth, p.m. dep.) | + 102.80 | + 68.50 | + 51.40 | + 34.25 |
| Melbourne-Mildura | ++ 37.50 | 27.50 | ++ 18.75 | 13.75 |
| Melbourne-Adelaide | † 59.00 | 42.00 | † 29.50 | 21.00 |
| Melbourne-Perth | ## 378.00 | ## 270.00 | ## 244.00 | ## 174.50 |
| Adelaide-Alice Springs | ## 182.00 | ## 131.00 | ## 111.50 | ## 84.00 |
| Adelaide-Perth | ## 296.00 | ## 228.00 | ## 191.50 | ## 153.50 |
| Kalgoorlie-Perth | / 40.10 | — | / 23.30 | — |

** First Class (FC) berths cost $A20 per night unless otherwise indicated.

*** Berth costs $A30. # Berth costs $A22.

† Berth costs $A23. 0 Meals included.

## Berth, meals included. ++ FC berth costs $A17.

+ Berths cost $A16 FC, $A8 EC for each additional night.

/ One class travel only; one meal included.

*Note:* Economy seats available on services between Adelaide-Perth, Adelaide-Alice Springs for lower fare (meals, berth *not* included).

**All prices subject to revision by mid-1985.**

### Railways of Australia Offices

Glendale, Ca. 91205—Tour Pacific / Australia, 116 S. Louise 818-247-4564

Toronto M5H 1P6—Thomas Cook, 111 Avenue Rd.

Peterborough, England PE3 65B—Thomas Cook, 22 Broadway, Thorpe Wood.

Frankfort 6000, Germany—Tourland Reisen, Broennerstrasse 11

Copenhagen 2200, Denmark—Hans Kristensen Travel, 56AA Boulevard

Tokyo 100—Japan Travel Bureau, 6-4 Marunouchi 1 Chome, Chiyoda-ku.

Wellington, NZ—New Zealand Railways.

## NEW ZEALAND

### New Zealand Railways Travelpass

**(Priced in New Zealand Dollars)**

8-day Pass — $120 (Feb. 1-Dec. 14)*
$180 (Dec. 15-Jan. 31)*

15-day Pass — $180 (Feb. 1-Dec. 14)
$240 (Dec. 15-Jan. 31)*

22-day Pass — $240 (Feb. 1-Dec. 14)
$320 (Dec. 15-Jan. 31)*

*Must be purchased outside New Zealand. Other periods can be bought at any NZ Railway Station or New Zealand Toursit Office.

Six extra days per pass may be purchased for $15 or $20 per day. Passes may be purchased in pairs; however, first date of travel must be given at time of purchase (no open dating) and it's advisable to make seat reservation at same time as Pass *does not* guarantee a seat at any time.

Passes can be bought abroad thru any travel agency; New Zealand Tourist Office will assist the agency. You receive a voucher; actual Pass is issued in Auckland or Christchurch upon your arrival. It's valid on all New Zealand Railway trains, buses and Cook Strait ferries (but not for berths).

### New Zealand Tourist Offices

Los Angeles 90024 — 10960 Wilshire Blvd. (213-477-8241)

New York 10020 — 630 Fifth Ave. (212-586-0060)

San Francisco 94111 — One Maritime Plaza (415-788-7404)

Vancouver BCV7 Y1B6 — 701 W. Georgia (210-455-186)

London SW1 Y4TQ — New Zealand House, Haymarket (01-930-8422)

Frankfurt / Main 6000 — Kaiserhofstrasse 7 (0611-288-189)

## JAPAN

### Japan Rail Pass

Good for unlimited travel on Japanese National Railways system (also certain buses, ferryboats), Rail Passes are valid for 7, 14 or 21 days at a cost of Yen 25,000, 41,000 or 53,000 respectively for ordinary (standard)[1] car seating, Y35,000, 58,000 or 76,000 for Green car seating. For comparison: ordinary RT Tokyo-Kyoto costs Y23,000 (about $92) on the bullet train.

Rail Pass Vouchers are sold in North America by Japan Air Lines or their agents (if traveling via JAL) or by the following: Japan Travel Bureau Int'l, 624 S. Grand, Los Angeles 90017; 5000 Birch St., Newport Beach, Ca. 92660; 360 Post St., S.F. 94108; 45 Rockefeller Plaza, N.Y. 10020. Nippon Travel Agency Pacific, 611 W. 6th St., L.A. 90017; 551 Fifth Ave., N.Y. 10176.

Dollar prices are calculated at time of voucher purchase based on current exchange rate. Vouchers can be exchanged for actual Rail Passes at National Railways ticket counters at Narita International Airport and 12 city locations, including Tokyo, Osaka and Kyoto.

One-way super-express fares out of Tokyo are not inexpensive — particularly so when returning to Tokyo (there are no reduced RT fares). Standard class fare to Kyoto is Yll,800; Green Car fare is Y17,200. Fares to Osaka and Hakata are Y12,200 and Y19,400 respectively; Y5,400 and Y7,800 more for Green Car. Domestic air fares from Tokyo to Fukuoka (Hakata) and Osaka are about the same as Green Car fares.

[1] Once purchased, an ordinary pass cannot be upgraded to Green. Should you wish to travel in a Green car, you must pay the difference between the two fares based on a one way ticket.



## GENERAL TRAVEL INFORMATION (Alphabetically by Countries)

## AUSTRALIA

### AUSTRALIAN TRAVEL-FACTS

**Bank Hours**—M-Th 10 am to 3 pm; F 10-5.
**Beauty Shops**—Called Hairdressing Salons. Closed Sat afternoon. Department stores more reasonable than hotels.
**Climate/Clothing**—Weather varies mainly north to south. From Brisbane and Alice Springs north, progressively warmer, more tropical. Cairns has average maximums of 89° in summer, 79° during winter (June, July, Aug.), minimums of 74° and 62°. Brisbane will be about 10% cooler. There are summer rains. Dress is very casual, lightweight; men wear bermuda shorts, long socks almost entirely — sports coats never. Anything but shorts okay for women's street wear. Not particularly buggy, though flies can be a problem in some spots during hot weather.
**Credit Cards** —All major cards accepted.
**Currency**—Banknotes in denominations of $1, $2, $5, $10, $20 and $50. Coins are 1¢, 2¢, 5¢, 10¢, 20¢ and 50¢. US dollar travel checks bring best exchange rate.
**Drive**—On left side; walk likewise (on sidewalks, too).
**Electricity**—220/240v, 50c; 3-prong plugs. All tourist hotels/motels in cities/resorts have built-in 110v razor converters except Cairns, Great Barrier Reef.
**Entrance Requirements**—Valid passport. Visa (free) required for U.S. and Canadian nationals; good for multiple entry (up to 6 months) for 48 months. Visa not required for stays up to 72 hrs. providing departure is from airport of entry.
**Film**—Readily available, expensive.
**Gambling**—Wrest Point Casino, Hobart, Tas; Alice Springs, Darwin. Legal lotteries, horse racing — both BIG. Slot machines in private clubs in N.S. Wales.
**Medical Facilities**—Australian Medical Assoc. has list of doctors, or consult your hotel. Many chemists (Pharmacies) open 24 hrs.
**Office Hours**—9 am-5 pm. Airline offices (some others) open Sat. 'til noon.
**Phones**—Local 10¢.
**Postal Rates**—Airmail to N.A. 50¢; postcard 30¢. Domestic letters 22¢.
**Taxis**—Metered. Additional charge if phoned for; none for additional passengers. Hail in streets or at public stands.
**Tipping**—Not done at all in most of the country. In Sydney and Melbourne, hotel porters, waiters and wine stewards in better hotels/restaurants are tipped (not over 10%) for good service only. Elsewhere, even in deluxe places, we were advised by Australians to keep our hand out of our pocket, particularly airport porters, taxi drivers, hairdressers — no tipping whatsoever.
**Water**—Pure.

## SOUTH AFRICA FARES

### The Blue Train

Johannesburg-Capetown (OW, per person):
Type A—$570; Type B—$420; Type C—$370; Type D—$315.

### Drakensberg Express

Johannesburg-Durban (OW, per person): $105.

If you want to 'sample' the *Blue Train,* South African Railways has a package (about $23) that tours Johannesburg in the morning, boards the train enroute for Pretoria for a light lunch, tours Pretoria and returns to Jo'burg by bus.

## EGYPTIAN FARES*

First class rail/sleeper fare to Luxor is L52.70 one way, to Aswan the same; second class is L30.70. First class coach fare Cairo to Luxor is L9+, to Aswan L11.5; second class is L5 and L6.10 respectively.

***In Egyptian Pounds (L), about on a par with US dollar.**

## ECUADOR TRAVEL-FACTS

**Bank Hours**—9-1:30 Monday thru Friday.

**Climate & Clothing**—Quito and the Central Valley, high astride the equator, have an equitable, Spring-like year 'round climate with cool evenings. Daytime temperatures average 70°, 50° or so at night. July to October are the dry months; rest of year showers and rain usually occur in afternoons for short periods. Always carry a raincoat then. A wool suit, dress and coat are needed as well as lighter clothing — sun can be delightfully warm and penetrating.

**Currency**—Monetary unit is the Sucre (S/), divided into 100 cents. Bills come in denominations of 5, 10, 20, 50, 100, 500 and 1000 sucres; don't bother with coins (largest is S/1). Money and travel checks are readily exchangeable at banks, cambios and hotels.

**Current**—110v AC.

**Entry Requirements**—Passport or proof of nationality, onward or return ticket. Minors under 19 traveling alone and with passport must have visaed authorization for travel signed by both parents.

No currency restriction. 300 cigarettes, a bottle of liquor can be brought in duty free.

**Gambling**—Quito has three nice casinos (open all night) in Hotels Colon, Quito and Humboldt. There are casinos in Guayaquil, Cuenca and Salinas. Parimutuel betting on horse racing.

**Shopping**—Colorful, interesting native handcrafts in markets, villages and city shops—possibly the best, most varied in South America: handcrafted rugs, handwoven cloth, wool blankets, ponchos, shawls, wall hangings; woven willow and straw baskets, place mats and coasters; charming costumes, dolls and balsa boats; leather goods, handcarved statues and masks; Indian beadwork, bows and arrows. "Panama" hats have always been woven in Ecuador of fine toquilla straw (Montecristi a top brand).

Silver jewelry and tableware, copper and brass ware range from inexpensive to expensive and excellent. Candles for religious fetes/processions are highly decorative, as are the many "bread dolls."

Ecuadorian modern art, both paintings and sculptures, is still an outstanding buy compared to the world market.

## ENGLAND TRAVEL-FACTS

**American Embassy** — Grosvenor Square, London W1A 1AE (499-8000).

**Banks** — Open M thru F 9:30 am to 3:30 pm; closed Sat., Sun. and public holidays. There are independent Bureaux de Change, exchange desks at hotels (for their guests), department stores and larger travel agencies. Heathrow and Gatwick airports have 24-hour banks; airport Green Line buses are allowed to exchange foreign currency for approximate amount of fare.

**Credit Cards** — Access (MasterCard) and Barclay (Visa) are universally accepted (including many gas stations), as are American Express and Diner's.

**Currency** — Based on the pound sterling (L) and divided into 100 pence (p). Prices may be written L7.70 or 770p, meaning 7 pounds 70 pence or 770 pence. Notes are in denominations of L1, 5, 10, 20 and 50; coins (pence) are ½, 1, 2, 5, 10, 50 and L1.

**Changing The Guard** — At Buckingham Palace daily at 11:30 am during summer, every other day in winter. Also at Horseguards Parade, 11 am M thru Sat., 10 am Sundays.

**Electric Current** — 240v AC thruout Britain.

**Emergencies** — Dial 999 for police, firemen and ambulance. In case of illness, National Health Service allows you to register with a General Practitioner as a temporary patient. Call Family Practioner Committee; in London, 723-3400.

**Entry Requirements** — Valid passport (no visa) for U.S., Canadian citizens. Landing card must be filled out and presented to passport control officer.

**Film** — Readily available though more expensive than at home. There are fast processing services.

**Hair Dressers (Beauty Shops)** — Generally their services are less expensive than at home (at least in Calif.). In summer of '84, paid as little as L2.30 for wash and set, L6.80 for touch-up, wash and set, L8.50 for wash, set, cut and conditioner at various times. A tip is expected.

**Liquor Licensing Laws** — In Central London, bars open from 11 am to 3 pm, 5:30 to 11 pm M-Sat; noon to 2 pm, 7-10 pm Sun. In Greater London and the Counties: 10:30 am-2:30 pm, 5:30-10:30 pm M-Th; to 11 pm on F & Sat; noon to 2 pm, 7-10:30 pm Sun. Guests in licensed hotels can buy drinks at any time.

**Post Offices** — Open from 9 to 5:30 M-F, to 12:30 or 1 pm on Sat. for mail, telegram and telephone services. Put letters in the Posting Box, inside or out. In London, branch at Trafalgar Square is open late at night, Sundays and Bank Holidays.

**Public Holidays** (England, Wales) — Jan. 1, Good Friday, Easter Monday, May Day, Springs Bank Holiday, Late Summer Holiday, Christmas and Boxing Day (Dec. 27). In Scotland, Jan. 1 and 2; other holidays are local.

**Shopping** — Most top stores participate in the retail export scheme which permits foreigners to receive from them a rebate of the 15% Value Added Tax (VAT) charged on all sales (VAT also applies to services, accommodations and meals but without rebate). There are two ways to go: 1) Mail the merchandise to your home, in which case VAT is deducted immediately but a shipping charge added. 2) Take merchandise with you, in which case the store completes an export form that you present, *with merchandise,* at a special counter at departure ferry dock or airport; when okayed by Customs, a copy of the form is mailed to the seller who then mails you a rebate for the amount of VAT. Transactions may take several months to complete.

**Shopping Hours** — London stores open at 9/9:30, close at 6 pm except on Thursdays when closing is 7:30/8. Hours are much the same in the rest of England except stores do not stay open later on Thursdays, may be closed one afternoon each week. All stores stay open thru the lunch hour, are closed on Sundays.

**Taxis** (not Cabs) — In London, those distinctive black boxes with open luggage compartment beside the driver are licensed and metered; extra charges (for luggage, late hours, etc.) are posted in the cab. In fact, meters show both rate and extra charge. "Blackies" can cruise the streets and be hailed. Mini-cabs (legal but unlicensed) may only be obtained by phone, do not have meters (get quotation when phoning). It's customary to step outside the taxi to pay the driver, not from the back seat; add a 10% to 15% tip.

**Telephones** — When making local calls from public booths *(kiosks),* raise receiver, listen for dial tone, then dial; when connected, you'll hear a series of rapid *bleeps* signifying it's time to feed the bleeper 5p or 10p coins (exact amount depends on distance of call). In stations, airports and large department stores, there may be 50p kiosks (blue). When calling outside your area, an area code must be dialed first; London's is 01. In London, dial 100 for operator, 142 for directory information (192 for outside London or 197 for international). For calls to U.S. and Canada not dialed direct, call International Operator on 107. For correct time, dial 123, for weather 246-8091.

**Time** — GMT (Greenwich Mean Time)

**Tipping** — Hotels, restaurants usually include a 10-12½ service charge (as well as VAT). 10-15% for taxi drivers; 15p or more for porters. It's customary to tip 30 to 50p for doing your hair, 10 to 20p for shampoo. Unlike the Continent, you do not tip theatre ushers; no tipping necessary in service stations.

**Transportation** — Bus fares run from 20p (short haul) to 80p; conductors collect exact amount after you're seated, will tell you where and when to get off if you need that information. At underground stations, buy a ticket on entering, surrender it at your destination.

### Airport Transportation From Heathrow

**Underground** — Picadilly Line to Gloucester Rd (38 min.), Picadilly Circus (46 min.), King's Cross Station (55 min.).

**Bus** — Airbus #1 (60 min.) to Victoria Station with stops at Cromwell Rd., Sloane St., Buckingham Palace Rd. Airbus #2 to Paddington Station (50 min.) with stop at Queensway Station. Flightline #767 goes to Victoria Coach Station. Buses run every 20-30 min. You can bus direct to Oxford (1:05) and many other cities. There's express bus service from Heathrow to Gatwick (#747).

**Weather**

| | Jan | Feb | Mar | Apr | May | Jun | Jul | Aug | Sep | Oct | Nov | Dec |
|---|---|---|---|---|---|---|---|---|---|---|---|---|
| *Average daily temperature* | 39° | 40° | 43° | 48° | 54° | 60° | 63° | 62° | 57° | 50° | 44° | 41° |
| *Average daily low* | 35° | 35° | 36° | 40° | 45° | 51° | 54° | 54° | 49° | 44° | 39° | 36° |
| *Average daily high* | 43° | 45° | 49° | 55° | 62° | 68° | 71° | 70° | 65° | 56° | 49° | 45° |
| *Average humidity* | 85 | 82 | 79 | 75 | 73 | 73 | 73 | 76 | 80 | 85 | 86 | 86 |
| *Average number of days with rain* | 15 | 15 | 14 | 13 | 12 | 12 | 13 | 13 | 12 | 16 | 16 | 16 |

Temperature scale: °F

### From Gatwick:

**Rail** — Four trains per hour to Victoria Station (3½ min.).
**Bus** — Green Line #777 to Victoria Coach Station, #747 to Heathrow.

### From Preswick

International Airport for Glasgow, 29 miles NE. Bus takes one hour; there are direct connections for Edinburgh (1:50 more). Also frequent rail service to Glasgow (1:00), from there to Edinburgh (0:47).

### From Edinburgh

Every 30 or 60 minutes to Waverly Bridge (0:25).

### Great Britain's Weather

On English "telly," newscasters (no need for weather specialists tracing satellite pictures) spend no more than 30 seconds on tomorrow's weather — presumably because it's so variable in different parts of the country there's not much to say except "variable." Caught as England, Wales and Scotland are by the vagaries of high and low pressures off the Atlantic and/or North Sea, that's another way of saying, "Honestly, we don't quite know what's going to happen tomorrow." One thing we learned; if you awaken to pouring rain, don't despair — the sun will probably be out before noon.

If anything, Scotland's weather is the more fickle. One time it was clear and cool as we went to bed, raining when we awakened; the rest of the day the clouds, the drizzles and brief stretches of sunshine played hide and seek, often within seconds of each other, while at times the wind blew strong and chilly. On another occasion, while driving, we encountered rain, overcast, darkened skies, patches of sunlight, sunlight and light rain, heavy rain followed by overcast — all in rapid succession.

Nights can be chilly, even in August, so that warm blankets, comforters or quilts piled on hotel beds are most welcome.

**Clothing** — For England and Scotland, one needs both light and medium weight clothing and, especially, an all-weather coat or jacket. If spending several weeks here, a small, fold-up umbrella comes in handy.

## FRANCE TRAVEL-FACTS

**Airport Transportation**—For central, eastern or southern sections of Paris, use Roissy-Rail service (F20) to Gare du Nord; for Left Bank hotels, stay on the train to St. Michel, then transfer to the Metro. Trains run every 15 minutes from Charles de Gaulle Airport.

Air France buses (F27) run every 20 minutes from 0600 to 2300 to Porte Maillot Air Terminal (western sector) in 30 minutes; unless your hotel is in the 16th or 17th district *(arrondissement),* the train is quicker.

At Terminal 1 of Charles de Gaulle, Air France buses and rail shuttle buses are near gates 30-32 on arrival level. Terminal 2 is on one level; at exit, look for directional signs to rail or bus service.

Similar services are available at Orly Airport. There's direct Air France bus service between the two airports; Roissy-Rail and Orly-Rail interconnect at St. Michel. There's helicopter service between the two airports.

From Charles de Gaulle, taxi fares range up to F120. From Gare du Nord or the Porte Maillot Terminal, fares depend on hotel location. Price-wise, it's more costly for an individual to take a taxi, about the same for a couple compared to rail-taxi or bus-taxi.

**Banking Hours**—M-F 9-12, 1:30-4:30. Close at noon day before holidays. There are currency exchanges at airports, train stations.

**Climate**—Since France is not subject to extremes, it's possible to vacation here just about any time of the year. Spring and fall are the best vacation times; in the south, notably Provence and the Riviera, summers are hot — even Paris can have some very hot days in July and August though usually pleasant enough, while September and October are delightful thruout France.

**Currency**—Bank notes come in denominations of 20, 50, 100, 200, 500 and 1000 francs; there are also 1, 2, 5 and 10-franc coins and 5, 10, 20 and 50-centime coins. *The French franc is the official currency of neighboring Monaco.* Banks, American Express and Thomas Cook take less of an *agio* (commission) and usually give a higher exchange rate than small Bureaux de Change (restaurants skim off even more if you're imprudent enough to pay in dollars or travel checks); your hotel will not charge a commission but gives less than going exchange rate.

**Embassies**—U.S. at 2 avenue Gabriel (296-1202; Canadian at 35 av. Montaigne (723-0101).

**Hospital**—American Hospital, 63 Blvd. Victor Hugo in Neuilly (747-5300) is associated with Blue Cross/Blue Shield.

**Public Toilets**—Available in all stations/airports, department stores, cafes and restaurants; also pay toilets (about F2) on some streets. In smaller towns, you may find coed facilities.

**Public Transportation**—In Paris, bus and metro tickets (for use on either or both) cost F2.50 for single fare over any distance, F24 for a *carnet* of 10 tickets. Or buy one- or two-day tourist tickets (2nd class) at any Metro station for unlimited travel by Metro, bus, RER (Regional Express Rail network) and French Railways in Paris area.

**Value Added Tax**—Exemption can be claimed by visitors over 14 providing the merchandise is taken with them when departing France and, further, that the amount purchased in any one store is 800 francs or more including tax; you may buy 800 francs or more from as many stores as you wish. Exempt from this provision are gold and unset precious stones, works of art and antiques of a value in excess of 10,000 francs,* guns, medicines, tobacco products and foodstuffs. The store fills out an export form in triplicate and gives same to you together with a stamped envelope. Present these to Customs at point of exit; authorities will detach the pink sheets and mail them to the store who will then mail you the amount of tax due; meanwhile, you're given the green sheet as a receipt. In many instances, stores may deduct the tax at time of purchase. You should also attempt to get a discount from regular prices when paying in U.S. dollars or travel checks.

Exemption of VAT should also be claimed on merchandise shipped to you back home or as duty free gifts to friends and relatives.
*Tax free purchases of works of art by living artists or artists deceased less than twenty years are authorized on production of a certificate issued by the Comite Professionnel des Galeries d'Art, 5 rue Quentin Bauchart, 75008 Paris.

## GERMAN TRAVEL-FACTS

**Airport Transportation** — Shuttle service from all major airports to city centers. Luggage can be checked to any rail station in Germany from DB (Germanrail) baggage counters in airports. Express bus service from Berlin's Tegel Airport to Zoo Station (14 min.). In Frankfurt, tickets for train from airport must be purchased in advance from automatic vending machines or from platform attendants at airport rail station.

When flying Lufthansa to Frankfurt, there's connecting train service from the airport to Dusseldorf, Bonn and Cologne at no extra charge.

**Banking Hours** — M-F from 8:30 to 1, 2:30 to 4 (5:30 pm on Th). Money exchanges at airports and border points usually open from 6 am to 10 pm daily. Exchanges at stations are open for int'l train arrivals.

**Currency** — West German Mark (DM) banknotes are in denominations of 5, 10, 20, 50, 100, 500 and 1000; coins are 1, 2, 5, 10, 50 pfennigs (cents) and 1, 2 and 5 DM.

**Doctors** — In case of emergency, call Arztliche Notdienst listed in all phone directories.

**Gambling** — Casinos (roulette, baccarat) in top spa resorts and a number of cities, including West Berlin.

**Shopping Hours** — Although varying from state to state, 9 to 6:30 M-F and 9 to 2 on Saturday (except first one of month when they may stay open until 6) are normal.

**Taxis** — Metered; rates vary from city to city. No surcharges for luggage.

**Tipping** — There's a service charge of 10% to 15% in all hotels and restaurantts. Otherwise tipping should be the same as back home.

## ITALY TRAVEL-FACTS

**Airport Transportation** — From Rome's Leonardo da Vinci Airport, it's a 55-minute bus ride to the Air/Rail Terminal; buses run every 15 minutes (7 am to 7 pm), 30 minutes thereafter. From Milan Airport, there are buses every 20 minutes for the six-mile run.

**Banks** — 8:30 am to 1:30 pm M thru F. There are foreign exchange offices in main rail stations and airports.

**Climate** — During spring and fall you'll find most of Italy to be delightfully temperate, but be prepared for hot weather during the summer from Florence south.

**Currency** — Notes are for 500, 1000, 5000, 10,000, 20,000, 50,000 and 100,000 lire. Coins are 10, 20, 50, 100, 200 and 500 lire. Foreign currency or travel checks are exchangeable at current exchange rate less a commission. Declare amount of money in your possession upon entering Italy so that the same or lesser amount can be taken out. Import and export of Italian currency cannot exceed 200,000 lire for denominations of 50,000 lire or less).

**Credit Cards** — All major ones accepted.

**Customs Regulations** — Luggage is examined on entrance and exit. Allowances for personal effects are liberal; one bottle of liquor, two of wine (seals broken), 400 cigarettes are allowed.

**Electric Current** — 115 or 220v, 50c AC. Better hotels have razor adapters when needed.

**Emergencies** — Dial 113 for Ambulance, Fire, Police. Every drug store *(Farmacia)* has a list of those open at night and on Sundays. First Aid Service *(Pronto Soccorso)* available at airports, stations and hospitals.

**Export Regulations** — No restrictions on gifts purchased here except antiques and works of art require authorization of Ufficio Esportazione di Oggetti d'Arte e d'Antichita, Minstero Pubblica Istruzione, Via Cernaia 1, Rome.

*Important:* By law, hotels and restaurants must give customers stamped receipts showing appropriate taxes (IVA) have been paid. *Save them* as they may be inspected on exit from Italy (checking up on the cheaters).

**Papal Audiences** — Usually held on Wednesdays in Vatican City or, in summer, at Castel Gandolfo outside of Rome. To participate, apply to the offices of the North American College, Via dell'Umilta 30. Catholics are requested to have a letter of introduction from their parish priest. For such audiences, women should dress modestly in dark or subdued colors (nothing flamboyant), have arms and head covered. For men, a dark suit and conservative tie are most suitable; though plain colored jacket, slacks and tie are okay.

**Telephone** — Overseas calls can be dialed direct. Local calls from public phones cost 100 lire; buy tokens *(gettones)* from newsstands or tobacco shops.

**Tipping** — A very complex situation as Italy is a very tip-conscious country. Generally, tip in lire the equivalent of what you would tip back home.

In restaurants, approximately 15% is added to the tab for service, but waiter expects 5% to 10% more, wine steward 10% of the wine cost. In cafes and bars, 15% if service not included in the tab; if standing at a bar or counter for an expresso or cappuccino, 100 lire — but 300 if having liquor, sandwiches or dessert.

Hotels add 15% to 18% service to room, restaurant and bar bills.

Taxi drivers expect 15% of fare, theater ushers 400-500 lire (more for opera). Porters rate 600 lire per bag *plus a small additional tip.*

**Value Added Tax (IVA)** — Well named as it's added to *everything* in varying degrees, usually around 15%; that's in addition to the service charge.

## NEW ZEALAND TRAVEL-FACTS

**Bank Hours** — 10 to 4 (3 pm for foreign transactions) Mon. thru Fri.

**Barber Shops** — Doesn't cost much to get clipped — generally about $4. If you require a hair stylist, no problem finding one.

**Beauty Shops** — Costs about $10 for wash, set and conditioner.

**Communications** — Cable, phone services operated by Post Office. International satellite dial service. Public phones in stores, street booths.

**Credit Cards** — American Express, Diner's, MasterCard, Visa are widely accepted, even in some gas stations.

**Currency** — Notes are in denominations of $1, $5, $10, $20 and $100. Coins are 1¢, 2¢, 5¢, 10¢, 20¢ and 50¢.

Hotels generally give less than official bank rate. Travel checks bring higher exchange rate than cash, both when exchanging currencies and paying hotel accounts.

Traveler's checks can be purchased at new Zealand banks with foreign currency.

Remember, you can't leave the country with more than $100 in NZ currency, and then only in $5 bills.

**Electricity** — 230v, 3-prong plugs — but all hotels / motels have built-in wall converters for 110v, 2-prong razors. Bring a round hole, European-style plug adapter as it fits converter better.

**Entry Requirements** — Valid passport. No visa required for Canadian / UK citizens, nor U.S. citizens for visits of 30 days or less.

**Film** — Readily available, but relatively expensive.

**Firearms** — Personal sporting arms admitted duty free; register with police upon arrival. *Handguns not admitted.* Buy ammo here.

**Gambling** — National lotteries; horse racing at track and off-track (TAB), greyhound at track only.

**Medical Facilities** — Doctors good, hospitals modern. Socialized medical system.

**Office Hours** — 9 to 5 M thru F. Airline offices, travel agents have extended hours.

**Taxes** — None for visitors except International Service Charge of NZ$2 (payable in NZ currency at airport on departure).

**Taxis** — Operate from stands or on call 24 hours daily.

**Tipping** — Normally, New Zealanders do not tip nor expect to be tipped. Light tipping *may* be in order for exceptional service.

**Time** — GMT +12. Daylight Saving in effect from last Sunday in October to last one in February.

**Water** — Pure. Perfectly safe to drink tap water.

## WHEN TO COME

In general, New Zealand's climate is moderate year 'round with no wet or dry seasons. However, winter in South Island — June, July, August — requires heat in the rooms, warm clothing. But that's when the mountains are gloriously mantled in white. Summer — December, January, February — can be hot anywhere. Peak demand for hotel/motel accommodations and plane reservations is from third week of December thru January (summer vacation), Easter and during the May and August school holidays.

Spring — September, October, November — is utterly delightful in all respects, a lovely time to see the burgeoning countryside, a time of pristine greens, gamboling lambs, leggy calves and foals, tiny piglets and todding pheasant chicks — a world born anew.

March, April and May when the leaves turn golden is equally satisfying and beautiful, although by the end of March, most of the snow has vanished from the mountain tops; thus, the scene, though still beautiful, is not as dramatic as in winter and early spring. During fall, winter and spring, hotel and plane reservations are usually readily available.

### WHAT TO WEAR

Dress as you would at home for the various seasons. Women will not require anything dressier than cocktail dresses. In all better hotels, men are asked to wear jacket and tie for dinner regardless of season.

### NORWEGIAN TRAVEL-FACTS

**Airport Transportation** — In Bergen, there's half-hourly or hourly bus service (30 min.) to DT bus station. In Oslo, SAS motorcoaches run every 15 minutes to Central Station and Scandinavia Hotel (25-min. run).

**Banks** — Generally open from 8:15 am to 3:30 pm M-F. May have later closing hour one day a week.

**Climate** — Due to the proximity of the Gulf Stream, the area enjoys a climate very similar to that of Central Europe, meaning April thru October is generally mild. However, be prepared for rain.

**Clothing** — Medium weight sportswear primarily plus rainwear and a topcoat for early spring and late fall.

**Credit Cards** — Although all major cards can be used in major hotels, restaurants and department stores, they're not as widely accepted in shops and smaller businesses as in most European countries.

**Currency** — Monetary unit is the krone (designated Nkr, pronounced *CROW-nuh*), divided into 100 ore. About 9 Nkr = $1 US, or one krone = 11¢. To approximate Norwegian prices in terms of US dollars, multiply krone prices by 11¢.

**Electricity** — 220v AC, 50 or 60c. Better hotels have 110v razor outlets.

**Language** — Each country has its own, but English is a second tongue, spoken in all stores, restaurants and hotels.

**Sales Tax** — Known as MOM, it's included in all prices and normally refunded on departure from the country and/or when shipped out of the country. Exact procedure varies in each country; same is noted under Shopping.

**Time** — Greenwich Mean Time +1.

**Tipping** — None expected. Service charge added to hotel, restaurant bills.

**Daylight in Scandinavia** — From early May until late August, the sun brightens the nights and lengthens the days; an average June day has over 17 hours of daylight in Copenhagen, almost 19 in Oslo, Stockholm and Helsinki — and even slightly more in July. Above the Arctic Circle, the sun is visible 24 hours a day from April 20 to August 21 in Spitsbergen, Norway, and from May 12 to August 1 around the North Cape of Norway; the number of sunlight days lessens as one approaches the Arctic Circle from the north, but even there you find 24-hour sun from June to mid-July.

### PERU TRAVEL-FACTS

**Airport Departure Tax**—About $10 for int'l flights *payable only in dollars or dollar travel checks.* No domestic flight tax if tickets purchased outside Peru.

**Bank Hours**—8:45-11:45 Jan.-March; 9:15-1 April-Dec.

**Climate**—Entire coastal area around Lima has nice year-round weather averaging 63°, never colder than 57° nor hotter than 80°. Slight humidity is relieved by cooling Pacific breezes. Cool evenings, even in summer. Don't worry about rain — only 1" annually — though fog and dampness may prevail April-Oct.

In Cuzco, April-May see the end of the rains, June is beginning of dry season, September is probably the best month for a visit. During the high season, December thru March is rainy — yet we hit rain in August and were drenched at the Machu Picchu station waiting for buses to take us to the ruins.

**Credit Cards**—Only American Express, Diner's and Visa are approved by the government.

**Currency**—Check current rate as Soles (S/) are steadily devalued. There are S/500, 1000, 5000, 10,000 notes. Banks, exchanges *(cambios)* and hotels exchange dollar notes/travel checks; passport required. Keep exchange receipts to convert soles to dollars upon departure.

**Electricity**—220v but better hotels have 110v shaver adapters.

**Entry Requirements**—Passport, onward or return ticket. Disembarkation Form, in *duplicate,* must be filled out *prior to* passing thru Immigration and Customs. Both *Cambio* and desk that gives out Disembarkation Forms are to your left as you approach Immigration.

**Shopping**—Excellent for native handcrafts, dolls, Indian fabrics, gold, silver and copper jewelry, silverware, leather goods, llama fur rugs, paintings and pottery.

**Water**—Perfectly okay in better hotels, restaurants. Natural or carbonated mineral water readily available.

### SWISS TRAVEL-FACTS

**Airport Transportation** — From Zurich, continuous rail service to downtown station (7 miles, 12 min.) with many going on to major cities without change of train. From Geneva, bus service every 15 minutes (15 min. to DT).

**Business Hours** — Banks usually open from 8:30 to 4:30 M-F. Currency exchanges at airports and major rail stations are open until 10 pm. Shopping hours usually 8 to 12:30, 2:30 to 6:30 pm M-F, Sat. 'til 4 pm. In larger cities, stores may be open during lunch, closed Mon. am. Post offices in large cities: 7:30 to noon, 1:45 to 6:30; Sat. 'til 11 am.

**Climate** — About the same as in northern U.S. but without extremes of hot or cold. During the summer, city temperatures are seldom above 80°, humidity is low. Southern part of country is subtropical, has year-round mild weather. Be prepared at any time for rain, usually brief showers — a small, foldup umbrella (Swiss make excellent ones) makes a good travel companion (as it does in Great Britain, Scandinavia).

**Clothing** — Lightweight wool sweaters, skirts, etc., are comfortable in the mountain areas and particularly appreciated at night.

**Currency** — Swiss Franc (SF) notes are in denominations of 10, 20, 50, 100, 500, and 1000. Coins are 5, 10, 20 and 50 centimes, also 1, 2 and 5 francs. *Swiss francs are official currency in Lichtenstein.* Official exchange rates, *which include commission,* are available from banks, exchange counters in stations and airports and some travel agencies.

**Language** — Multi-lingual. German is spoken in Central and Eastern parts, French in the West, Italian in the South and Romansch in Southeast. English might be called a fifth language.

**Museums** — Usually open from 10 to 12 and 2-5.

**Taxis** — Rates somewhat higher than in U.S. In most major cities, tip is included. From international airports in Zurich, Geneva and Basel, approx. rates to city center are SF40, 24 (tip not included) and 30 respectively.

**Tipping** — Service is included on all hotel and restaurant charges. *An extra tip is neither necessary nor expected* (what a relief).

# WORLD TIME CHART

## ATLANTIC TIME ZONES (Eastward from Honolulu/Alaska)[1]

| PST | MST | CST | EST | -4 | -3 | -1 | GMT |
|---|---|---|---|---|---|---|---|
| 0900 | 1000 | 1100 | 1200 | 1300 | 1400 | 1600 | 1700 |
| 1000 | 1100 | 1200 | 1300 | 1400 | 1500 | 1700 | 1800 |
| 1100 | 1200 | 1300 | 1400 | 1500 | 1600 | 1800 | 1900 |
| 1200 | 1300 | 1400 | 1500 | 1600 | 1700 | 1900 | 2000 |
| 1300 | 1400 | 1500 | 1600 | 1700 | 1800 | 2000 | 2100 |
| 1400 | 1500 | 1600 | 1700 | 1800 | 1900 | 2100 | 2200 |
| 1500 | 1600 | 1700 | 1800 | 1900 | 2000 | 2200 | 2300 |
| 1600 | 1700 | 1800 | 1900 | 2000 | 2100 | 2300 | 2400 |
| 1700 | 1800 | 1900 | 2000 | 2100 | 2200 | 2400 | 0100 |
| 1800 | 1900 | 2000 | 2100 | 2200 | 2300 | 0100 | 0200 |
| 1900 | 2000 | 2100 | 2200 | 2300 | 2400 | 0200 | 0300 |
| 2000 | 2100 | 2200 | 2300 | 2400 | 0100 | 0300 | 0400 |
| 2100 | 2200 | 2300 | 2400 | 0100 | 0200 | 0400 | 0500 |
| 2200 | 2300 | 2400 | 0100 | 0200 | 0300 | 0500 | 0600 |
| 2300 | 2400 | 0100 | 0200 | 0300 | 0400 | 0600 | 0700 |
| 2400 | 0100 | 0200 | 0300 | 0400 | 0500 | 0700 | 0800 |
| 0100 | 0200 | 0300 | 0400 | 0500 | 0600 | 0800 | 0900 |
| 0200 | 0300 | 0400 | 0500 | 0600 | 0700 | 0900 | 1000 |
| 0300 | 0400 | 0500 | 0600 | 0700 | 0800 | 1000 | 1100 |
| 0400 | 0500 | 0600 | 0700 | 0800 | 0900 | 1100 | 1200 |
| 0500 | 0600 | 0700 | 0800 | 0900 | 1000 | 1200 | 1300 |
| 0600 | 0700 | 0800 | 0900 | 1000 | 1100 | 1300 | 1400 |
| 0700 | 0800 | 0900 | 1000 | 1100 | 1200 | 1400 | 1500 |
| 0800 | 0900 | 1000 | 1100 | 1200 | 1300 | 1500 | 1600 |

## EUROPE/FAR EAST TIME ZONES (Eastward)

| GMT | +1 | +2 | +3 | +4 | +5 | +6 | +7 | +8 | +9 |
|---|---|---|---|---|---|---|---|---|---|
| 1700 | 1800 | 1900 | 2000 | 2100 | 2200 | 2300 | 2400 | 0100 | 0200 |
| 1800 | 1900 | 2000 | 2100 | 2200 | 2300 | 2400 | 0100 | 0200 | 0300 |
| 1900 | 2000 | 2100 | 2200 | 2300 | 2400 | 0100 | 0200 | 0300 | 0400 |
| 2000 | 2100 | 2200 | 2300 | 2400 | 0100 | 0200 | 0300 | 0400 | 0500 |
| 2100 | 2200 | 2300 | 2400 | 0100 | 0200 | 0300 | 0400 | 0500 | 0600 |
| 2200 | 2300 | 2400 | 0100 | 0200 | 0300 | 0400 | 0500 | 0600 | 0700 |
| 2300 | 2400 | 0100 | 0200 | 0300 | 0400 | 0500 | 0600 | 0700 | 0800 |
| 2400 | 0100 | 0200 | 0300 | 0400 | 0500 | 0600 | 0700 | 0800 | 0900 |
| 0100 | 0200 | 0300 | 0400 | 0500 | 0600 | 0700 | 0800 | 0900 | 1000 |
| 0200 | 0300 | 0400 | 0500 | 0600 | 0700 | 0800 | 0900 | 1000 | 1100 |
| 0300 | 0400 | 0500 | 0600 | 0700 | 0800 | 0900 | 1000 | 1100 | 1200 |
| 0400 | 0500 | 0600 | 0700 | 0800 | 0900 | 1000 | 1100 | 1200 | 1300 |
| 0500 | 0600 | 0700 | 0800 | 0900 | 1000 | 1100 | 1200 | 1300 | 1400 |
| 0600 | 0700 | 0800 | 0900 | 1000 | 1100 | 1200 | 1300 | 1400 | 1500 |
| 0700 | 0800 | 0900 | 1000 | 1100 | 1200 | 1300 | 1400 | 1500 | 1600 |
| 0800 | 0900 | 1000 | 1100 | 1200 | 1300 | 1400 | 1500 | 1600 | 1700 |
| 0900 | 1000 | 1100 | 1200 | 1300 | 1400 | 1500 | 1600 | 1700 | 1800 |
| 1000 | 1100 | 1200 | 1300 | 1400 | 1500 | 1600 | 1700 | 1800 | 1900 |
| 1100 | 1200 | 1300 | 1400 | 1500 | 1600 | 1700 | 1800 | 1900 | 2000 |
| 1200 | 1300 | 1400 | 1500 | 1600 | 1700 | 1800 | 1900 | 2000 | 2100 |
| 1300 | 1400 | 1500 | 1600 | 1700 | 1800 | 1900 | 2000 | 2100 | 2200 |
| 1400 | 1500 | 1600 | 1700 | 1800 | 1900 | 2000 | 2100 | 2200 | 2300 |
| 1500 | 1600 | 1700 | 1800 | 1900 | 2000 | 2100 | 2200 | 2300 | 2400 |
| 1600 | 1700 | 1800 | 1900 | 2000 | 2100 | 2200 | 2300 | 2400 | 0100 |

## PACIFIC TIME ZONES (Westward from North America)[1]

| +10 | +11 | 12 | -11 | -10 | HST | -9 |
|---|---|---|---|---|---|---|
| 0300 | 0400 | 0500 | 0600 | 0700 | 0700 | 0800 |
| 0400 | 0500 | 0600 | 0700 | 0800 | 0800 | 0900 |
| 0500 | 0600 | 0700 | 0800 | 0900 | 0900 | 1000 |
| 0600 | 0700 | 0800 | 0900 | 1000 | 1000 | 1100 |
| 0700 | 0800 | 0900 | 1000 | 1100 | 1100 | 1200 |
| 0800 | 0900 | 1000 | 1100 | 1200 | 1200 | 1300 |
| 0900 | 1000 | 1100 | 1200 | 1300 | 1300 | 1400 |
| 1000 | 1100 | 1200 | 1300 | 1400 | 1400 | 1500 |
| 1100 | 1200 | 1300 | 1400 | 1500 | 1500 | 1600 |
| 1200 | 1300 | 1400 | 1500 | 1600 | 1600 | 1700 |
| 1300 | 1400 | 1500 | 1600 | 1700 | 1700 | 1800 |
| 1400 | 1500 | 1600 | 1700 | 1800 | 1800 | 1900 |
| 1500 | 1600 | 1700 | 1800 | 1900 | 1900 | 2000 |
| 1600 | 1700 | 1800 | 1900 | 2000 | 2000 | 2100 |
| 1700 | 1800 | 1900 | 2000 | 2100 | 2100 | 2200 |
| 1800 | 1900 | 2000 | 2100 | 2200 | 2200 | 2300 |
| 1900 | 2000 | 2100 | 2200 | 2300 | 2300 | 2400 |
| 2000 | 2100 | 2200 | 2300 | 2400 | 2400 | 0100 |
| 2100 | 2200 | 2300 | 2400 | 0100 | 0100 | 0200 |
| 2200 | 2300 | 2400 | 0100 | 0200 | 0200 | 0300 |
| 2300 | 2400 | 0100 | 0200 | 0300 | 0300 | 0400 |
| 2400 | 0100 | 0200 | 0300 | 0400 | 0400 | 0500 |
| 0100 | 0200 | 0300 | 0400 | 0500 | 0500 | 0600 |
| 0200 | 0300 | 0400 | 0500 | 0600 | 0600 | 0700 |

[1] In United States and Canada, all time zones except Hawaii (−10) have Daylight Saving Time (one hour earlier) from last Sunday in April to last one in October.

Hawaii time zone includes central Alaska, French Polynesia (except Marquesas, which is −9½) and Cook Islands.

[2] Having passed International Dateline (at 180° latitude), it's now a day earlier than in North America; if you left on the 1st, it's now the 2nd.

−9 zone is Skagway, Alaska while Yukon Territory is on PST time.

Turning westward, −11 includes American / Western Samoa, Tonga and Kwajalein.

+12 covers Fiji, New Zealand, Marshall & Wake Islands.

+11 — New Caledonia, Solomon Islands, Vanavatu.

+10 — Australian East Coast. South Australia, Alice Springs and Darwin are +9½, Australia West Coast +8. New Guinea (including Bougainville) and Guam are +10.

Returning to the Pacific Coast, Mountain Standard Time (MST) includes Baja California Sur, Easter Island. CST covers central Mexico, Central America.

EST includes southeast Mexico, Cuba, Colombia, Ecuador, Peru, Panama, Haiti, Jamaca, Bahamas, Caymans.

−4 — Atlantic Canada, Thule (Greenland); Bolivia, Chile, Paraguay, Venezuela; Bermuda, Puerto Rico, Virgin Islands; Barbados, Dominican Rep., Guadelupe, Leeward & Windward Islands, Martinique, Netherlands, Antilles, St. Vincent, Trinidad & Tobago.

−3 — Argentina, Brazil, French Guiana, Guyana, Uruguay; St. Pierre; Greenland (west coast). Newfoundland and Surinam are −3½.

−1 — Azores, Cape Verde Islands, Greenland (east coast).

GMT — Iceland, Ireland, Portugal, United Kingdom, Canary, Faero, Orkney and Shetland Islands; Algeria, Morocco; Gambia, Ghana, Guinea, Ivory Coast, Liberia, Mali, Mauretania, Senegal, Sierra Leone, Togo, Upper Volta.

+1 — Albania, Austria, Belgium, Czechoslovakia, Denmark, France, Germany (East & West), Gibraltar, Hungary, Italy, Luxembourg, Malta, Monaco, Netherlands, Norway, Poland, Spain, Sweden, Switzerland, Yugoslavia; Angola, Cameroon, Chad, Eq. Guinea, Gabon, Niger, Nigeria, Tunisia, Zaire (Kinasha).

+2 — Bulgaria, Finland, Greece, Romania; Egypt, Israel, Jordan, Lebanon, Libya, Syria; Botswana, Burundi, Malawi, Mozambique, Namibia, Rwanda, South Africa, Sudan, Swaziland, Zambia, Zimbabwe (Rhodesia).

+3 — Russia (West), Turkey; Iraq, Iran (+3½), Kuwait, Qatar, Saudi Arabia, Yemen; Bahrain, Djibouti, Ethiopia, Kenya, Madagascar, Somali, Tanzania, Uganda.

*Note:* Most European countries have Daylight Saving Time between the last Sunday of March to last one of September (Ireland & United Kingdom last Sunday in October). The dissenter is (you guessed it) — USSR (Moscow time); April 1 to September 30. Turkey does not have DST.

+4 — Mauritius, Oman, Seychelles, United Arab Emirates.

+5 — Maldives, Pakistan; India, Sri Lanka (+5½); Nepal (+5⅔).

+6 — Bangladesh; Burma (+6½); +7 — Indonesia (west), Laos, Thailand.

+8 — Brunei, China, Hong Kong, Indonesia (central), Malaysia, Mongolia, Philippines, Singapore and Taiwan.

+9 — Japan, Korea, Indonesia (east).

## TIPS ON PLANNING YOUR TRIPS

### Check The Weather Before You Go

Bad weather is a waste of time and money, a fun spoiler. More trips are ruined by it than any other factor. And, within reasonable limits, it's avoidable — by checking what's happened in prior years. In the U.S., National Weather Service has complete statistics. Our *Travel Digests* tell you when, when not to go to Mexico, South America, South Pacific and Far East. To get World Climate Charts covering 24 areas of the globe, join IAMAT, the non-profit medical advisory organization (see Healthful Travel for addresses); these detail monthly climatic and sanitary conditions in 1440 cities, suggest proper weight clothing. Excellent, invaluable for world globe-trotting.

Generally, spring and fall, anywhere in the world, are ideal travel times — you'll rarely go wrong following that guideline. Summer may be too hot, too humid (and too crowded), winter too cold (except for skiing). But remember, seasons do not occur in the same months around the world. Below the equator, seasons are the reverse of ours. In Chile and Argentina, Australia and New Zealand sheep are lambing in September, you're skiing in July, sunbathing in December and watching the leaves fall in April-May.

Here, though, are more general guidelines:

*Far East:* Can be visited year 'round though rainy season in the tropical countries (Indonesia, Malaysia, Philippines, Thailand) is usually May-October period (exact months vary country to country); in Singapore, rains come in Oct-Feb. In China and Hong Kong, rains usually heaviest in summer. There's snow in the mountains of Japan, Korea and China during winter.

*South Pacific:* May thru November is best period in the tropical zones. December-March is no time to visit Australia's Great Barrier Reef (possible hurricanes); in same period, it's hot along New Guinea's coast (excessive rain, too), in northern and central Australia. South of Brisbane, Australia, and Auckland, New Zealand, June thru August (winter) is a period that sees the most rain, coolest temperatures with snow in the mountains (but not in cities).

*South America:* Fold back a map of South America across its northern coast so that the southern tip of Chile rests in Arctic North America. Resulting correlations are generally valid for broad purposes of comparisons (remember, seasons are reversed). Travel is good thruout the year in most areas. At the equator, it's temperate or hot, depending on altitude. Snow level is about 16,000 ft. in the Andes so that temperatures are usually moderate in Andean cities like Cuzco, Peru. South of the Amazon jungles, weather becomes cooler, finally colder; north to the Caribbean it remains tropical and warm, often hot (except in Bogota, Caracas and the northern Andes).

*Mexico:* Coastal resorts are always warm, summer hot; June into October is the rainy season. In Mexico City and other highland areas, it's mild and bracing year 'round with winter months equivalent to nippy fall weather back home (days are usually warm); you'll need a lightweight coat, particularly at night. Rainy season, May-October (heaviest during summer) consists of brief showers (usually in afternoon).

European weather is generally similar to corresponding areas in North America; seasons, of course, are the same.

In the Middle East and North Africa, it's hot during the summer, can be cool during the winter (as in Cairo), even chilly at nights in the deserts. In Egypt, April brings sandstorms (last up to 50 days). Seasons the same as ours.

In South Africa, seasons are reversed — but only in the Capetown area is it cold during winter.

There's this to say about off-season travel: it's cheaper. If you like really hot weather, summer's the time to see places like the California, Arizona and Egyptian deserts, other hot spots around the world. On the other hand, ski resorts can be delightful in spring and summer.

### Do You Wish To Travel With A Group Or Individually?

Group travel is the way to go for all but experienced travelers who prefer being on their own. But individual travelers (known as FITs when traveling to foreign countries) have to cope with expensive transfers (except by airport bus) between airport and hotel. Group tours, however, have a tour manager, invaluable when claiming luggage, getting it and you thru customs — usually quite a hassle when several 747s disgorge passengers at the same time. Local sightseeing, by car or seat-in-bus, is expensive for FITs, especially full day or longer excursions.

Group travel has other advantages: hotel and plane reservations are confirmed, rates usually less than for individual bookings. Local transportation and sightseeing is less expensive. But main advantage is it makes travel comparatively hassle-free — all decisions, arrangements, baggage transfers and tipping are taken care of by the tour manager.

There are, of course, some disadvantages: possible incompatibility or annoyance with other group members, less freedom of individual movement, frequent times of "hurry up and wait," not spending as much time as you'd like in certain places, too much at others. Careful selection of the tour best suited to your needs and desires is paramount. Travelers who enjoy doing things on their own should pay special attention to how much leisure time is available in each city.

When comparing similar tours, check the following:

1) Land cost *per night* (not including nights on a plane).
2) Included number of breakfasts, lunches and dinners. Are breakfasts continental or American? Other meals table d'hote or a la carte? Are meals included at restaurants outside hotels?
3) Class of hotels being used. Some brochures claim deluxe when actually first class. Check that out with your travel agent.
4) What class rooms in those hotels — standard, superior, deluxe?
5) Is tour fully escorted thruout (plus local guide service) or is it a guided tour (services of local tour operators without a tour manager)? Former is preferable albeit more expensive.
6) How physically strenuous is the tour? Avoid one that has too many late evening arrivals, early morning departures. Most adventure-type tours are graded by degree of activity, physical condition required.
7) Reputation of tour operator, number of years in operation.
8) Beware of the fantastic bargain. We've never seen a miracle, especially in the travel business.

It is particularly important to check how much sightseeing is included in the tour and what important "optional excursions" are listed as extra expenses. Same applies to cruises; on one we checked recently, shore excursions were not included in the cruise price.

Always read *carefully* the fine print of any tour or cruise contract *before* you sign it, particularly the cancellation and refund clauses. *Never* pay in advance more than is necessary — and do it at last possible moment. Payments by credit card gives extra time in which to draw interest on your bank accounts.

### On A Group Tour, Can I Fly Back Independently?

Depends on which airline is being used by the group. Some fares permit independent return (with stopovers), some do not. Others may permit an extended stay in the last destination (but possibly no other stopovers).

### What About Independent Travel?

It can be, and in our case is, very rewarding. More advance preparation is needed. And it might prove more costly, though if you arrange to travel with a compatible couple your sightseeing and transfer costs are halved. You will, in any case, have the untold satisfaction of discovering new worlds of your own.

## PRE-DEPARTURE REQUIREMENTS

### What Documents Do I Need?

A *passport* for which a birth certificate or notarized affidavit of birth (vouched for by a relative or person who has known you for a long time) is needed, plus two passport photos (front view, 2" x 2" on white background). Passports for U.S. adults (18 and over), valid for *10 years*, cost $42 if obtaining one for the first time, or $35 if you submit with your application a previous passport that was valid during the past eight years. Those under 18 pay $20 (for *five-year* validity) plus a $7 execution fee — a total of $27.

### How & Where Is A Passport Obtained?

Apply in person to Passport Agencies (see following list) or process applications thru Clerks of Federal, State or County Courts and larger Post Offices; allow four weeks. If you've had a passport within past eight years (issued after your 18th birthday), you can apply by mail after obtaining pink application form DSP-82 from nearest Passport Agency; return it with old passport, the $35 fee (personal check or money order) and two photos. In cases of emergency, Passport Agencies may issue a passport in 24 to 48 hours when you appear in person. Each family member, including minors, must have a passport.

Always keep a copy (in purse or wallet) of your passport number, date of issue and expiration so that in case of loss, a duplicate can be obtained from nearest embassy or consulate. By registering at one or the other upon arrival in a foreign country, you're entitled to an on-the-spot replacement (instead of waiting for one from Washington).

#### U.S. Passport Agencies

Boston 02203—John F. Kennedy Bldg., Room E123
Chicago 50504—230 S. Dearborn, Rm. 380
Honolulu 96850—300 Ala Moana Blvd., Rm. C-106
Los Angeles 90024—Federal Bldg., 11000 Wilshire Blvd.
Miami 33130—51 SW First Ave., Rm. 804
New Orleans 70130—2 Canal St., Rm. 400
New York 10020—630 Fifth Ave., Rm. 270
Philadelphia 19106—600 Arch St., Rm. 4426
San Francisco 94102—450 Golden Gate, Rm. 1405
Seattle 98174—915 Second Ave., Rm. 906
Washington, D.C. 20524—1425 K St., N.W.

### Canadian Passports

Costs $21 for five years, is non-renewable. Persons born in Canada must have birth certificate or proof of citizenship (voter registration, expired passport, armed forces ID) and signature of guarantor. Persons not born in Canada must have guarantor and documentary proof of citizenship. Applications available from travel agencies and carriers. Passports are issued in Ottawa, Montreal, Toronto and Vancouver.

### What Are Visas And Do I Need Them?

A visa is an official form stamped in your passport indicating you have been granted entry into that particular country for a stated number of days. Some countries issue single entry or multiple entry visas (or both); a single entry visa means that after you enter and depart the country, you must have another visa if you wish to re-enter. Life of a visa varies, usually from a month to as much as 4 years for multiple entry. There may/may not be a fee involved (up to as much as $13 or so).

Visas (and visa applications) are issued by consulates and embassies of countries requiring same; in some countries, a visa may be obtained at port of entry (but that holds up departure from the airport). Most tour operators provide applications, process them for members of group tours at minimum cost. Individual travelers are best served by a visa service company (unless traveler lives in Washington or a city served by major consulates); your travel agent undoubtedly has contacts with visa service companies in Washington, New York or other cities.

Entries into all countries are invariably predicated on your having an onward or return airline, train or ship ticket (although we can't recall ever having been asked for same).

### What Countries Do Not Require Visas?

Canada, Mexico, Caribbean and South American countries (except Argentina,[2] Brazil[3]), Western European countries (including Turkey), Israel. In the South Pacific, only Australia and Papua New Guinea require a visa for U.S. citizens, New Guinea only for Canadians. For the Far East, Bangladesh, Hong Kong, Macau, Malaysia, Philippines, Singapore, Sri Lanka and Thailand do not require them, all other countries do (except India for Canadians). In Central America, passport and visa are needed for Honduras and Nicaragua; proof of citizenship only for Belize, Costa Rica (plus Tourist Card; Canadians passport only), El Salvador, Guatemala.

All East European, Middle East and African countries (except Botswana, Malawi, Morocco, Tunisia and Zimbabwe-Rhodesia) require visas.

The following countries refuse entry to those whose passport has a valid or expired Israeli visa: Bahrain, Iraq, Jordan, Saudi Arabia, United Arab Emirates (Abu Dhabi and Dubai are two of the better known sheikdoms), Yemen Arab Republic. However, since Israel does not require visas from Americans and Canadians, this does not apply to them — except those countries would undoubtedly deny entry to those whose passport showed Israeli entrance/exit stamps. A new passport would circumvent that — or visit Israel after leaving Islamic countries.

The same situation vis-a-vis some African countries could apply to South Africa. Here the remedy is to have South African officials issue a "loose-sheet" visa — one that can be taken out of your passport after leaving South Africa.

In South America, Tourist Cards are required for each entry to Bolivia, Chile, Colombia (2 photos), Panama ($2) and Paraguay ($1); Venezuela accepts a Tourist Permit. Cards and Permits are issued by airlines, some shipping companies.

### What's Needed To Visit Canada, Mexico?

**Canada** — No passport nor visa. Native-born U.S. citizens should have proof of citizenship; naturalized citizens should carry naturalization certificate or other evidence of citizenship. Permanent U.S., non-citizen residents should have their Alien Registration Receipt Card (Form 1-151 or 1-551). Unaccompanied minors (under 18) must have a letter from parent or guardian giving permission to travel in Canada.

**Mexico** — Tourist Card only. Entrant fills in own form; issuing office merely check *proof of citizenship.* Valid up to 180 days but void if unused within 90 days of issue. Tourists cannot stay more than 180 days on any single trip unless incapacitated by illness.

No card required for visits of less than 72 hours to Mexican border towns or within 60 miles of border.

*Proof of Citizenship* is a passport or one of following: birth certificate, voter's registration, naturalization certificate, military ID card. *While in Mexico, always carry proof of citizenship as well as Tourist Card.* Children under 15 years of age can be included in parents' Single Entry Card; if there's a likelihood of their returning without parents, then obtain separate cards.

Minors (under 18) traveling alone or with any person other than parents must obtain a Tourist Card, plus notarized letter of consent by *both* parents or guardians (must be validated at office where Tourist Card is obtained). If minor is accompanied by only one parent, notarized letter of consent from other parent is required.

*Types of Tourist Cards:* Single Entry (no photos) or Multiple Entry (three 2"x2" passport photos). No charge for either type.

[2] Visa costs $5; one photo. [3] No charge, no photo. Good for 90 days after entry.

## BUY THE "BIBLES" THOUSANDS OF AGENTS USE

**Tell How To Plan Trips, When & Where To Go, How To Get There, What To See & Do. Also Where To Eat, What To Buy. Hotel/Resort Directories, Currency & Tipping, Entry Requirements, Climate & Clothing, Motoring, Air & Sea Travel. Profusely mapped, illustrated. Like having personal escorts wherever you go.**

**MEXICO TRAVEL DIGEST**

As good as having your personal guide to and thru Mexico — from just below the Border all the way to the fascinating Lands of the Mayas (a special 32-page feature) and on to the Caribbean resorts — by air, bus, car and rail. Motoring section alone is indispensable. Resort Roundup covers entire gamut from Baja California, across Sea of Cortez to the famous, glittering resorts of the mainland west coast and on to Cancun and Cozumel in the Caribbean. Complete sections on Mexico City and environs, Oaxaca, the Colonel Circle and little-known, offbeat spots. Comprehensive Hotel Directory for entire country (with current price ranges, authors' recommendations). "Used the *Digest* to plan four trips — it's our Bible," says one reader. 176 magazine-size pages, heavily illustrated.
$9.95 postpaid

**SOUTH PACIFIC TRAVEL DIGEST**

Latest data, plus the romance, history and allure of these regional areas: Australia, New Zealand, Polynesia (American & Western Samoas, Tonga, Tahiti, Cook Islands, Fiji), Melanesia (New Guinea, Solomon Islands, New Hebrides, New Caledonia). Special features: Easter Island and the Enchanting Galapagos as part of a South Pacific-South America circle tour. Each area, each country is treated as: 1) A destination in its own right; 2) Part of overall South Pacific routings. Diagrams concisely illustrate how to route trips within and between the various countries. Makes travel planning automatic. Detailed South Pacific Map plus Air Map showing all routings. 160 magazine-size pages, 260 photos and maps.
$9.95 postpaid.

**SOUTH AMERICA TRAVEL DIGEST**

Designed for travel agents (as are all Digest titles), it is considered by the travel trade as the "bible" of South America, for no other writers know the continent as well as the Jacobs. Actually 12 books in one, it details latest information on Argentina, Bolivia, Brasil, Chile, Colombia, Ecuador, Panama, Paraguay, Peru, Surinam, Uruguay, Venezuela. Covers all exciting adventure tris: Amazon, Easter Island, Galapagos Islands, Machu Picchu/Lake Titicaca, Argentine-Chilean Lakes, Strait of Magellan, Iguassu Falls and others. Special feature: Cruising Around and in South America. Used as text for tourism courses. Lavishly illustrated. 168 magazine-size pages.
$9.95 postpaid.

**FAR EAST TRAVEL DIGEST**

The best ever published for the Orient. No other guide attempts such extensive, inclusive coverage: Peoples Republic of China, Japan, South Korea, Taiwan, Hong Kong, Thailand, Malaysia, Singapore, Burma, Brunei, Indonesia, Philippines — PLUS India, Sri Lanka, Nepal, Bhutan, Sikkim and Ladakh. Provides all essential travel data plus background material on life styles that helps visitors understand what they're seeing — like the religions, art and customs of the Far East, festivals, Japanese and Chinese (also Indian) cuisines. Tells you how to plan trips to and between the countries (with route diagrams) for varying lengths of time. Hotel Directory for each country. Well illustrated, mapped. 176 magazine-size pages.
$9.95 postpaid

## WE HELP YOU MAKE DREAMS COME TRUE!

Travel to faraway places with strange sounding names is a lifetime dream for most people. So, by bringing all those wondrous places into sharp focus, in relating one to another, in suggesting innovative routings and advising when to go, Travel Digests collaborate with you in making dreams come true. Not only that but when you give, loan or sell Travel Digests to your clients, you're creating extra dreams by which to travel . . . and extra profits for you.

**DESTINATION: GREECE**

Live again that Golden Age when Greece gave birth to Western art, architecture and mythology . . . when gods inhabited Mt. Olympus and Delphic Oracles foretold the future. You'll find it entertainingly retold in 32 magazine-size, beautifully illustrated pages. $3.95 postpaid.

**DESTINATION: EGYPT**

Crammed with photos, drawings of the gods and basic information about Egypt's pharaohs, gods, mythology and history. Makes Ancient Egypt come alive, adds an extra dimension to your trip. 32 magazine-size pages.
$3.95 postpaid.

**DESTINATION: INDIA**

Completely covers India in depth plus Sri Lanka, Nepal, Bhutan, Ladakh and Sikkim. Comprehensive what to do and see information . . . descriptions of the religions and art of the region. 32 magazine-size pages.
$3.95 postpaid.

**DESTINATION: ENGLAND**

With this Travel Planner, you quickly, easily plan trips to the most interesting parts of England by car, rail, bus and boat. Gives details of BritRail, Brit Express (bus) Passes, tells how to drive the Roundabouts, locate inexpensive Bed & Breakfast lodgings. 32 well-mapped, magazine-size pages make your next trip a B-R-E-E-Z-E.
$3.95 postpaid.

**DESTINATION: CHINA**

This 16-pg, magazine-size brochure gives detailed answers to what life in China is all about, how China evolved over the ages, how history is repeating itself today—PLUS vital tourist information, Tourist Map, How To Pronounce Chinese Names and Spell City Names.
Just $1.95 prepaid.

**BEAUTIFUL GALAPAGOS MAP**

Precisely scaled replica of all islands (with their Spanish and English names) surrounded by drawings of a Giant Tortoise, Iguana, Galapagos Gull, Seal, Penguins and Galapagos Owl. Handsomely lithographed in sepia brown and sea green on 17½ × 22½" heavy, textured white stock. Ideal for framing or mounting in office or den.

Specially Priced . . . . . . . . . . . . . . .$4.95 postpaid.

Mail Check or Money Order to
**TRAVEL DIGESTS, 30695 Ganado Dr., Rancho Palos Verdes, Ca. 90274**
*For Calif. Deliveries:* Add 6% Tax (6½% L.A. Area)
*Canadians:* Remit in US $$$, checks drawn on US Banks